THE MARXISM OF REGIS DEBRAY

THE MARXISM OF REGIS DEBRAY

Between Lenin and Guevara

Hartmut Ramm

THE REGENTS PRESS OF KANSAS
Lawrence

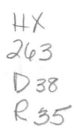

Copyright © 1978 by The Regents Press of Kansas
Printed in the United States of America

Library of Congress Cataloging in Publication Data

Ramm, Hartmut, 1942–
The Marxism of Régis Debray.
Bibliography: p.
Includes index.
1. Debray, Régis. 2. Guevara, Ernesto, 1928–1967.
3. Lenin, Vladimir Il'ich, 1870–1924. 4. Communism.
I. Title.
HX263.D38R35   335.43'092'4 [B]   77–17915
ISBN 0–7006–0170–8

Publication of this book was assisted by the American Council
of Learned Societies under a grant from the Andrew W. Mellon
Foundation.

Permissions have been granted by the publishers for quotations from
these works:

Prison Writings, by Régis Debray, copyright © 1973 by Random
House, Inc.

"Régis Debray and the Brazilian Revolution," by Joao Quartim, copyright © 1970 by *New Left Review*.

Revolution in the Revolution?, by Régis Debray, copyright © 1967,
English Translation, by Monthly Review Press. Reprinted by permission of Monthly Review Press.

Strategy for Revolution, by Régis Debray, copyright © 1967, 1968,
1969 by Librairie François Maspero. Reprinted by permission of
Monthly Review Press.

Contents

Preface

On January 1, 1959, Fidel Castro and Che Guevara entered Havana at the head of the victorious Rebel Army, ushering in a new era of international political relations. For the next decade, relations between Cuba, on one hand, and the United States and its Latin American client states, on the other, were marked by irreconcilable differences and considerable hostility. The Soviet Union—which had been pursuing a policy of peaceful coexistence with the United States when, almost in spite of itself, it adopted the beleaguered revolution and spread its nuclear and economic umbrella over it—found detente poisoned by the U.S.-Cuba confrontation. U.S. policymakers were obliged to rush into Latin America to close the barn door with massive doses of economic and military aid to encourage reform and counterinsurgency.

Until his death in late 1967, the principal architect of Cuban policy both foreign and domestic was Che Guevara, one of the few Marxists in the Rebel Army during the insurrectionary period and the principal pole of attraction for Castro and Cuba in their drift toward socialism. To the dismay of Soviet policymakers Guevara did not believe in the possibility of peaceful coexistence; instead, he accepted confrontation as the proper relation between an aggressive alliance of Socialist states and a faltering empire of underdeveloped and developed capitalist states. He regarded the liberation of the underdeveloped capitalist world, in the manner of Cuba, as the only viable mechanism for resolving the capitalist-Socialist antagonism and as the only solution consistent with socialism's moral commitment to bring a speedy end to generalized human misery. Thus it was that Cuban foreign policy during the decade of Guevara's stewardship concentrated on exhorting the would-be revolutionaries of Latin America to take up arms against their socially and politically repressive governments. To back up his exhortations Guevara developed a theory of revolution, purportedly grounded in the lessons of the Cuban experience, which sought to justify rationally the moral imperative of immediate and uncompromising intervention in an intolerable world order. The cornerstone of the theory was the roving rural guerrilla band, or *foco*; the theory itself came to be referred to as *foquismo*.

The theory which Guevara sketched out, however, collided with all traditional Marxist-Leninist conceptions of revolution, as espoused by pro-Peking, pro-Moscow, and Trotskyist parties. Since all of these groups appealed to Lenin for confirmation, it was natural for Guevara to question their claims and assert his own ties to Lenin's heritage. But because Guevara's acquaintance with Leninist thought was scanty and because he embarked on the odyssey that ended in Bolivia just as this debate was beginning to heat up, the burden of the theoretical struggle passed to a brilliant, young French intellectual, Régis Debray.

The principal focus of this study is the nature of the Guevarist theory of revolution and its similarities and differences with the Leninist theory; the principal vehicle for the investigation is Régis Debray. Debray is ideally suited for this role. He came to Guevarism as a confirmed devotee of Lenin and became Guevara's most articulate and rigorous interpreter, systematizer, and adherent. When his involvement in Guevara's fateful Bolivian *foco* put him in prison for three years, Debray began a retreat from Guevarism that quickly brought him back to an orthodox Leninist conception of revolution. After he was released from prison, a stream of events—including the course of revolution in Chile and Uruguay—led Debray to a creative, if not altogether persuasive, synthesis of Lenin-

ism and Guevarism. In examining this evolution the prominent features of Guevarism and Marxism-Leninism are brought
into view, as are their relationships to the anarchist and social
democratic traditions of political theory.

Acknowledgments

It was my good fortune to have received generous doses of aid and encouragement at every stage of this study. Special thanks is due Donald Clark Hodges for first turning my attention to the Debray controversy, for giving me the frequent benefit of his challenging ideas, and for demonstrating an ongoing interest in my work. Vincent V. Thursby, Gilbert Abcarian, and Ross Gandy read the manuscript during its difficult adolescent stage and made scores of helpful comments. I would like to express my thanks to Pierre Nagel for help in preparing the index. Most of all, I must thank my wife, Barbara, for the many hours she contributed to this effort as midwife of my thoughts, editorial assistant, and typist.

1

Leninizing Guevara:
Foquismo I

Jules Régis Debray was born in Paris on September 2, 1940,
into the well-to-do middle-class household of Georges and
Jannine Debray. Both parents were prominent attorneys,
future members of the Resistance, and politically to the right
of center. At age sixteen, Debray received the philosophy
prize in the annual Concours Général. In 1959 he graduated
first in his class from the prestigious Lycée Louis-le-Grand
and received the highest mark on the entrance exam to the
Ecole Normale Supérieure, a very exclusive university whose
distinguished graduates include Louis Pasteur, Jean Girau-
doux, and Jean-Paul Sartre.[1] That summer, his parents re-
warded Debray's scholastic achievements with a trip to the
United States; he returned, unexpectedly, by way of Cuba,
which had just been liberated from the Batista dictatorship.
At the Ecole Normale Debray studied with Louis Althusser,
the renowned Marxist philosopher and militant of the Parti
Communiste Français (PCF). It was Althusser who introduced young Debray to Marxism and to the PCF student
organization, to which he belonged until 1963.[2]

Debray has since written with considerable disenchantment about this period, depicting himself and the group of
students around Althusser as clever apologists of the Moscow
line, well schooled in Lenin, expert in construing the illogical
to appear logical, and approaching all criticism of the PCF

line with the haughty and unshakeable assurance that it would reflect the naive interpretations of "poor things" who were not privy to the secrets of the ideological codes in which the "oracles" of the PCF were wont to speak.[3] This alienation from reason to which Debray confesses was coupled with the students' complete isolation from the working class and from the practical, everyday work of the party. This arrangement was mutually agreeable to the party and the students, saving both from embarrassment and reinforcing the students in their one-sided obsession with theory. "For in fact," he admits,

> we were only really at ease with Marx's writings, and the complete works of Lenin whose twenty-odd volumes . . . lined our shelves. Those we read, underlined, quoted, reread. That precise and cumbersome style of Lenin's with its well-structured framework, its unemotional and meaningful sentences . . . established for us the norm for all possible political writing, and gave us a model to copy. We could barely conceive the possibility that other cultures, climates or temperatures might ever produce models of any other kind.[4]

The fact that Debray read Lenin under the tutorship of PCF theoreticians[5] and supported the easy-going reformist strategy of the PCF, which confined itself to the electoral road to power and to activities bearing the stamp of legality, indicates that his reading of Lenin was, on balance, a reformist one—one which played down Lenin's persistent revolutionism and emphasized his polemics against anarchism and other variants of ultraleftism. Referring to the most important of these works, *Left Wing Communism—An Infantile Disorder*, in which Lenin inveighs against the uncompromising stance of certain anarchist elements in the Third International,[6] Debray writes how he used it perversely to abuse the "woolly left-wing moralists who were always excited, always ready to fall in love with the first revolution they met, as long as it was good and far away. . . ."[7]

During his summer vacation in 1961 Debray escaped from this sterile academic milieu when he again visited Cuba and witnessed the great literacy drive which was being carried out that year. Two years later, after receiving his degree in philosophy, Debray returned to Latin America; this time he remained for one and one-half years, until the end of 1964. During this third visit he traveled in every country of the South American continent except Paraguay, making contact with numerous revolutionary organizations—most notably the Venezuelan rural guerrillas, the Armed Forces for National Liberation (FALN), at whose camp he stayed for several days. (The FALN was the armed wing of the Frente de Liberación Nacional [FLN], a front group composed of the pro-Moscow Communist party [PCV], the Revolutionary Left Movement [MIR], a group of young Fidelista dissidents who had split off from the ruling Acción Democrática [AD] party, and leftist dissidents from the Democratic Republican Union [URD].) There Debray obtained a long interview with Douglas Bravo, who was both a member of the PCV Politburo and commander of the FALN's Leonardo Chirinos Front in the state of Falcón. This meeting was recorded in Debray's first essay on the Latin American revolutionary movement, "Report from the Venezuelan Guerrilla."[8]

In Bravo, Debray encountered a new kind of Communist militant, one whose experience with political violence dated back to the struggle against the Jiménez dictatorship in 1957 and 1958.[9] Bravo led the forces within the PCV for a hard-line of armed struggle against the harshly anti-Communist, rightist regime of Rómulo Betancourt, a leader of AD. It was this meeting with the Venezuelan guerrillas that influenced most strongly the first phase of Debray's development as a theoretician of Latin American revolution. The synthesis of Castroism and Leninism that Bravo achieved in practice is attempted by Debray in theory in his long essay "Castroism: The Long March in Latin America," which appeared in *Les Temps Modernes* shortly after his return to France at the end of 1964.[10] It was followed by a companion essay, "Problems of Revolutionary Strategy in Latin America," published in March 1965.[11]

In a later effort to blunt the criticism directed at his works, Debray explains what he did not intend to accomplish in these essays:

As for the two articles on Latin America, they were written

3

long ago alongside literary studies which, in deference to the bourgeoisie, I valued more highly at the time. It is unnecessary to stress that these were simply review articles—rough sketches intended for European readers. All this light baggage [including *Revolution in the Revolution?*] has never pretended, nor could it pretend, to be a body of "theses," rigorously deduced one from the other, an established system or the final definition of a "blue-print." With regard to revolutionary action, such terminology is so frightening that it makes one smile.[12]

There is an element of distortion in this disclaimer (as Debray openly concedes in the last sentence) that invites an attempt to articulate what these essays, taken together or singly, can and do purport to be. They do not constitute a deductive system and they do not pretend to give a complete set of rules for revolutionary action. But they do constitute highly structured, rigorous arguments and a body of empirical theses (the listing of chains of "theses" is a favorite literary device of Althusser's) which purport to proscribe rationally certain forms of political behavior and to prescribe others.

A more accurate account of the limitations of these essays is found in an introductory passage added in 1967 to "Castroism: The Long March in Latin America." Having declared his intention to develop some general theses about "Castroism" or "Fidelism," Debray explains how they must be regarded logically:

As a revolutionary tactic Castroism has proved itself irreversibly: its proof is Cuba [this sentence is also in the original version]. But as Louis Althusser has reminded us recently, "Marxists know that no tactic is possible which does not rest on some strategy and no strategy which does not rest on some theory." The notes published here seek only to discuss a tactic and a strategy which is today on trial throughout Latin America—hence they are deliberately incomplete. It remains to be seen how Castroism as a tactic for insurrection and the seizure of power will adjust to the system of contradictions peculiar to each Latin American country, and in what way it will form a part of Marxist-Leninist theory.[13]

In other words, because ultimately the truth or falsity of his

4

theses can be established only when they become integrated into a larger theory, they must be regarded as extremely tentative.

The reminder by Althusser is nothing more than an elaboration or variation on Lenin's dictum, well known to all Marxists: "without revolutionary theory there can be no revolutionary movement."[14] What Debray does is to define an extant movement, called "Castroism," by its strategy and tactics alone, apart from any theory but in anticipation of it. He then assumes that in each country the movement will elicit its own conceptual foundations in the form of a Marxist-Leninist theory; the theory will rise up to meet the practice. The theory in question would presumably (because it is a Marxist-Leninist theory) meet Lenin's conditions for a revolutionary theory: "a strictly exact and objectively verifiable analysis of the relations of classes and of the concrete features peculiar to each historical situation."[15]

Superficially, this program appears to be not only reasonable but wholly Marxist-Leninist in inspiration. How reasonable it is will be discussed later. For the moment, it should be noted that however much Debray may pay his respects to Marxist-Leninist theory by positing it logically prior to tactics (and their implementation by a movement), he stands Lenin on his head methodologically by positing tactics and movement temporally prior to their full integration into the Marxist-Leninist theoretical tradition. For Lenin, theory was not only a necessary condition for strategy and tactics but a precondition. This is evident in the changing character of Lenin's writings between the onset of his revolutionary activity in 1893 and the middle of 1905, at which time "Bolshevism as a tendency took definite shape" with the formulation of a specific strategy for revolution.[16] Like Debray, Lenin found little of immediate value in the theorizing of his predecessors and contemporaries. Like Debray, it was necessary for him to make a beginning: Russian Marxism under Plekhanov's leadership (during the ten years prior to Lenin's entry into politics) had been disposed to defer to Karl Kautsky and the German Social Democratic party in all matters of economic and political theory.[17] But unlike Debray, Lenin began with

5

Marxist political economy and "class analysis," gradually shifting the center of his thinking to forms of organization and alliances. The same pattern can be found in the works of Mao Tse-tung.[18]

It is also worth noting that Lenin's 1905 strategy was conceived in the heat of a revolutionary struggle, its final formulation coming only after the largely spontaneous and unexpected revolutionism of the workers and peasants, and the timorousness of the liberal bourgeoisie, had revealed more clearly than was possible in peacetime the political forces alive in Russia. This strategy was updated in 1917, again in the midst of revolution, with the revision reflecting the lessons and insights of the previous twelve years of theoretical ferment (particularly with regard to the relationship of various classes to imperialism and the war) as well as the "amazingly unique situation" of dual power in which Russia found itself after the February-March revolution.[19] To use a hackneyed metaphor, the Bolshevik strategy was forged in the heat of revolution, with the theoretical pieces carefully prepared in the prerevolutionary period. As for tactics, or forms of struggle, Lenin avers that these

> . . . arise of themselves in the course of the movement. Absolutely hostile to all abstract formulas and to all doctrinaire recipes, Marxism demands an attentive attitude to the mass struggle in progress, which, as the movement develops, as the class-consciousness of the masses grows, as economic and political crises become acute, continually gives rise to new and more varied methods of defense and attack.[20]

When the tactics do arise out of the mass struggle, then

> Marxism demands an absolutely historical examination of the question of the forms of struggle. . . . To attempt to answer yes or no to the question whether any particular means of struggle should be used, without making a detailed examination of the concrete situation of the given movement at the given stage of its development, means completely to abandon the Marxist position.[21]

To extend our metaphor, tactics are to be selected and pulled from the fire and then shaped into more effective revolutionary tools. Under no circumstances is any tactic to be judged on any criterion other than its efficacy in making the existing flames burn hotter.

No student of the Cuban Revolution and of its long polemic with traditional Latin American Communist parties could be in doubt about the influences that motivated Debray's methodological denial of Leninism. First, in Cuba a revolution had triumphed in the virtual absence of Marxist theory, while the strategies devised by Communist theoreticians had failed consistently in Cuba and everywhere else in Latin America. Second, prior to the Cuban Revolution it had been possible to argue that Latin America was not ripe for revolution. Two factors frequently cited by Communists were, first, the persistence of feudal economic structures and the uneven, immature level of capitalist development and, second, the low level of political awareness among the masses, especially in the dominant rural sector. A third factor, less openly admitted but probably even more decisive, was geographical fatalism—the awful assurance that any anti-imperialist upsurge in the backyard of the North American colossus would be swiftly and mercilessly crushed. The seemingly reasonable conclusion to be drawn was that in Latin America even the bourgeois revolution lay in the distant future. Consequently, revolutionaries should focus on more or less routine, peaceful action ("mass struggle") in quest of limited, immediate political gains in support of Moscow's current soft line of peaceful transition to socialism[22] and seize the opportunity to undertake the time-consuming theoretical tasks that Leninists held as fundamental. The predominantly peasant revolution, however, which had progressed beyond capitalism towards socialism, in a country only ninety miles from U.S. shores, shattered this line of reasoning.

The rude assault by Cuban revolutionaries on "theorists" had not yet reached its high point when Debray was composing his first essays, but the denigration of theory was an early feature of Cuban revolutionary rhetoric. In a speech less than a month after the seizure of power, Che Guevara remarked sarcastically that "the example our Revolution has set in Latin America, and the teachings implied in it, have de-

7

stroyed all coffee-shop theories." Contrary to these theories, the strategic lessons of the Cuban Revolution were, first, that "a small group of determined men with the support of the people and without fear of death . . . can defeat a regular and disciplined army" and, second, that "agrarian revolutions can be made; we must struggle in the countryside, in the mountains, and from there take the revolution to the cities."[23] Che reformulated the same conclusions in an April 1959 interview and credited them with causing "the mere talk of the coffee houses to be dispersed like smoke." Che appealed to his Latin American brothers to absorb these lessons.[24] In a speech made at the First Congress of Latin American Youth on July 28, 1960, he described the development of the ideology of the Rebel Army as a series of lessons from experience, first with peasants and then with workers. The dominant theme of the speech was that the truths of Marxism are not understood solely through books; they can be rediscovered in the revolutionary process. This was the Cuban way, and he clearly recommended it to his audience whom he addressed somewhat sardonically as "studious youth of Latin America."[25] In an article dated October 8, 1960, Guevara repeated these arguments even more forcefully, openly acknowledging his divergence with Lenin:

> This is a unique Revolution which some people assert contradicts one of the most orthodox premises of the revolutionary movement expressed by Lenin: "Without a revolutionary theory, there is no revolutionary movement." It would be suitable to state that a revolutionary theory, as the expression of a social truth, is beyond any enunciation of it, that is to say, the revolution can be made if the historical realities are interpreted correctly and if the forces involved are utilized correctly, even if the theory is not known.[26]

In other words, Guevara believed that Lenin was wrong: Cuba had shown that there can be a revolutionary movement without a revolutionary theory. But to say that, Guevara notes, is not to say that theory cannot be useful, since "an adequate understanding of the theory simplifies the task and prevents us from falling into error as long as the theory corresponds to the reality."[27] Moreover, the lesson of Cuba was not that no theory is needed, for while the principal actors were not theoreticians, neither were they completely ignorant of social theory. What had been shown was that "with some theoretical knowledge as a base and a profound understanding of reality, it was possible to create a revolutionary theory with the passing of time."[28] In short, theory is not a precondition for revolutionary action; it is not a high priority item. It will evolve in time along with the practical conduct of the revolution.

In this article Guevara describes the Cubans as "practical revolutionaries."[29] In an interview a month later he is clearly pleased at being called a pragmatic revolutionary and reaches a new high point in his tribute to practice, explicitly endorsing the trial-and-error method:

> You use the phrase "pragmatic revolutionary," and I like it. . . . I am of a practical turn of mind. I speculate little and do not characterize myself as a theorist. I myself have been in Guatemala, Bolivia, and Mexico, and in actual study of conditions in various countries. You learn more than anything else how to avoid error. Where one really learns is in a revolutionary war; every minute teaches you more than a million volumes of books. You mature in the extraordinary university of experience.[30]

After late 1960 the antitheory position was taken up by Fidel Castro, whose polemics were, if anything, even more direct and biting than those of Guevara. While Che had questioned only the relative efficacy of theory, Fidel lambasted the theorists themselves. In his celebrated "Second Declaration of Havana," the now-famous slogan coined by Fidel—"the duty of every revolutionary is to make the revolution"—is directed primarily at the Latin American Communist parties as are his sarcastic comments that "the role of Job doesn't suit a revolutionary" and "it is not for revolutionaries to sit in the doorways of their houses waiting for the corpse of imperialism to pass by."[31] A few months after the October 1962 missile crisis, when relations with Moscow were at a low ebb, Castro slurred the pro-Moscow CPs with a thinly disguised reference to theorists who are expert at compiling data but don't do their duty, intimating that their behavior was a sign that they feared the revolution. This brought heated replies from the leaders of the Brazilian and Argentine CPs, but despite a month-long visit in the U.S.S.R. designed to smooth over differences, the traditional July 26 address in 1963 brought a fresh assault. Fidel taunted Latin American Communists for "gorging on theoretical knowledge" and "forgetting the practical realities of the revolution" and asserted that what had happened in Cuba could happen in exactly the same way in many other Latin American countries.[32]

Though the years 1964 and 1965 brought no new abuses of CP theorists, neither did they bring a retreat from the lines established earlier. The hostility that characterized Cuban relations with the Soviet Union in 1963 was followed by a two-year period of detente in which open recriminations ceased but the clash along theoretical lines continued unabated. On one side, Latin American and Soviet theorists defended the peaceful road and cautioned against initiating armed struggle in advance of a thorough study of local conditions; on the other, "pragmatic revolutionaries" insisted on the timeliness of immediate and generalized guerrilla action.

In his early essays Debray was already leaning strongly towards pragmatism in methodology as in doctrine. There is a self-conscious attempt, however, to root his new outlook in what is best in Leninism. In methodology, Debray puts tactics before class analysis without denying the fundamental role of the immediacy of theory. Debray's attitude is more moderate than Guevara's or Castro's, yet it remains unmistakably Guevarist. The same may be said of Debray's doctrine, as we shall now see.

Forms of Struggle

In the literature of Castroism-Guevarism, Debray's essay "Castroism: The Long March in Latin America" can be viewed as a successor to Guevara's 1960 work Guerrilla Warfare. The latter is a guerrilla leader's summary of the tactical and strategic lessons of the Cuban Revolution on the morning of its success; the former is an attempt by a nonparticipating but close and well-traveled observer to summarize those lessons for the next five years of armed struggle on the South American continent.

Debray's essay is written in defense and support of "Castroism" or "Fidelism," which Debray defines as a form of revolutionary nationalism and as a particular strategy and tactic for insurrection and the seizure of power. The strategy called for is protracted war against the oligarchies allied with U.S. imperialism; the distinctive tactic is that of the insurrectional guerrilla foco.

The premise that the development of the Latin American states requires insurrection is justified in Debray's later essay, "Problems of Revolutionary Strategy." The argument takes the form of a refutation of the reformist CP argument. According to the CP view as portrayed by Debray, the principal contradiction (or antagonism) in Latin America is not between socialism and capitalism but between developing national states and imperialism, which stifles independent development. This makes the national bourgeoisie a natural enemy of imperialism and a potential ally of the Socialist states. Given the decline of capitalism and the increasing power and prestige of socialism, the bourgeoisie of Latin America could be nudged out of the clutches of North American imperialism through the gradual substitution of disinterested Socialist developmental aid. The role of the Communist party was to mobilize the masses to apply popular pressure on the progressive wings of the bourgeoisie. For this it was necessary to perpetuate the party's legality. Given possibilities for peaceful struggle in a national-democratic state, armed struggle was counterproductive: it would throw the most progressive elements of the bourgeoisie into the hands of reaction; it would lead to the reversal of progressive land reforms and nationalization; and it would prompt the U.S. to demand that the Soviet embassy be shut down.

Debray has no quarrel with the premises of this reformist argument. He too considers the contradiction between nationalism and imperialism to be fundamental, and he does not doubt the existence of a sizeable, progressive, anti-imperialist national bourgeoisie. But because of the economic weakness of this class, Debray denies that independent development can be achieved under its leadership; he denies the viability of the progressive national-democratic state. In the absence of an infrastructure of economic power on which to base its rule, only two outcomes are possible: self-betrayal or betrayal by the armed forces—i.e., either the road of Mexico, Venezuela, and Bolivia or that of Brazil and Guatemala. If the bourgeois party uses the state to consolidate its own political power, exchanging public employment for party loyalty and thus creating a strata of state-supported parasites, then the regime becomes unable to carry out the promised reforms and the "revolution" is an empty one. If the bourgeois regime attempts to carry out its promises, it is driven by pressure from the U.S. ambassador, journalistic campaigns, and judicial obstacles to seek the support of the popular masses—thereby provoking a military coup. Either the bourgeois state allies itself with the preponderant forces of agrarian feudalism and foreign capital, or it is overthrown by the army in their control.[33]

Thus does Debray pour cold water on leftist strategies which aim to ride to power on the coattails of the national bourgeoisie. He is no less skeptical about strategies, such as the one pursued in Chile, which rely on the vote-getting strength of left-wing electoral blocs. In analyzing the failure of the Popular Action Front (FRAP) in the 1964 elections, Debray makes three basic criticisms: First, the electoral supremacy of the dominating classes was guaranteed from the start by their control over the media, their vote-buying power (thanks to the Alliance for Progress), and the conservative influence of the Church; second, under these conditions it was politically regressive to bank everything on the elections and suspend traditional activities in an effort to woo the middle classes; and third, in the face of proliferating military putsches, to harbor hopes for a durable and meaningful electoral victory was to underestimate imperialism.[34]

In "Castroism: The Long March in Latin America," insurrection is taken for granted. The need for a guerrilla *foco* is inferred in part by elimination of other common tactics, in part by direct consideration of its inherent virtue. Debray considers first the military coup or *golpe*—lightning action taken at the top by an isolated military minority. From an examination of the abundant post–World War II experience with this tactic, he concludes that no insurrection basing itself on the actions of the existing army can fulfill the promise of social revolution. The army is and will remain an army of the dominant classes, an instrument of the semicolonial state. In order to transform its armed might into a popular revolutionary power, one would have to transform the reactionary consciousness of a majority of its soldiers—their belief in military honor, caste solidarity, and unreasoning anticommunism—into a revolutionary consciousness. While cautioning against underestimating "the revolutionary or nationalist politicization of some sectors of the army and the aid they can give to the revolutionary movement," Debray asserts that "it is an absolute law that one cannot base a strategy, or even a tactical episode of the struggle, upon the decision of a regiment or a garrison."[35] Even less can one base an entire revolution on the army as a whole.

Another defect that dooms the coup d'état tactic to failure is that it is not based on and supported by the organization and revolutionary consciousness of the masses. Consequently, the new government is unable to elicit from them the sacrifices that national independence would demand; nor is it able to count on the people's support for far-reaching structural reforms of the economic, political, and military systems. Thus, Debray argues, reform-minded populist regimes, such as those of the late Vargas in Brazil and Perón in Argentina, were limited to "social reforms which seem revolutionary, but are in fact merely demagogic, since they are not based on any solid economic foundation." And for this thin fare they risk succumbing in turn to a coup d'état by the reactionary core of the army.[36] In sum, a nationalist military government is no better equipped for survival than is a nationalist democratic government.

On the opposite extreme from the military coup is the CP tactic of "pure mass action"—the nonmilitary action of organized and awakened masses, e.g., a general strike. Debray argues, in effect, that this tactic is plausible only to those who rule out insurrection beforehand or who close their eyes to its violent aspects.

> ... any general strike which does not pave the way for some kind of insurrectionary strike tends to be blunted or broken by violence. But an insurrectionary strike presupposes arms and an organization of militia and of leadership which are not going to rise up from the mass action by a miracle of spontaneity. . . .
>
> The entire apparatus of organized violence belongs to the enemy. The violence with which the people can strike back, "mass action," is easily dismantled by the enemy's organized violence. A military can overnight pulverize democratic parties, trade unions, the combativity of the masses and their hopes: the Brazilian example is valid for the whole continent.[37]

Furthermore, Debray deduces from the ill-fated ventures of peasants organized by the Trotskyists Hugo Blanco in Peru and Francisco Juliao in Brazil that action by the masses without armed support is as hopeless in the countryside as it is in the cities. Both of these peaceful peasant organizers raised the hopes and combativeness of peasants through successful mass struggle against the latifundist-dominated power structures, but the two were unable to defend the peasants against the forthcoming repression. The result was that the peasant unions in Peru and the peasant leagues in Brazil were smashed and the peasants slaughtered wholesale.[38]

Debray concludes his analysis of aberrant tactics by posing Lenin's question: "What, then, is to be done?"[39] The answer has been partly determined by his preceding discussion, which, as we have seen, makes the following general points: 1) the regular army is the main prop of the semicolonial state and must be destroyed; 2) it must be destroyed from without by an irregular revolutionary army; and 3) the masses of people must be made aware of the importance of this struggle. (Of these preconditions, the first and the third also played an important role in Lenin's insurrectional theory, as did the direct denial of the second.)

The need for a revolutionary army follows directly from, or is an integral part of, the central defining property of

Leninism—the insistence that all revolutionary strategies establish the unrestricted power of the victorious masses over the
vanquished few. According to Lenin, any strategy which aims
for less is less than revolutionary. Lenin's basic strategy called
for the creation of a dictatorship of the proletariat and the
whole peasantry over the tsar and his top bureaucrats—the
landed nobility and the upper bourgeoisie. This was to be
followed, in due time, by a dictatorship of the proletariat over
all remaining bourgeois elements in the city and countryside.
The task of each successive dictatorial stage was to abolish the
economic classes whose representatives it had supplanted and
excluded from power. Since, from the standpoint of those
adversely affected, such a government was the ultimate catastrophe, they would resist its imposition and, failing that, its
consolidation. The revolutionary army was needed to crush
this resistance. In general terms Lenin averred that "the revolutionary army is needed because great historical issues can be
resolved only by force."[40]

Thus, Debray and Lenin agree that a revolutionary army
is a necessary condition of revolution. Where they disagree
substantively is in their conceptions of the origins of this
army. For Debray, as we have seen, the Latin American
soldier is a soldier first and a member of a downtrodden class
second. Lenin viewed the Russian soldiers in the opposite
fashion; for him they were "peasants in soldiers' uniforms";
being a soldier was part of being a peasant.[41] Although he
found soldiers and sailors to "stand closest to the politically
least developed peasantry,"[42] the numerous mutinies and garrison revolts during the 1905-7 revolution left Lenin secure in
the conviction that the soldier could be expected to manifest
the discontent of the masses and could be won over to the
revolution. Until the revolution "assumes a mass character
and affects the troops," Lenin wrote in summing up the
Moscow uprising of December 1905, "there can be no question of serious struggle."[43] This does not mean that he saw no
role for partisan combat by rural guerrillas or barricade fighters,
only that these constituted a lower level of struggle. The
creation of the revolutionary army through the defection of
large segments of the regular army and their reconstitution

into a revolutionary army was the last and highest stage of the insurrectionary phase of the revolution: "outbreaks—demonstrations—streetfighting—units of a revolutionary army—such are the stages," Lenin wrote, "in the development of the popular uprising."[44]

The directive force of the uprising in all of its stages was mass struggle: political organization, agitation, and propaganda among all sectors of the people—first and foremost the industrial proletariat, then the peasantry in and out of uniform, and then the exploited marginal sectors. Under conditions of autocratic rule by tsarist officials and police, these activities had to be conducted underground, requiring an organization of dedicated people skilled in clandestine work. In answer to his own question, "What is to be done?" (also "Where to begin?"),[45] during 1902 when spontaneous outbreaks in the cities were occurring with increasing frequency, Lenin broke with the loose organizational structure of the West European Social-Democratic parties and their purely legal struggle to demand that Russian Social-Democrats adapt to Russian conditions. He argued that in a police state a party could be effective in educating the masses and leading them in advancing their struggle only if it was successful in penetrating the wall of silence thrown up around them by the secret police. This was possible only if the command posts of the party were in the hands of "people who are professionally engaged in revolutionary activity and who have been professionally trained in the art of combatting the political police."[46] Only a tight organization consisting of a narrow circle of professional revolutionaries—political guerrillas, as it were—commanding a wide network of local organizations which drew support from the broad masses of people could lead the people to the seizure of power. Only such a party could be an effective vanguard of the working class.

In offering his answer to the question "What is to be done?" Debray pays lip service to Lenin, saying that "Fidelism replies in terms which are similar to those of Lenin"[47] without bothering to concern himself with the more prominent differences. Instead, Debray turns for his answer to Guevara's three famous lessons of the Cuban Revolution, in the final form in which they appeared in the preface to *Guerrilla Warfare:*

1. The popular forces can win a war against the army.
2. It is not always necessary to wait until all the conditions for revolution are fulfilled—the insurrectionary centre can create them.
3. In under-developed America the terrain of armed struggle must basically be in the countryside.[48]

The first proposition is directed against the assumption of Latin American CPs, resting on Lenin's authority, that a regular army can be defeated only by mutinous units of that army —i.e., from within. Guevara inferred from the Cuban experience (as Debray had done from the broader Latin American experience) that the regular army could be disposed of by popular forces alone. What is needed, Guevara asserted in the second and third theses, is a rural insurrectional center or *foco*.

These last two theses likewise refute central tenets of Moscow-oriented communism which, in turn, are also founded on Lenin's writings. Debray wholeheartedly affirms the third thesis—the importance of the rural struggle—but seeks a compromise with Lenin on the matter of creating revolutionary conditions. In doing so Debray does not seem to be aware of his differences with Guevara. Taking up the third thesis first, for Lenin the principal terrain is wherever the advanced workers are to be found, which can only be the cities. Debray not only supports Guevara's denial of that tenet, he adds a great deal to Guevara's supporting argument.

Guevara argues that the urban guerrilla is situated on the most unfavorable ground because repressive forces are strongest in the cities. This severely limits the scope of urban activities. It limits the size of a fighting squad to four or five men; it forces guerrillas to operate only at night; and it compels them to operate close to their refuges.[49] Such an army, he argues, can never successfully engage the enemy army in frontal battle; it cannot, therefore, achieve the aim of the revolutionary army. Nor can the revolutionary leadership reside in the urban underground because of the ease with which a single betrayal could disrupt the continuity of command.[50] In the remote countryside, however, the repressive forces are weakest; the terrain favors the highly mobile guerrilla; the central command enjoys greater permanence; and the guerrilla force can swell into a popular army capable of defeating the regular one. Guevara also cites Castro's contention in the "Second Declaration of Havana" that the peasantry is the most exploited, oppressed, and numerous sector of the population. Though he refers to the putatively "more and more explosive nature of their struggle," Che notes that the peasantry is not a live political force but a dormant one. Its explosiveness is not actual, only potential. Nevertheless, he considers the population of the countryside a favorable factor, more so than the inhabitants of the cities.[51] The crucial element is the objectively miserable conditions of the peasants; the experience of this misery can be transformed by a guerrilla catalyst injected into their midst.

Guevara notes a final, important advantage of the countryside over the cities: in the countryside the guerrilla can begin the transformation of society and do it on two fronts. He begins to structure the future governmental apparatus,[52] and, more importantly, he is transformed through contact with the oppressed people and his near-total dependence upon them. He becomes at once their servant and their leader, and his identification with and feelings of duty toward them grow into a lifelong commitment. Che refers in several places to this process of inner change as "proletarianization."[53] The fact that this process did not reduce the antipathy felt for communism by a majority of Cubans in the Rebel Army does not seem to matter, indicating that proletarianization involves something other than indoctrination into the truths of Marxism. What Che valued highly, and what apparently constitutes the essence of the spiritual transformation in question, is the development of a spirit of self-sacrifice for the revolution. This is proletarianization.

Debray calls Che's arguments "irrefutable" and repeats them in large part, adding his own trenchant analysis using the 1962 Venezuelan urban guerrilla campaign to illustrate concretely the problems faced by the urban commando. Debray's major contribution to the discussion lies in his penetrating insights into the political liabilities of urban combat and his adroit delineation of the mechanisms by which they are engendered by military contingencies.[54] In order to minimize the enemy's vast technical and material superiority, the urban guerrilla has no choice about the time and place of combat; the time must be night and the place must be the sprawling slums that gird every Latin American city. To reduce the omnipresent danger of encirclement it is necessary to disperse. These factors plus the danger of betrayal lead to atomization—the near total isolation of combatants from each other, solitude, anonymity, and the confinement of human relationships to a minimum. These conditions carry an inherent threat of depoliticization on all levels—of the guerrilla, the guerrilla movement, and the people at large. Under conditions of extreme dispersion, control and coordination become difficult, so that the tactical initiative falls to the militant. The result is that the youth of many of the combatants, their lack of sophistication and prudence, the absence of group restraint, and the general oppressiveness of guerrilla life readily lead to a climate of voluntarism and subjectivism. The movement loses its political harmony, coherence, and thrust in a rash of single, anarchic heroic actions. Consequently, the political impact of these actions on the people is lost. Worse still, every action immediately comes to the attention of the press, which can be counted on to lay down a barrage of harmful propaganda that cannot be effectively countered; the necessity of dispersion denies the militants an economic and social base among the people and thus the possibility of winning popular support through social reforms; and finally, armed action robs the cities of their traditional political importance inasmuch as it makes legal mass action and audacious alliances impossible.[55] In short, it is Debray's view that the city suffers heavy political losses when it becomes the stage for armed action.

Debray also expands on Guevara's account of the positive features of the rural terrain. He repeats Guevara's assertion that the countryside is militarily the most vulnerable zone and that social contradictions are most explosive in the countryside,[56] while admitting that the dispersion, illiteracy, and mistrust of the peasantry pose great problems for the fledgling foco.[57] He also says a great deal about the proletarianization of the guerrillas; but his account, which appears to owe more to Venezuela than to Cuba, is markedly different from Guevara's. For Debray, proletarianization is a direct consequence of "the distinguishing characteristic of a rural guerrilla movement"—that is, the need for "constantly creating and re-creating its conditions of existence."[58] The rural guerrillas cannot seal themselves off from human contacts as the urban fighter must. The struggle for physical survival demands more or less immediate integration with the peasantry, socially and economically; the guerrilla must not only befriend the peasant, but must in the beginning do as the peasant does—clear forests, work the soil, harvest crops, hunt, and so forth. This produces "a profound transformation of men and their ideology"; it forces the guerrilla to proletarianize himself morally and ideologically. This transformation explains the ideological disparity that developed both in Cuba and in Venezuela between the urban and rural leaders—with the former tending to remain "petty bourgeois revolutionary intellectuals."[59] And it indicates that the naive illusions and romanticist and militarist tendencies fostered by city combat and city life are alien to the mountains.[60]

There is no disagreement between Debray and Guevara with respect to either the importance of the countryside or the ability of a popular force to defeat an army. The same cannot be said of Guevara's second thesis: "It is not necessary to wait until all the conditions for revolution are fulfilled; the insurrectionary centre can create them." Debray's Leninism is too strong to allow him to accept its full consequences. To understand this we must examine the conditions which Lenin believed were necessary for the successful preparation of an insurrection, i.e., conditions that constituted a "revolutionary situation." The conditions in question are "objective": favorable or unfavorable conditions which are beyond the power of a revolutionary organization to produce or prevent, be that organization ever so scientific, skillful, and energetic. For Lenin there were basically two favorable conditions, one involving the revolutionary class and the other involving the remaining classes. Lenin formulated these conditions on several occasions, each time changing the wording but not the essential thought. The formulation which is of special interest here is the one found in "Marxism and Insurrection" (published in 1917), since it is quoted approvingly by Debray.[61] In defending Bolshevism against accusations of Blanquism (a nineteenth-century anarchist doctrine), Lenin cites three important distinctions; the last two of these reappeared in subsequent definitions of a revolutionary situation.

> To be successful, insurrection must rely not upon conspiracy and not upon a party, but upon the advanced class. That is the first point. Insurrection must rely upon a revolutionary upsurge of the people. That is the second point. Insurrection must rely upon that turning point in the history of the growing revolution when the activity of the advanced ranks of the people is at its height, and when the vacillations in the ranks of the enemy and in the ranks of the weak, half-hearted and irresolute friends of the revolution are strongest. That is the third point. And these three conditions for raising the question of insurrection distinguish Marxism from Blanquism.[62]

Now, which of the conditions (the latter two "points") for a revolutionary situation can be created by an insurrectional foco? Che rejects both as they stand, dismissing the necessity for a "revolutionary upsurge" altogether and retaining only the bare bones of a reliance on the advanced class. Since the enemy is understood to be the ruling class and strong vacillations within it indicate an unstable government, a turning point at which this instability is maximized can be nothing short of a profound national political crisis. Che's rejection of this as a necessary precondition for declaring war against the Latin American oligarchies can be inferred by elimination. None of his conditions, objective or subjective, had to do with the behavior either of the ruling class or the intermediate "half-hearted and irresolute friends of the revolution," with political matters, or with turning points. The only condition necessary for revolution which Guevara cites is of an economic and sociological character:

HUNGER OF THE PEOPLE: weariness from being op-

> pressed, abused, and exploited to the maximum; weariness
> from selling one's labor day after day for fear of becoming a
> part of the great mass of unemployed—all so that the maxi-
> mum of profit is squeezed from each human body only to be
> squandered in the orgies of the owners of capital.[63]

Guevara believes this sole condition to be fully satisfied in
Latin America, especially in rural areas, coming as the inexorable product of underdevelopment; therefore anytime was a
good time to declare war on the oligarchy and U.S. imperialism. All that was necessary was willing and determined combatants—the subjective condition.[64]

The misery of the people was also cited by Lenin in an
earlier formulation, but misery was not an independent condition for him as it was for Guevara. It was only when the
suffering and want had "grown more acute than usual" and
had given rise to the "revolutionary upsurge of the masses,"
only when the multiplicity of personal crises had been con-
verted into mass action, when individual "weariness" had become organized anger—it was only then, Lenin contended,
that the time for insurrection had come.[65] In Guevara's estimation this transformation could be performed by the foco;
all essential political conditions (at least those Lenin considered essential) could be created by military means.

In Guerrilla Warfare Guevara added the proviso that a
guerrilla outbreak is not feasible against a government which
maintains the appearance of constitutional legality and against
which all legal forms of struggle have not been exhausted.[66]
But he dropped this qualification after the Latin American
democracies backed Cuba's expulsion from the Organization
of American States in 1962. Henceforth Guevara extended the
meaning of dictatorship to cover all Latin American states
whether autocratic or democratic, defining dictatorship as the
domination, direct or indirect, of one class over another.
Bourgeois legality was no longer treated as a barrier to the
initiation of armed struggle but as a hypocritical "disguise" for
violent or direct dictatorship which armed insurgency could
strip away.[67]

So much for political considerations at the national level.
At the local level, in the zone of guerrilla operations, Guevara

shows the same disregard for questions of timing. Here is how he describes the initiation of guerrilla action:

> Relatively small nuclei of individuals choose places [but not times] favorable for guerrilla warfare, . . . and there they begin to operate. . . . At the beginning the relative weakness of the guerrilla force is such that it must only wish to establish itself in the area in order to become acquainted with the environment, establishing connections with the populace and reinforcing the places that may possibly be converted into their support bases.[68]

Debray's position on the question of when to initiate armed action can be described as a compromise between Lenin's and Guevara's. It could also be described as an attempt to save Guevarism from Blanquism. But in attempting to Leninize the theory of the foco, Debray adds something alien to Guevara, which he erroneously calls the "Leninist theory of the weakest link."[69] According to Debray, this theory requires that a foco be "installed as a detonator at the least guarded position, and at the moment most favorable to the explosion."[70] According to Debray, the least guarded position is invariably somewhere in the countryside, either in the jungles or the mountains. Debray defines the most favorable moment in terms of Lenin's two conditions. In his illustration, however, of what these conditions signify when applied to guerrilla warfare in Latin America, Debray subscribes to them only in a diluted form. On a national level the most favorable moment did not mean that a catastrophic economic and political crisis was a necessary condition of revolution, only that a propitious political turn was a desirable condition. Such a turn could create a climate in which the launching of a rural guerrilla band "could set the psychological conditions for a mass insurrection . . . or, in any case, for a massive movement of solidarity."[71] Debray praises the Venezuelan guerrillas who created a new front in the Bachiller district in the state of Miranda for not going into action "haphazardly but at the exact moment (July 1964) when the Leoni regime had demonstrated by its actions that 'the broadly based Government' was betraying its promises and that repression was acquiring a new lease on life in the country."[72]

On the local level, Debray again urges careful timing, preceded by a period of on-the-spot preparation. During this period the group of future guerrillas cultivate support among the peasantry through good works (assisting in cultivation, caring for the sick, teaching reading, etc.), establish an underground politico-military infrastructure, familiarize themselves with the terrain and the social climate of the area, and otherwise educate themselves in the skills of their profession. Then, when "a sharp social conflict which is easily 'politicizeable'" comes along, the group can burst into action. By way of example, Debray notes approvingly, the Ejército Guerrillero del Pueblo (EGP) waited for the sugar harvest, at which time a latifundist-peasant confrontation could be expected over crops raised on unused land that had been expropriated by the peasants. The fact that the organization was exposed and crushed before it could move to the offensive did not dampen Debray's enthusiasm for its tactics.[73]

Debray defends the *foco* theory against charges of Blanquism by citing another characteristic which, in addition to the two outlined by Lenin, purportedly differentiates Leninism (and Castroism) from Blanquism. Debray argues that Blanquism aims to win over the masses after the seizure of power, after a lightning victory. The *foco*, in contrast, represents only the first stage of a protracted war which eventually involves the broad masses. The *foco*

> establishes itself at the most vulnerable zone of the national territory, and then slowly spreads like an oil patch, propagating itself in concentric ripples through the peasant masses, to the smaller towns, and finally to the capital. . . . From the towns themselves there comes a movement of mass strikes, demonstrations in defense of public liberties, fundraising campaigns, and an underground resistance movement galvanized by the exploits of the rural guerrilla.[74]

It is interesting to note this characteristic was not mentioned by Lenin as being among the many that distinguished Blanquism from Bolshevism, and it was not a feature of the October Revolution. The Russian seizure of state power required less than a day; and at the time the Bolshevik party did not have a formal majority among the troops or the politically active masses organized in soviets, though it had a near majority. Furthermore, by Lenin's own admission, the Bolsheviks had not yet achieved any significant success in mobilizing the largest sector of their own class constituency—the poor peasantry. This sector, composing about 65 percent of the rural population and consisting of the rural proletariat and semiproletariat, was under the domination of the Kulaks (capitalist farmers).[75] Thus, if Lenin's characterization of Blanquism brands Guevara and badly singes Debray, so does Debray's characterization brand Lenin, although this was surely unintentional.

In any case it is inaccurate to label Debray's version of the *foco* theory as the product of a conscious or unconscious ideological exercise, as a witting or unwitting adaptation of Guevarism to Marxism-Leninism. Debray's expressed aim of reevaluating *foquismo* in the light of five years of experimentation across a continent must be accepted as the basic aim of his essay; the wealth of data he marshals and the depth and independence of his subsequent analysis brook no doubt on this score. What cannot be accepted, or must be severely hemmed in by qualifications, is Debray's claim that "only Venezuela at present [late 1964] provides an example of the *foco* as Guevara conceives it."[76] It would be more accurate to say that Venezuela provided Debray with an example of the *foco* as he, Debray, conceived it.

Broadly speaking, the main distinction between the two theories is that Debray's is more concerned with the political problems of guerrilla warfare, especially those which have or appear to have serious military ramifications. The main body of Debray's first major essay, "Castroism: The Long March in Latin America," is taken up by eight lessons for future *focos*. With the possible exception of the fifth lesson, which concerns the viability of pure mass struggle in the countryside (which has already been discussed), and the first, which emphasizes the need for greater care in the selection and training of combatants, all of the "lessons of the long march" are, at bottom, political.

Forms of Organization

Of the remaining six lessons, four are concerned to a greater or lesser degree with the preparation of the *foco*, i.e., with organizational matters. The reason for this preoccupation is that, for Debray, organization holds the key to eliminating inadequate security, to diminishing the effectiveness of informers and infiltrators, the primary cause of the repeated failures of the "long march." Debray prefaces his itemized list of theses with two measures which would serve to reduce the susceptibility of *focos* to these dangers. The first is better political education of the organization's members. The second has already been mentioned in connection with the question of timing—thorough political preparation in the zone of operations. Three of the Venezuelan guerrilla fronts served as examples in this regard. The *foco* in the Bachiller district of the state of Miranda is cited for "installation of a social, economic and political infrastructure on the basis of existing conditions—long in advance of the launching of the guerrilla centre properly speaking."[77] The behavior of Bravo's front in the state of Falcón as reported by Debray in his 1963 "Report from the Venezuelan Guerrilla," also fits this description. Debray relates that Bravo's guerrillas had initiated their struggle in the countryside during a period in which they refused all contact with the enemy, using the opportunity to befriend the peasantry by working with them, building a library and a school, and reaping the political fruit of the government's massive repressive response. The duties of the guerrillas were as purely ideological and political as circumstances would allow.[78] One can infer from Debray's discussion of rural guerrilla warfare in his seventh thesis that a considerable amount of energy also went into the struggle for survival, which through the process of proletarianization prepared the guerrillas ideologically and physically. One learns also that this stage, in which all military conflict is avoided, is "the longest stage of the struggle."[79]

In his 1963 "Report" Debray quotes Bravo to the effect that this purely defensive stage had been completed and that the Falcón Front had moved on to the second stage, one of strategic defense and tactical offense.[80] But in "Problems of Revolutionary Strategy" Debray discloses that the exertions of the guerrillas both in Falcón and Lara continued to be predominantly political. Debray's description of these activities is worth reproducing at length, since they are the key inspirations for Debray's strictures on organization:

> Anyone who went to the rural fronts before the elections of 1964 [Debray is referring to the national elections which were, in fact, held December 1, 1963] could testify to the strategy of Douglas in Falcón and Urbina and Gabaldón in Lara: *guerrilla struggle in depth, taking political more than military forms* [emphasis added]. The patient creation of support cells among the peasants in each hamlet or village, the daily talk of propaganda and contacts, the cultivation of new lands in the jungle, the methodical campaign to achieve literacy among the combatants and peasants, the reinforcement of the organization to maintain contact with villages and towns, the supply and information networks—all this work of political organization culminated in the creation of a fixed revolutionary base with its school, its own jurisdiction and its own radio centre. . . .[81]

Debray generalizes the experience of the Venezuelans in his fourth thesis. "Politico-military organization cannot be postponed," he writes. "The work of setting it up cannot be left merely to the momentum of the struggle itself."[82] In supporting this thesis Debray makes the valuable point that the Cuban Revolution had created new difficulties for the guerrillas, so that "post-Cuban conditions . . . do not allow the same degree of empiricism as was possible for Cuba."[83] In "Problems of Revolutionary Strategy" he identifies two obstacles: first, antiguerrilla forces, well trained by the U.S. in the special school in Panama and by military missions; and second, greatly expanded political police forces, well trained in the art of infiltration and espionage. The creation of these repressive apparati was one important way in which the Cuban experience had "revolutionized" counterrevolution.[84] The revolutionary response, Debray says, must be better preparation, less empiricism, and fewer illusions about the self-sufficiency of guerrillas. To illustrate what kind of organization and organizational process the new conditions demand, Debray employs the metaphor of a pyramid. At the apex of the pyramid is the *foco*. Extending down from the mountainous, sparsely populated zone in which the *foco* furtively operates there must be a continuous network of contacts serving as conduits for arms, funds, supplies, and recruits from the towns. With regard to the construction of these organizations Debray writes:

> Certainly this pyramid will not appear in *advance* of the installation of the *foco*, or one would wait two thousand years to begin the revolution. The pyramidal formation is created from its two extremities, the base and the summit, and will never be anything other than the dialectical process of its destruction and reconstruction on a wider base.[85]

In other words, the establishment of a politico-military infrastructure does not precede the installation of the *foco*; it is the *foco's* first task, discharged during the long initial phase together with city-based coconspirators. After that, the organization is altered as required to accommodate the growth of the military unit.

The important question of leadership occupies the second, third, and sixth theses. Debray affirms the Leninist doctrine that armed struggle must be subordinated to the political direction of a national political organization. To illustrate the futility of revolutionary warfare without politics, he points to two examples: *La Violencia* in Colombia and the wave of Argentine terrorism from 1958 to 1960.[86] Debray's conception of the nature and role of the organization runs counter to that of Lenin and finds no support in Guevara. In one of the few direct appeals to the lessons of the Cuban Revolution Debray avers that

> *The presence of a vanguard party is not . . . an indispensable pre-condition for the launching of an armed struggle.*
> Here the Cuban revolution has established that *in the insurrectional phase of the revolution,* while it is indispensable to have some sort of organization and a firm political leadership (July 26th movement), it is possible to do without a vanguard Marxist-Leninist party of the working class. It should be emphasized that this applies only to the preparatory stage of the seizure. An anti-imperialist national liber-

ation struggle in a colonial or semi-colonial territory cannot be conducted under the banner of Marxism-Leninism or the leadership of the working class for obvious reasons: *de facto* "aristocratization" of the relatively small working class, the nationalist character of the anti-imperialist struggle. As for the party, this will be formed and its cadres will be selected through the natural processes of the liberation struggle, as happened in Cuba.[87]

In this passage Debray shunts aside the working class and its vanguard during the initial stage of the revolution. From the standpoint of traditional Marxism-Leninism, this is a major, if not the greatest, heresy. There are, to be sure, many examples of revolutionary war in which the proletariat played a negligible role. In China the Communist party found its base of support among the peasantry, while the proletariat was imprisoned in the cities by the Japanese and the Kuomintang. In Portuguese Guinea the proletariat played no role because, very simply, there was no black proletariat to speak of except a few dock workers and river-boat men; the bulk of the proletarians were Portuguese.[88]

But in these cases, and in similar situations in Vietnam, Mozambique, and Angola, the hub of the revolutionary political and military apparatus was still the local Communist party. And these parties were able to put a Socialist stamp on their respective wars of national liberation without an active proletariat. Debray wishes to go one step further and forego even the party during the early phases of the revolution. The Cuban Revolution had, after all, shown that this was possible.

There is a difficulty in interpreting Debray because he uses Cuba as an example. The main point he wants to make is that a vanguard party is unnecessary; the role of such a party is undermined by the guerrilla army. But then one must ask what the political composition of the support organization should be. If a Communist party is not needed, will a July 26th Movement still do? Is the example of Cuba still relevant in this regard? There are reasons for believing that Debray did not think so. First, the July 26th Movement did not openly challenge North American imperialism, which Debray in his characterization of the struggle as an "anti-imperialist national liberation struggle" singles out as the primary enemy. Furthermore, the July 26th Movement was a Latin American variant of social democracy known as *Aprismo*, which had been inspired by the writings of Victor Raúl Haya de la Torre, who was, in turn, inspired by Marx but not by Lenin. Since 1924, when Haya de la Torre formed the Alianza Popular Revolucionaria Americana (APRA), Aprista parties have played prominent roles in most Latin American countries. Before the Cuban Revolution their characteristic features were, defined negatively, antifeudalism, anticommunism and anti-imperialism. In concrete terms this meant agrarian reform without destroying private ownership of land, and it meant the reform of industry to break up foreign domination without, in principle, opposing foreign investment. It also meant expansion of the internal market under the aegis of the national bourgeoisie independent of foreign concerns. The promise of national development was the basis for the formation of mass parties, allying the national bourgeoisie as the senior partner with all sectors of the population. During the anti-Batista struggle, several of these parties expressed their solidarity with the July 26th Movement with shipments of arms. But after Cuba's turn to socialism, the anticommunism of the Social Democrats greatly outweighed their anti-imperialism. In Debray's words, they were first used by the Cuban Revolution and then unmasked by it, "expelled . . . from the revolutionary stage on which, until quite recently, they awakened popular illusions."[89] Thus, it is hardly credible that Debray would counsel that "firm political leadership" be entrusted to a Social Democratic party, even if, after Cuba, such a party could be found.

Finally, wherever else the question of a political organization attending the installation and development of a *foco* is raised, political leadership is assigned to an anti-imperialist front. One might wonder why Debray chose to overlook the Venezuelan guerrillas, whose FLN he surely considered more relevant under prevailing conditions than the July 26th Movement. The most likely answer is that the FLN was organized and dominated by a CP that had chosen to take the road of armed struggle. One cannot make the point that a Marxist-

Leninist party is not necessary by citing an example where such a party is present and is successful. Just as the July 26th Movement actually lies to the right of Debray's political guidelines, the FLN lies to the left; the former is not adequate, the latter is more than adequate. What Debray is arguing, in effect, is that the anti-imperialist struggle can accommodate a large measure of ideological diversity. The triumph of a proletarian ideology is, after all, assured by the sociology of guerrilla warfare and by the fact that the political and military leadership is united in the countryside. (The necessity of this union is the sixth lesson of the long march, which Debray infers from the experience of the Venezuelan FLN with divided leadership—political in the city and military in the countryside.) The anti-imperialist struggle can also do without the political experience of established Marxist-Leninist parties and their ties to the working classes. This experience is irrelevant to the armed struggle which the Communist parties have consistently shunned in theory and in practice. Debray has use only for their Fidelist-inspired youth, whom he calls "the most valuable element for the future."[90]

How this differs from Guevara is difficult to say because Guevara is characteristically silent on this, a political question. It is evident that Guevara's contempt for bourgeois parties was at least as great as Debray's[91] and that he had no illusions about winning over large numbers of Latin American Communists to the *foco* strategy. Whether Guevara attached any importance to the idea of anti-imperialist front groups, created by young leftist dissidents from a wide variety of quiescent parties, is difficult to determine, but one may infer from the fact that he remained mute on this point that he certainly did not consider such groups "indispensable," as Debray did. To go beyond this observation it will be necessary to address the question of alliances in class terms. On this level several differences between the two men are perceptible.

Alliances

Every revolutionary strategy depends on a conception, more or less clear, of the nature of a given revolution, which

31

determines the all-important questions of alliances and programs. It is here, more than anywhere else, that theory—defined as concrete historical analyses of class relations—is obligatory if a revolutionary strategy is to be Leninist. And it is here that the antitheoretical bias of Debray shows itself most clearly. In his last lesson of the long march he declares that

The present controversy over the revolutionary programme—bourgeois-democratic revolution or socialist revolution—poses a false problem and in fact inhibits engagement in the concrete struggle of a united anti-imperialist front.[92]

Debray labels this classical problem of Marxism-Leninism a "false" one based on two lessons of the Cuban experience: first, because the revolution is an "indefinite process, without 'separable phases,' which if it cannot start from socialist demands, inevitably leads to them"; and second, because "*the nub of the problem lies not in the initial programme of the revolution but in its ability to resolve in practice the problem of state power before the bourgeois-democratic stage, and not after.*" By "resolv[ing] in practice the problem of state power," Debray means destroying the existing state machinery, notably its armed agencies. "Cuba," he notes, "could only become a socialist state because at the moment of realizing its democratic national reforms, political power was already in the hands of the people."[93]

It is interesting to note that both of these statements could have also been made about the Russian Revolution.[94] It too was an "indefinite process," marked by much disagreement in Bolshevik ranks over its character, particularly after Lenin's arrival from exile in April 1917. And in this case also the people, through their soviets of Workers' and Soldiers' Deputies, held the balance of military power, thus making possible the Bolsheviks' quick seizure of power and their institution of a dictatorship of the proletariat.[95] But these circumstances did not lead Lenin to Debray's conclusion in his strategic recommendations to the Third International. The fact that a revolution was "uninterrupted" and at an intermediate stage characterized by a condition of "dual power" in which the bourgeoisie held the reins but did not have a monopoly on organized violence did not suggest to Lenin that future revolutionaries could dispense with revolutionary programs.

If the lesson of the Russian Revolution had been that such programs were indispensable instruments for victory, it was because the Bolshevik strategy was not primarily military, but a political one. It was a strategy that ultimately depended for its success on the "revolutionary upsurge of the masses" and on the ability of the Bolsheviks to channel this upsurge into an acceptance of their leadership by the masses. This process required indoctrination. The weapons of indoctrination were and are organization, agitation, and propaganda; their bullets were revolutionary programs and timely slogans. The potency of the ammunition depended on the depth of the understanding of the contradictions and harmonies between the various classes and strata of classes. Furthermore, since the primary constituency of the Bolsheviks—the industrial proletariat—constituted a small minority of the population, effectiveness demanded the conclusion of alliances with other, bourgeois classes. Different results would be achieved with different allies. For example, a victorious alliance of workers with the big industrial bourgeoisie against the tsar and feudal landlords- the Menshevik strategy—would produce a less radical outcome than the Bolshevik strategy of an alliance between the proletariat and the peasantry (i.e., both proletarians and lower bourgeois elements) against the tsarist state, feudal landlords, and the upper bourgeoisie. As Lenin pointed out, there are many different forms of bourgeois-democracy—from the regime of Kaiser Wilhelm to those in Switzerland and America. For this reason he demanded that a revolutionary program not only define itself in general terms as bourgeois-democratic or Socialist but more specifically in terms of the particular form of transitional regime to which it aspired, e.g., as a "revolutionary-democratic dictatorship of the proletariat and peasantry."[96] For Lenin, this was where the nub of the problem lay.

The fact that Debray finds the nub elsewhere reflects in part the fact that his strategy is tied, in the first instance, not to a mass upsurge but to a particular military tactic. This tactic obviates a certain amount of class analysis by directly and indirectly predetermining questions of alliance that would otherwise have to be resolved theoretically. The choice of rugged mountainous or jungle terrain, dictated by military considerations, determines who will be the initial ally of the "proletarians" in the *foco*. The residents of these inhospitable regions are generally *conuqueros* or *sitiantes*—peasant squatters who have been pushed into marginally productive areas by expanding estates.[97] From this base, if successful, the *foco* will encounter peons and agricultural workers in the valleys and plains and industrial workers in the towns. This fact of geography, plus the irreconcilable differences between the Fidelistas and parties of the working classes on questions of strategy, limits the role of the working class to a kind of urban fifth column which sees significant action only on the eve of the victory.

To a great extent Debray's disparagement of this theoretical question is simply an instance of his Guevarist predilection for pragmatism, for solving problems as they arise with "a profound knowledge of reality" and common sense. For Debray, it is enough to know that ultimately the revolution "will end by confronting American imperialism, and by developing into socialism"[98] and that first it will have to confront the regular army of the semicolonial state; what happens in between is anyone's guess. The important thing is to begin. The immediate task is, after all, clear without any further theoretical ado: install a *foco* and form an anti-imperialist front.[99]

Debray takes a strong position with respect to one ally not imposed upon the *foco* by geography: the national bourgeoisie. Even though such an alliance is much more difficult after Cuba, Debray argues that "to integrate any sizeable fraction of the national bourgeoisie in an anti-imperialist front . . . can and must be the prime objective."[100] Here, and in his conception of the nature of the Latin American revolution, Debray is strongly at odds with Guevara.

According to a reconstructed account of Guevara's first political article, "I Saw the Fall of Jacobo Arbenz," whatever confidence Guevara might have had in the sincerity of anti-imperialist sentiment among the nationalist bourgeoisie was shattered in Guatemala in 1954, when it refused to take up arms to defend its revolution. Fidel Castro's movement inspired confidence only because of its manifest commitment to armed struggle.[101] Guevara's postrevolutionary assessment of the national bourgeoisie goes through three major changes, none of which gives it any significant role. And the closest approximation to Debray's views is to be found in Guevara's first strategy corresponding to the first three years after Batista.

In his earliest pronouncements, Guevara's model for Latin American revolution was Cuba.[102] Before linking up with the Socialist camp, he argued that the revolution for which Latin America was ripe was the overthrow of dictatorships not the bourgeoisie.[103] In April 1958 Guevara described Fidel Castro and his movement in the same terms as Debray described Fidelism in 1965—as "national revolutionary."[104] In late January 1959 he declared, in language similar to Debray's description of Fidelism, that the Cuban Revolution did not "belong to any one group in particular."[105] A few months later Guevara denied that it was a "class revolution," declaring that its only enemies were those who opposed the land reform—latifundists and the reactionary bourgeoisie.[106] And in a still later interview, he identified the reactionary bourgeoisie not with the bourgeoisie in general, but with businessmen who derived their wealth from foreign investment and public corruption.[107] In all of these statements the national bourgeoisie received no mention as an ally of the Cuban Revolution, nor was it singled out as an enemy; it was simply ignored. On one occasion when Guevara did explicitly mention it, the national bourgeoisie was credited with helping the revolution to power but, at the same time, was classified as a nonrevolutionary force which had sought ways to decelerate the revolution.[108]

In 1962, however, a new attitude became evident. Coinciding with Cuba's rejection by the national bourgeois governments on the continent, Guevara began to express his own rejection of the national bourgeoisie. He did this indirectly, by forecasting the objective and outcome of the revolution as Socialist, and directly, by declaiming the weakness of the national bourgeoisie, its fear of revolution, and its alliance with American imperialism.[109] Nothing could be more inimical to

Debray's position than the following condemnation expressed in Guevara's 1963 article, "Guerrilla Warfare: A Method":

> The national bourgeoisies have joined American imperialism and must meet the same fate as the latter in each country. Even in cases where there are pacts or common contradictions shared by the national bourgeoisie and other imperialisms with American imperialism, this occurs within the framework of a fundamental struggle, which will, in the course of its development, necessarily encompass all the exploited and all the exploiters.[110]

In short, the antagonism between the national bourgeoisie and imperialism had become irrelevant to the contradiction between exploiters and exploited. Guevara's final strategy, which he attempted to implement first in Africa and then in Bolivia, defined this conflict in continental terms, with all exploiting classes joining in open alliance with the imperialist United States—which would be forced, as in Vietnam, to intervene—to crush the revolutionary wave unleashed by *focos* in one country after another. In the most unmistakable terms, this strategy declared the choice to be "either a socialist revolution or a make-believe revolution."[111]

Clearly, Debray was lagging behind Guevara in his conception of class conflict and the ideology of revolution in Latin America. There is also room for suspicion that Debray was more captivated by the Cuban model than Guevara, despite his repeated protestation that Fidelism is opposed to all revolutionary models "whether Soviet, Chinese, or even Cuban."[112] However much Debray may have tried to renew the *foco* theory, his vision of the course of the revolution remains solidly Cuban. His adherence to this model extends even to the genesis of the movement. His hopes for a renascence of Fidelism are pinned on well-known, honest, and charismatic leaders who, like Fidel, will have captured the imagination of the masses before going into the mountains. Even more striking is the firmness of his belief that the new revolutionaries must or will stumble upon socialism as Castro did. "Fidel," he notes,

> read Marti before reading Lenin; a Venezuelan revolutionary

nationalist will have read the correspondence of Bolivar before *The State and Revolution*, a Colombian the constitutional projects of Nariño, an Ecuadorian Montalvo, and a
Peruvian will have read Mariátegui and reflected upon
Tupac-Amaru.[113]

What Debray forgets is that pragmatism is no guarantee
against doctrinairism and schematism; or, to put it another
way, it is as easy to make a cult of pragmatism as of Marxism-
Leninism. To recommend the same measure of trial and error,
learning from experience, and acting out of practical necessity,
to insist that others seek alliances where Castro sought them
and stumble where he stumbled is to impose a new model
distinguished from the others not by its flexibility but by its
primitiveness.

We have, however, no cause for complaint, for we were
told to expect primitiveness at the outset. There is a limit to
the structure that a few blocks of theory will support. But we
may well question whether Debray has successfully joined the
existing blocks to the superstructure. At every stage of his
attempt to synthesize Lenin and Guevara, Debray is repulsed
by one or the other; at times he is repulsed by both, as on the
question of alliances. He attempts to show that what he calls
Castroism is merely Leninism adapted to Latin American conditions. Instead, however, he develops a shaky Leninization
of Guevara. He affirms the Leninist methodology, which insists that strategy and tactics be based on class analysis (a dynamic theory of the power relations between principal socio-
economic groups), but he ignores class analysis in his essays.
He dilutes the objective conditions required by Lenin for beginning an insurrection in order to accommodate Guevara's
foco theory, which accents subjective conditions. He discards
the Leninist party and, unlike Guevara, retains the liberation
front. And as opposed to Guevara and, even more strongly, to
Lenin, Debray offers the command posts of the revolutionary
movement to non-Socialist takers.

Clearly, if Guevara and the Cuban Revolution are to be
integrated into the Marxist-Leninist mainstream, a better way
must be found. By now it should come as no surprise that the
"better" way passes through the tragedy and carnage of war.

2

The Revolutionary Ferment, 1964-67

Debray remained in France throughout 1965. While there, he resumed his studies, receiving a diploma in July 1965 as agrégé in philosophy; and for a few months he taught at the University of Nancy. In January 1966 he returned to Cuba as professor of the history of philosophy at the University of Havana, under the terms of a Franco-Cuban technical and cultural cooperation agreement.[1]

It is fitting that Debray should have come to Havana in time to attend the Tricontinental Conference, for this conference signaled the beginning of a new phase in Cuban relations with Latin American communism. More specifically, it sounded the tocsin for Castro's renewed offensive to wrest the hegemony of the Latin American revolutionary movement from its traditional claimants, an offensive in which Debray's *Revolution in the Revolution?* was to figure prominently.

The Cuban Offensive in Foreign Policy

Castro's problems with the left wing of Latin American Marxism had already begun in 1965. Prior to the secret conference of Latin American CPs (held in Havana during December 1964 and January 1965) at which a shaky truce had been reached with the pro-Moscow parties, Castro had largely ignored the Maoist and Trotskyist tendencies, supporting neither them

39

nor Moscow in their heated polemics. This informal truce was broken for several reasons. On the one hand the Chinese, for whom the threat of Soviet revisionism to Third World revolution was as dangerous as U.S. imperialism, took the dimmest possible view of the secret Havana Conference. There is a report that shortly thereafter the Cuban Carlos Rafael Rodríguez led a group of Latin American Communists to placate the Chinese, only to be treated to one of Mao Tse-tung's rare exhibitions of anger. Mao accused Castro of caving in to revisionism because of his fear of imperialism and the atomic bomb.[2]

Castro, on the other hand, had little understanding of or sympathy with the Sino-Soviet quarrel. Cuba sided with North Vietnam, which the U.S. had commenced bombing in February 1965, in deploring the Sino-Soviet split as division in the face of an enemy aggressor. In a speech delivered March 13, 1965, Castro called for an end to the "byzantine battle" which only served to encourage imperialism to more violent aggression against Vietnam and other small countries. While maintaining an air of neutrality in the face of the split, he denounced any attempt (presumably by Maoists) to plant "the apple of discord" in Cuba or to lecture Cuba on revolution.[3] Whatever the merits of the Chinese criticism of Soviet policy (which, in denouncing peaceful transition and advocating armed struggle, had much in common with the Cuban line) might be in other parts of the world, Castro seems to have been warning that in Cuba it was superfluous; Cuba could guard its own left flank.

Because Castro regarded the Chinese and Trotskyist splinters as equally superfluous on the Latin American continent, he was not opposed to joining the pro-Moscow CPs in their efforts to combat factionalism, as had been resolved at the Havana Conference. His low opinion of these factions was undoubtedly reinforced by their conduct in the abortive Peruvian guerrilla campaigns of 1965. While Fidelistas fought and died, Trotskyists and Maoists remained on the sidelines denouncing the guerrillas as adventurers.[4] Worse still, in mid 1964, a Trotskyist faction led by J. Posadas had managed to effect an ideological capture of the Guatemalan guerrillas under Yon Sosa when the latter lost patience with the vacillations and lukewarm support of the Guatemalan Communist party. In April 1965 when the Bolivian CP split into a Maoist faction under Oscar Zamora and a pro-Soviet faction under Mario Monje, Castro supported the latter. Other Maoist groups also began to complain of Cuban hostility.[5] As 1965 wore on, this new attitude by Castro provoked increasing criticism from Maoist and Trotskyist circles.

On January 2, 1966, on the eve of the Tricontinental Conference, Castro counterattacked, sharply criticizing the Chinese for cutting back on their rice shipments to Cuba.[6] The conference saw the clash between Cuba and the traditional Left reach a new level of vituperation. Fidel's closing speech included a sensational attack on Trotskyism in general and the Posadas faction in particular, as well as a transparent rebuke of those who criticize theorists "and at the same time set themselves to theorizing."[7] Less than a month later Castro again denounced China's commercial policy and charged political meddling in the Cuban civil service and armed forces.[8] Criticisms by the pro-Peking Belgian and Ceylonese CPs elicited yet another diatribe, remarkable for its abusiveness. Fidel labeled his Maoist critics "paper revolutionaries" and added gratuitous insults against the Chinese government and Mao Tse tung, whom he suggested had succumbed to senility. In addition, Castro hotly disputed Chinese claims to a great victory at the Tricontinental, declaring that "the victory of this conference was a victory of the revolutionary movements . . . not a victory of the powerful, not a victory of the 'great ones' but of the 'small ones'. . . ."[9]

The "small" movements which Castro felt had won the greatest victories at the Tricontinental were those in Cuba, Vietnam, and North Korea. All gained key positions in the executive secretariat of the new tricontinental organization (Organization of Solidarity of the Peoples of Africa, Asia, and Latin America—OSPAAAL), which became the concrete organizational expression of their mutual desire for more independence from the "great ones." Osmani Cienfuegos, a Cuban, became OSPAAAL's secretary-general and Havana became its home. By contrast, China and the Soviet Union were excluded from the secretariat. By its participation in a conference whose leitmotif was the advocacy of armed struggle, the Soviet Union had outwardly given its approval to a degree of radicalism that jeopardized its efforts toward rapprochement with Western governments.[10] Nor was this the extent of the Cuban victory. Immediately after the close of the conference, Fidel gathered together the Latin American delegates at the instigation of Salvador Allende and organized, against the resistance of wary CP leaders, the Organization of Latin American Solidarity (OLAS). The design of the new organization was to coordinate the struggle in Latin America along Cuban lines.[11]

A controversy over the meaning of the Tricontinental Conference was the most immediate sign of a widening gulf in relations between Cuba and the Soviet camp. Under pressure from Latin American governments incensed over the conference's interventionist implications, Soviet diplomacy began quietly to disavow its connections with the more controversial aspects and to minimize the significance of the conference. The Cubans vigorously denounced this effort. This was not the only controversy. The Soviets complained about Cuba's unorthodox and radical domestic doctrine of the "parallel construction of socialism and communism."[12] Castro expressed his growing displeasure with Moscow by resuming his duel with the official theorists of Marxism-Leninism. In his 1966 May Day speech he decried the "stagnation" and "rot" that characterized the thinking of those who opposed Cuba's bold domestic initiatives.[13] One month later, Fidel's metaphor was picked up by the Cuban delegate to the World Federation of Democratic Youth in Sofia, Roberto Ogando, who concluded his criticism of that conference's meager accomplishments with a lecture on the necessity of avoiding "thinking which becomes putrid."[14] In Castro's speech there was also a disparaging reference to "readers of manuals."[15] The manuals which he mocked here and again, even more bitingly, in a speech on August 29 were Marxist theoretical textbooks published primarily by the U.S.S.R.'s Academy of Science. These texts were mandatory in the cadre training schools of pro-Moscow CPs and had been used in the Cuban Communist party's Schools of Revolutionary Instruction

(EIR). The manuals soon became objects of ridicule and the focus of Cuba's diatribes against Soviet theory. For the last half of 1966 a polemic against the manuals raged in the pages of the EIR journal, *Teoría y Practica*, and in *El Caimán Barbudo*, a publication founded by students of the Philosophy Institute of Havana University who were dissatisfied with the Soviet-oriented interpretation of Marxism.[16]

The most significant bone of contention, however, emerged on the political front. Here the peaceful orientation of the Soviet camp and Cuba's advocacy of armed struggle put the two at odds on the questions of aid to Vietnam, relations with reformism in general and the Chilean brand of Christian Democracy (CD) in particular, and attitudes towards the guerrilla movements. In short, Cuba censured the Soviet Union for not doing enough for Vietnam, for making friendly overtures to the Frei regime in Chile instead of flatly opposing it, and for giving only half-hearted support to the guerrillas. The latter two issues lay at the heart of the two countries' irreconcilable views.

The verbal exchange between the Frei regime and the Cuban government began shortly after the Tricontinental Conference, with Fidel doing everything in his power to prevent the Soviet Union and the Communist party of Chile (PCCh) from lending credence to the boastful Christian Democratic claim that it represented an alternative to the Cuban road, one which could bring the masses to revolution without taking away traditional liberties. In his July 26 speech Fidel expressed his sharp disagreement with Moscow for its technical and economic aid to the Frei regime, adding a sharp slap at the PCCh.

> . . . It is our duty to warn the Socialist countries against Frei's flirtation, since the prostitute will not become a virtuous woman simply because her flirtation elicits a response. Let Frei first show that he does not obey the dictates of Yankee imperialism. . . .
>
> Lamentably there are times when countries of the Socialist camp are mistaken; but one should not blame them for their mistakes so much as the pseudo-revolutionaries who advise them and counsel them in a mistaken manner.[17]

In the same speech Castro rated the "pseudo-revolutionaries" as the "most important allies of imperialism" and pointedly insulted a PCCh leader and member of the Chilean parliament who was present. When the latter protested and left Cuba in a huff, Castro added injury to insult by making a point of further ridiculing him in his August 29 speech.[18]

The Guerrillas Fight Tradition

However irritated the Chileans were, the Cubans were equally galled (if not more so) by the attitude of the Soviet Union and the behavior of its affiliated parties in those countries where guerrilla warfare was being waged. Just as Cuba's support for the Moscow line was strongest immediately after the secret Havana Conference, so was the Soviet support for armed struggle. The conference had urged "active support" for the combatants of Venezuela, Colombia, Guatemala, Honduras, Paraguay, and Haiti.[19] On January 14 *Pravda* carried a rare front-page editorial endorsing the armed struggle in Venezuela, Guatemala, and other countries.[20] In those two countries, as well as in Colombia, detachments of rural guerrillas were actively fighting under the auspices of the Moscow-oriented CPs. In late March 1965, the Venezuelan government's interception of two Communist couriers who were bringing into the country $330,000 ostensibly earmarked for the FALN guerrillas furnished proof that Moscow's commitment was more than verbal. It was not, however, as unequivocal and unqualified as Cuba would have liked. The dominant themes of Soviet foreign policy remained peaceful coexistence and a peaceful transition to socialism; only where tactics of peaceful mass struggle were made impossible by government repression could armed struggle be sanctioned. Anywhere else, the support of violence would only jeopardize the Soviet bloc's painstaking efforts to end its diplomatic and economic isolation.

The pacifist inclinations of Latin American communism faithfully reflected these foreign policy imperatives, as well as a certain sociological characteristic of the local parties: to a greater or lesser extent, party leadership tended to be in the hands of elderly veterans of decades of Popular Frontism and peaceful transition. In many cases the activity of these venerable old men dated back to the founding of their parties during the 1920s in the days of the Comintern. The Cuban Revolution, with its turn toward socialism and its alignment with the Soviet Union, came as a mixed blessing. On the one hand, it brought the Latin American CPs greater influence in the political life of their respective countries and greater popular prestige, especially among youthful admirers of Castro. As the young swelled party ranks, however, their pressure on the leaders to imitate Cuba increased. Failure to respond to this pressure, in word or deed, carried the danger of costing the CPs more in factional splintering than they had gained in the heyday of the Cuban celebration. Thus, the tension between Russia and Cuba was reproduced in microcosm within each party as a more or less pronounced generation gap.[21]

If the impulse to armed action came from Castro and Guevara, the justification for it continued to be borrowed from Lenin and from Soviet doctrine. That is to say, the "old guard" generally retained ideological hegemony within the parties. Guerrilla warfare was not hailed as a categorical imperative or as the touchstone of commitment to revolution or as a ploy to attract the visible intervention of the U.S. Rather, it was included in the revolutionary armory as but one of the many forms of mass struggle which a vanguard party might find useful, along with other tactics, under certain circumstances. This flexible policy had been formulated by Lenin late in 1906 in the face of heated opposition to guerrilla warfare as a tactic; sixty years later the same formula was invoked in Latin America to counter heated advocacy of this same tactic to the neglect of all others.

Lenin had conceded that "the party of the proletariat can never regard guerrilla warfare as the only or even the chief method of struggle," but he had defended it as "natural and inevitable" when an insurrection had reached its highest stage, that of civil war:

> It is absolutely natural and inevitable that the uprising should assume the higher and more complex form of a prolonged civil war embracing the whole country, i.e., an armed

45

struggle between two sections of the people. Such a war cannot be conceived otherwise than as a series of a few big en-
gagements at comparatively long intervals and a large number
of small encounters [guerrilla warfare] during these intervals.[22]

In short, Lenin defended guerrilla action as a "filler" for the
lulls in a sustained popular uprising. In Venezuela, Guatemala, and Colombia the Communist parties were propelled
into guerrilla warfare under far less propitious circumstances.
In Venezuela, something approaching a revolutionary situation was thought to be at hand, and armed struggle was officially viewed as a means of bringing on a crisis and a truly
revolutionary situation, but nothing of the sort was or could
be claimed for Guatemala and Colombia.[23] There the rationale for resorting to arms was self-defense against official repression.

Undoubtedly this breach of Leninist orthodoxy affords a
measure of the strength of the Cuban impulse, but at the
same time it lessened the CPs' commitment to guerrilla struggle. The absence of a revolutionary situation, which a decade
earlier would have constituted grounds for avoiding armed
confrontation altogether, could now be used as grounds for
limiting its scope or for abandoning it when the preferred
peaceful road was again opened up by a change in government.
In fact, it was used to hamstring armed struggle in the three
countries Debray chose as a basis for launching his polemic in
Revolution in the Revolution?

Colombia

In Colombia the Tenth Congress of the Communist party
(PCC), meeting in January 1966, admitted in an offhand
way that it had undertaken guerrilla warfare as a secondary
form of struggle before a revolutionary situation could be said
to exist.[24] The decision to fight had been forced on it by an
aggressive government determined to wipe out the independent peasant republics in the Andes, which had been organized
during *La Violencia* (1948-57) and had resisted disbandment
thereafter. The most famous of these, the republic of Marquetalia, under the leadership of Manuel Marulanda, was
crushed in mid 1964. When all the republics had been up-

rooted, the partisans regrouped as mobile guerrilla forces under the rubric of the Southern Guerrilla Blocs. At the Tenth Party Congress the PCC agreed to unify its units through the formation of the Colombian Revolutionary Armed Forces (FARC).[25] The congress emphasized, however, that guerrilla warfare is only another form of mass struggle (if "one of the highest"), which should be combined with other forms and assigned a role, preeminent or subordinate, as the immediate situation demanded.[26] In June 1966, the secretary-general of the PCC, Gilberto Vierra, stated flatly that there was not as yet a revolutionary situation in Colombia, adding as a corollary that the guerrilla struggle was not yet the principal form of struggle.[27] The party continued to focus its attention on political activity to awaken and mobilize the urban masses.

This was in marked contrast to the pronouncements of an independent Guevarist guerrilla *foco*, the National Liberation Army (ELN), which had begun operations in Colombia in 1965 under the leadership of Fabio Vásquez (and, for a few short months before his death in February 1966, had included the revolutionary priest Fr. Camilo Torres). The ELN position was that armed struggle was the principal form of struggle which all other tactics must complement. Consistent with Guevarist principles, the ELN viewed guerrilla warfare not as a transitory expedient but as the first stage in an implacable insurrectionary conflict, limited only by the offensive capabilities of the guerrillas. The gulf that separated the PCC and the Soviet Union from the ELN and Cuba was sharply accentuated on this score when the Soviet Union moved to reestablish diplomatic, cultural, and economic ties with the Colombian government, since this had the effect of limiting the scope of FARC guerrilla activity.[28] Another closely related issue that served to divide the ELN and FARC was the role of the party. Given ELN priorities, the logical focus for the revolutionary command was the countryside; given PCC priorities, only the party could lead. It was this difference which the PCC singled out as preventing the unification of the two guerrilla movements and as obliging it to rebuff repeated ELN attempts to bring such a unification about.

Guatemala

The conduct of the Guatemalan Workers' party (PGT) had much in common with that of the Colombian party although conditions were very different. The guerrillas to whom the PGT was organizationally tied had been united independently, originating from an abortive barracks uprising launched on November 13, 1960, in protest over the use of Guatemala as a U.S. training and staging ground for the Bay of Pigs invasion. The defeated conspirators had regrouped in exile under the leadership of their former officers, among them Marco Antonio Yon Sosa and Luis Auguste Turcios Lima, forming the Alejandro de Leon 13th of November Revolutionary Movement (MR-13). In September 1962 a delegation of the MR-13 went to Cuba, where they met with Jacobo Arbenz, the reformer who had been deposed from the presidency in 1954 by a CIA mercenary army. Arbenz greeted them emotionally and declared his willingness to take up the sword and join them. The guerrillas also met with Che Guevara. When they returned to Guatemala in December 1962, "they no longer thought in terms of coups d'état but of revolutions, they no longer thought about pronouncements but about guerrilla warfare."[29]

The guerrillas' search for a political base ended with the PGT, which, because of its short history, had a relatively youthful membership and leadership. In May 1961 the Central Committee had defined armed struggle as the principal revolutionary tactic and, with the formation of military commissions, began to move toward military involvement. In March and April 1962 the political order of Guatemala was shaken by a semi-insurrectionary, mass uprising of students and workers to oust the right-wing President Ydígoras. The MR-13 did much to spark these demonstrations with its first burst of guerrilla fighting during the previous two months. During the heat of the uprising the PGT launched a poorly prepared column of thirty guerrillas in the mountains of Baja Verapaz; the band was promptly and unceremoniously annihilated.[30] Clearly the time had come to join forces. In December 1962 the MR-13 and PGT jointly created the Rebel

Armed Forces (FAR), which, in accordance with the traditional Marxist-Leninist model, assigned military leadership to the MR-13 while the PGT assumed full political leadership within the zones of operation.

It was not long before the FAR proved to be an uneasy marriage of incompatible conceptions of guerrilla warfare. The PGT did not share the Guevarist view that guerrilla war was the principal aspect of a protracted struggle. The PGT saw guerrillas as pawns in a larger political game. The party continued to search for political formulas to regain legal status and a share in the government. The guerrilla front was just so much more capital for any future joint venture. In the 1964 elections the party pinned its hopes on José Arévalo, but a preventive coup by Col. Peralta Azurdío wiped the election slate clean. The Communists thereupon joined with pro-Arévalo groups and formed a United Resistance Front (FUR) to direct the struggle against the new dictatorship. The only role foreseen for the FAR was to exert political pressure on democratically minded army elements to restore the constitution.[31]

All of this proved too much for Yon Sosa, whose disenchantment with the PGT dated from the party's support of a pro-U.S. candidate (Jorge Toriello) over the more progressive Villagrán Kramer in the 1962 Guatemala City mayoralty elections.[32] In June 1964 Yon Sosa and one of the two functioning guerrilla fronts defected to Trotskyism, specifically to Posadas' Latin American Bureau in Buenos Aires; Yon Sosa's group retained the name MR-13. The Edgar Ibarra Guerrilla Front (FGEI) under Turcios Lima remained loyal to the PGT but, together with the Communist youth organization, began to demand a greater voice. In January 1965 the party, faced with the prospect of a massive revolt of Fidelista dissidents rallying around the FGEI, agreed to reorganize. A Provisional Center of Revolutionary Leadership (CPDR) was created to provide a single politico-military command and an unambiguous revolutionary war orientation. In March a new FAR was formed (without the MR-13) which endorsed the line of protracted war. In May the Central Committee ratified "Ten Theses of Organization" which called for extraordinary organizational changes amounting to the full integration of the PGT into the armed movement and the integration of the youth organization into the party.[33]

These sweeping changes did not, however, leave the Fidelistas in control. The leadership maintained a centrist position between the FGEI and conservative elements who opposed the changes.[34] And, as soon became clear, the party's priorities remained unaltered. An October 1965 Central Committee resolution reveals the tentative nature of the PGT's commitment to armed struggle:

> Since opportunities for political struggle by peaceful and legal means are lacking, the revolutionary forces have taken the only road left to our people. They have resolved to oppose revolutionary to counter-revolutionary violence. . . . In present conditions, the road of our revolution does not lead through elections.[35]

Within three months after making this statement the PGT began scheming to reroute the revolution through elections once more. When Peralta decided to attempt to legitimate his regime by decreeing elections for March 1966, the PGT entered into secret negotiations with the candidate of the liberal opposition party, Méndez Montenegro. The PGT offered its support, its services as an intermediary in promoting the sale of coffee to Socialist countries, and the demobilization of its men in arms in exchange for the legalization of its organizations and the legal possibility of coming to power in the future. The final decision to back Méndez was taken in January 1966 while Turcios Lima and Fidel Castro were lambasting the Communists' traditional Trotskyist foes at the Tricontinental Conference.[36] Turcios Lima came out firmly against participation in the elections, but in vain.[37] A new PGT-FAR crisis was in the making.

The crisis sharpened when the PGT's election strategy proved to be a great debacle. That strategy was predicated on the mistaken belief that antagonisms within the ruling circles between advocates of democratization and of continued military dictatorship exceeded the differences between the Left and moderate democrats. The opposite proved to be the case.

Méndez allowed himself to be blackmailed by the military into making a secret deal that canceled out the one made with the FAR and gave the military a free hand in dealing with the guerrillas after the elections.[38] In the meantime the army and Méndez collaborated in a masquerade of conciliation. The army withdrew from the guerrilla zones while Mendez called for a truce. The unwitting CPDR reciprocated with a declaration virtually suspending guerrilla activity. With military pressures off and harboring illusions about a pacific future, the FAR lowered its guard. Security in the guerrilla zones melted away at the very moment when the army was preparing for the kill, organizing paramilitary "death squads," infiltrating the guerrilla zones, and preparing for a massive "pacification" program which was organized, trained, and equipped by the U.S. Military Assistance Program and the Agency for International Development (AID) with the latest techniques and technology tested in Vietnam.

As a prelude to the offensive, twenty-eight leaders of the PGT were rounded up two days before the election and summarily executed. The offensive began on October 3, 1966; on October 2, the hazards of a city-based politico-military command were highlighted when Turcios died in an automobile crash while returning from a CPDR function. Leaderless, heavily infiltrated, outmanned thirty to one, outgunned, and surprised, the guerrillas were badly mauled. Before the elections, the FAR and MR-13 guerrillas could boast of a support base among the peasantry unequalled in Latin America. By August 1967 all that was left was a handful of survivors hiding in the capital.[39] These heterogenous elements were regrouped late in 1967 by Camilo Sánchez through the imposition of iron discipline and on the basis of total opposition to the PGT. Politicism formally gave way to militarism in January 1968 when the guerrillas repudiated the PGT as a decrepit and reactionary parasite on the guerrilla movement.[40]

However much the wavering attitude of the Colombian and Guatemalan CPs must have rankled the Cubans, they were inhibited in the volume and intensity of their criticism as long as these parties were still formally bound to a guerrilla movement and publicly advocated armed struggle. There are indications, however, that private criticism did take place between 1965 and early 1967. And, at least in the case of Guatemala, Cuban organs were made available to critics of the Communist policies. In October 1966 Orlando Fernández, a collaborator of Debray's and a PGT-FAR official, published a sharp criticism of pre-1965 PGT policies in the Cuban literary journal *Casa de las Américas*. In addition the first issue of *Pensamiento Crítico* in early 1967 carried an exposé of the 1966 election deals between Mendez and the PGT. The article, submitted by a dissident PGT regional committee, included a polemic against the PGT faction which had opposed earlier concessions to the Left.[41]

In giving dissident Communists access to media so that they could air their complaints, while refraining from anything which could be construed as direct interference, Cuba was preserving the last shreds of the tattered Havana Conference agreements. The spectacular developments in Venezuela demolished these agreements altogether.

Venezuela

Guerrilla warfare in Venezuela[42] evolved out of the insurrectionary period between 1960 and 1962, which witnessed the radicalization of the Venezuelan Communist party (PCV), of the Movement of the Revolutionary Left (MIR), and of leftist military men; the catalyst was the increasingly repressive regime of the head of Acción Democrática (AD), Rómulo Betancourt. In 1958 the AD had joined with the PCV, Christian Democrats, and Unión Republicana Democrática (URD) to overthrow the dictatorship of Pérez Jiménez. Once installed in power, Betancourt excluded the PCV from the ruling coalition and became an ardent anti-Communist and adherent of the Alliance for Progress. The opposition raised by the MIR (a splinter of the AD) to Betancourt's regime was grounded in the glaring contrast that the Cuban Revolution posed to the half-hearted Venezuelan process: the difference was perceived by MIR militants as a betrayal by the AD of the national revolution. Between 1960 and 1962 the PCV and MIR began to combine forces, taking part in a number of urban uprisings and garrison revolts.

The first outbreaks of guerrilla warfare occurred in 1962. By the end of the year twenty guerrilla fronts had been organized in half of the departments in Venezuela, but their dispersion and lack of contact with each other or with the Urban Tactical Commandos (UTCs) led to severe losses. In an effort to coordinate the struggle, dissidents of the PCV, MIR, and URD, along with leftist defectors from the military, set up the FLN/FALN, with PCV members having the decisive voice.

But during most of 1963 the PCV concentrated on the elections scheduled for December 1. Then on October 1, PCV and MIR members in Parliament lost their immunity from prosecution, and by the end of the month several hundred had been arrested. After that, the FLN/FALN worked to obtain the release of prisoners. A FLN call for a general strike to disrupt the elections received only half-hearted support from the working class; and the FALN abstention campaign failed miserably, with 90 percent of the registered electorate going to the polls. The election results were a serious blow to the movement.

The president-elect, Dr. Raul Leoni, took office in March 1964 and announced in his inaugural speech that the ban on the PCV's activities would be removed if the party would renounce violence. In May the party's Central Committee manifested its desire to withdraw from the fighting in a message to the Venezuelan people emphasizing that an end to the fighting was negotiable. That fall, the FALN drew up its conditions: amnesty for political prisoners, legality of the PCV and MIR, reinstatement of pro-FALN officers in the army, guarantees of constitutional liberties, and adoption of a national economic policy. But since these demands amounted to capitulation by the government, no real grounds for negotiation existed. Within a year, however, the PCV was ready for unconditional withdrawal. The earliest indication that a major change of strategy was in the offing came at the party's Seventh Plenum, held in April 1965, with the endorsement of a program calling for a popular frontist campaign to establish a government of "democratic peace." For a time the PCV leaders denied any intention of dismantling the guerrilla movement (though this was obviously implied by the new line), but after a number of serious military setbacks in the fall of 1965, the wisdom of such a move could be avowed in indirect but unmistakable terms. Simultaneously, financial support for the guerrillas began to dry up, indicating that the Soviet Union was throwing its weight behind the democratic-peace line.

The guerrillas were not, however, prepared to lay down their arms. Douglas Bravo began to rally about him those revolutionaries who were opposed to the new line. On December 10, Bravo, Fabricio Ojeda, and others sketched a tentative reorganization of the FLN/FALN as a revolutionary movement independent of the PCV politbureau and directed by a single political-military command. This initiative to gain independent status received a tremendous boost from the Tricontinental Conference, where the FLN became one of the four Latin American members of the Executive Secretariat of OSPAAAL. The conference majority also pressured Moscow to continue its financial aid, and efforts were made to create a special fund to enable guerrilla movements to meet such emergencies as the one in which the FALN found itself. In April the FLN/FALN reorganization was completed and presented to the PCV as a fait accompli. MIR approval was obtained one month later, and a triumvirate leadership composed of Bravo, Ojeda, and an MIR leader was designated. The non-Communist Ojeda became the new leader of the FLN.

Despite their desire to end their involvement with violence, the PCV soft-liners viewed this development with alarm. The resolute breach of discipline committed by Bravo and his followers set a precedent that was all the more dangerous because the new FLN/FALN existed as a formidable rallying center for middle-level and rank-and-file cadres with strong Fidelista sentiments. Thus it was not enough for the PCV to expel all guilty parties and thoroughly wash its hands of the guerrillas; it was necessary to discredit them as antiparty factionalists and unwitting counterrevolutionaries. This offensive began in May 1966 with the suspension of Douglas Bravo from the Politbureau and the outright expulsion of an important aide, Alberto Pasquier. The reorganization was denounced as divisive and as an usurpation of authority.

It was at this point that Cuba began to intervene openly on the side of the guerrillas. Here, as in Guatemala, Cuban support at first (for about eight months) was restricted primarily to offering the dissidents the use of Cuban media to publicize their case. The severity of the Venezuelan crisis, however, and the correspondingly greater Cuban concern, was reflected in the material published and in the place of publication.[43]

The first item published, on June 11, 1966, was a letter from the unified FALN general command to Fidel Castro in Granma, the organ of the Central Committee of the Cuban CP. It referred indirectly to the PCV, noting that "many [members] are hesitating in the face of sacrifices and difficulties," and justified the formation of a "real revolutionary leadership" on the grounds that "conciliation with imperialism can only act as a brake on the popular struggle, encourage illusions among the masses and perpetrate the exploitation and scorn suffered by our peoples."[44] On the anniversary of the Bolsheviks' October Revolution the Cubans edged closer to active participation with an editorial in Granma which compared Lenin's battles against "pseudorevolutionary currents" (by then, a generic name for Latin American CPs) to the present conflicts in Latin America. The editorial then praised Douglas Bravo as a "symbol of the attitude which the Latin American Communists should adopt."[45] In December 1966, by way of responding to harsh PCV criticism of the Venezuelan "factionalists" and the party's provocative description of the Tricontinental Conference as a "farce,"[46] Cuba gave Radio Havana over to the broadcast of a series of sensational attacks on the PCV by Mario Menéndez Rodríguez (Menéndez was editor of Sucesos para todos, a pro-Cuba Mexican periodical, and a brother of the editor of the Havana daily El Mundo.) After interviewing Castro in August, Menéndez had interviewed the FALN leaders in the mountains of Falcón. Several of his broadcasts consisted of interviews with Bravo, who complained mildly of "errors," "deviations," and "regrettable mistakes."[47] Menéndez, by contrast, unloaded a barrage of accusations and expletives. He accused the PCV leaders of treason, sabotage, economic blackmail, attempting to climb to power by way of a military coup, plotting with the government to liquidate Douglas Bravo, and having been infiltrated by the CIA.

On January 2, 1967, Castro publicly entered the fray in his annual address, saluting Douglas Bravo and his forces and crediting them with having saved the Venezuelan revolution. This was met by an immediate and lengthy public statement by the PCV rejecting Fidel's intervention in Venezuelan affairs and censuring the Cuban news media for its "cowardly" attacks on the struggling PCV and for its support of "vile anti-CP groups."[48] In January Debray's *Revolution in the Revolution?* appeared, filled with direct and indirect condemnations of the PCV, among other targets. In March the polemic neared its climax with the FALN's kidnapping and subsequent assassination of Dr. Julio Iribarren Borges, an extremely unpopular former government official and brother of the Venezuelan foreign minister. On March 4 *Granma* published a statement by the new FLN president, Elías Manuitt Camero, justifying the act and taking credit for it. This brought on a flood of protests and vigorous calls for sanctions by the Leoni government.

What finally tore the cloak of civility from the PCV-Cuba polemic was the fact that the PCV joined in the loud condemnation not only of the assassination, but also of the Cuban CP for its publication of Manuitt's statement. For this, Fidel excoriated the PCV soft-liners on March 13 in terms scarcely less inflammatory than those of the Menéndez broadcasts. In blasting its unrevolutionary conduct, Castro goes back to the beginning of the Venevuelan conflict to give a step-by-step historical critique of the guerrilla struggle as it was waged under PCV leadership. It will be useful to quote Castro's views, as presented in this speech, at some length because they present his conception of revolution in Latin America shortly after the publication of *Revolution in the Revolution?*

[Underestimation of the Peasantry] . . . the revolutionary

movement was strong in the capital, and on the other hand —as has happened or had happened in many other countries of Latin America through the fault of the Communist Parties—the revolutionary movement was very weak in the countryside. Why? Because the Marxist parties preferred to concentrate their attention on the cities, on the workers' movements, which is, of course, quite correct. But in many cases . . . they greatly underestimated the importance of the peasantry as a revolutionary force.

[Underestimation of the Guerrilla Movement, Overestimation of the Military] . . . for a long time the leadership of the Venezuelan revolutionary movement overestimated the importance of the capital and the struggle in the capital and underestimated the importance of the guerrilla movement. . . . Venezuela was one of the countries—or the country in recent times—where the revolutionary movement achieved major penetration into the ranks of the professional army. . . . And this led to another conceptual error: to downgrading the guerrilla movement and pinning great hope on the military uprising.

[Direction of the Guerrilla War from the City] . . . the guerrillas found themselves abandoned, deprived of the most elementary resources; . . . the revolutionary leadership of the Party tried to lead the guerrillas from the plain, from the capital. . . . What an audacious and truly revolutionary leadership would have done . . . [is to] march to the mountains with the guerrillas, to direct the guerrillas from the field of battle. . . .

It is absurd and almost criminal . . . to try to direct the guerrillas from the city. The two things are so different, so distinct, the two settings so completely dissimilar, that the greatest insanity—a painfully bloody insanity—that can be committed is to want to direct the guerrillas from the city.

[Using Guerrillas as Political Tools] And the guerrillas were not really viewed as a force capable of developing to the conquest of power in countries like ours, but as an instrument of agitation, as an instrument of political maneuvering, as an instrument of negotiation.

[Truces] . . . And in Venezuela the guerrillas were constantly ordered to cease fire, and that is insanity! The guerrilla that

57

does not fight perishes from starvation; the guerrilla that does not fight does not develop; the guerrilla that concludes a truce in combat is a guerrilla condemned to defeat.

The guerrilla can make a truce of a day or two days, as ours did in some sectors of our front, to return prisoners to the Red Cross. A guerrilla, as a matter of principle, must never conclude a truce of any other kind. The men become accustomed to the quietude of the camp, a debilitation and demoralization of the forces set in.

[Role of the Communist Party] Our position with respect to Communist Parties will be based on strict revolutionary principles. We will support parties which have a non-vacillating and noncapitulationist line, parties which in our opinion have a resolutely revolutionary line, under all circumstances; but parties which entrench themselves behind the name of Communists or Marxists and believe themselves to have a monopoly on revolutionary sentiment—and are really monopolizers of reformism—we will not treat as revolutionary parties. And if in some country those who call themselves Communists do not know how to do their duty, we will support those who, without calling themselves Communists, comport themselves as real Communists in action and in struggle.

. . . What will define the Communist is his attitude toward oligarchies, his attitude toward exploitation, his attitude toward imperialism; and in this continent his attitude toward the armed revolutionary movement. . . .

[The Importance of Theory] . . . Many times practice comes first and then theory. And our people are also an example of this, because many, the vast majority of those who today proclaim themselves Marxist-Leninists, arrived at Marxism-Leninism by way of revolutionary struggle. . . . Whoever denies that it is precisely the road of revolution which leads the people toward Marxism is not a Marxist though he may call himself a Communist.[49]

As we shall see, these themes sketched by Castro in his March 13, 1967, speech are also major themes of *Revolution in the Revolution?*

During the spring and summer months the dispute between Cuba and the PCV spread throughout Latin America and beyond, with the New Left all over the continent supporting the FALN and Fidel and the traditional CPs coming to the defense of the PCV. It was in this atmosphere of confrontation that the OLAS convention was convened on July 31 in Havana's Hotel Libre.

The high point of the conference, as well as of the dispute, was Castro's speech delivered at the closing session on August 10. Along with a good deal of entertaining invective, Fidel again laid bare some of the conceptual issues involved.

[Propaganda] There are those who believe that it is necessary for ideas to triumph among the masses before initiating action, and there are others who understand that action is one of the most efficient instruments for bringing about the triumph of ideas among the masses.

Whoever hesitates while waiting for ideas to triumph among the greater part of the masses before initiating revolutionary action will never be a revolutionary. For, what is the difference between such a revolutionary and a rich landowner, a wealthy bourgeois? None whatsoever!

[Forms of Struggle] . . . Different terms have been employed: whether this is the only way or not the only way, whether it is exclusive, or not exclusive. And the Conference has been very clear about this. It has not used the term the only way, although it could be called the only way. It has referred instead to the fundamental way, and the other forms of struggle must be subordinated. And, in the long run, it is the only way.

[Conditions for Armed Struggle] . . . essentially, it is not that difficult to decide if it is possible, if conditions are ripe, to take up arms or not.

. . . We prefer that they make the mistake of trying to make the revolution although immediate conditions may be lacking than that they make the mistake of never wanting to make the revolution.

[Role of Political Parties] . . . The guerrilla is bound to be the nucleus of the revolutionary movement. This does not mean that the guerrilla movement can rise without any previous work; it does not mean that the guerrilla movement is something that can exist without political direction. No! We do not deny the role of the leading organizations, we do not deny the role of the political organizations. The guerrilla is organized by a political movement, by a political organization. What we believe incompatible with correct ideas of guerrilla struggle is the idea of directing the guerrilla from the cities.[50]

Despite appearances, the object of OLAS was not merely to take the traditional Left to task for its passivity or treachery. The campaign against the CPs was a means to a higher end —the continental revolution, and then not just any hypothetical continental revolution but the one unfolding at that very moment (or so it was hoped) in Bolivia under Che Guevara's direction.[51] In his annual July 26 message to the Cuban people, delivered five days before the opening of the conference, Fidel singled out for attention the "magnificent example" of the Bolivian Army of Liberation whose "victories" a scant four months after beginning hostilities were thought to show that "professional armies become ineffective in the face of patriotism."[52] The mood of the OLAS convention itself was dominated from beginning to end by the absent guerrilla chief. The convention hotel was decked with huge posters of Simón Bolívar and Guevara. In the main assembly hall huge portraits of Che and Bolívar were superimposed on a map of Latin America, and an empty chair for Guevara, the OLAS chairman, stared out at the delegates from the rostrum. The Cuban report to Commission One endorsed Che's strategy of "many Vietnams" and declared that it was the obligation of revolutionaries in countries where there was no guerrilla struggle to support armed struggles in other countries.[53] The conference ended with the passage of a resolution saluting Che "wherever he may be."[54]

3

Orthodox Guevarism: *Foquismo* II

Like OLAS, the purpose of Debray's *Revolution in the Revolution?* was not only to popularize armed revolution and to stigmatize vacillation among self-professed revolutionaries, but to drum up support for Guevara's project in advance of its exposure.[1] Unlike Debray's two earlier works, *Revolution in the Revolution?* was not written for an academic audience. Nor was it written in isolation; Debray had many collaborators.

The editor of the Cuban publishing house Casa de las Américas, Roberto Fernández Retamar, reports that Debray had a number of long conversations with Castro and with members of Castro's inner circle, who made available to him numerous unpublished documents, including military correspondence. "No one else," Fernández Retamar claims, "has had access to such a wealth of materials for historical research."[2] The unofficial view appears to have been that Castro was Debray's most important collaborator. K. S. Karol, who arrived in Cuba in July 1967 to research a voluminous book on the Cuban Revolution, reported that "in Havana everybody knew that he [Debray] had written his book after long private discussions with Fidel Castro, who had himself revised and corrected the proofs."[3]

Jean Lartéguy, a French correspondent, reported his talks with highly placed Cuban officials, concluding that "Debray was the pen, Fidel the thought."[4] The latter claim, if taken at face value, is too extravagant, underestimating as it does not only Debray's role but the importance of other collaborators such as the Guatemalan Orlando Fernández. Debray describes the work as a collective effort of many like-minded revolutionaries.[5] Nevertheless Lartéguy's overstatement does draw attention to an oddity—that Debray should have been "chosen" to speak for the Cubans.[6] In accounting for it, we should note first of all that Debray was no stranger to the Cuban people when he arrived in early January 1966. Shortly thereafter he was asked to speak to the students of Havana University on the subject of revolution in Latin America. The questions put to him (he declined to give a speech) indicate that his two essays, particularly "Problems of Revolutionary Strategy," had already given him a solid reputation. This is further borne out by the fact that Debray was invited as an observer to attend the important Tricontinental Conference being held in Havana. In a short time, Fernández Retamar tells us, "the subtlety of his concepts, his great analytical ability, and the originality of his approach, already revealed in the earlier articles, awakened the interest of the leading circles of the Cuban Revolution."[7]

Besides the qualities cited by Fernández Retamar, Debray brought another important competency to the task—a thorough grounding in the Marxist-Leninist tradition. The hallmark of Guevara's writings, as we have already seen, is the studious avoidance of politics in the Leninist sense. Thus Guevarism arose as a doctrine paralleling orthodox Marxism-Leninism but never actually locking horns with it over fundamental issues. The same can be said for Castro's sole effort in this genre, "The Second Declaration of Havana." Both Guevara and Castro had decried the dogmatic and mechanical character of Moscow-oriented theory, but they had not challenged it effectively beyond pointing to their own experiences and successes. What was needed was a more direct challenge on theoretical grounds, one which could find anchors in traditional Marxism-Leninism while standing, in its freshness, audacity, and originality, as an exhibit of Leninism unfettered in style and content by archaic formulas. There was no one better suited for this assignment than the talented stylist and author of the remark, "Fidelism is only the concrete process of the regeneration of Marxism and Leninism in Latin American conditions."[8]

The interest of Fidel and other Cuban revolutionaries in Debray's work made itself felt most strongly in the weight now placed on the Cuban insurrection. The primary force behind the transformation in Debray's thinking on strategy and tactics—the transformation of "foco I" into "foco II"— must be sought here. If, however, the impression Debray gave in a February 1967 Granma interview is factually accurate, his decision to research the Cuban Revolution for insights into the burning issues of the moment was reached independently.[9] This suggests that it was not only Debray's analytical ability and originality that brought him together with Fidel, but also the shared belief that the lessons of the Cuban Revolution continued to have a far greater relevance to contemporary Latin America than was generally supposed. It was this deep-seated conviction that the Cuban Revolution warranted setting aside the strategic and tactical formulas developed in other times and places that sustained Fidel in his bold challenge to orthodox Marxism-Leninism. The writings of Che Guevara, particularly "Cuba: Exceptional Case or Vanguard in the Struggle against Colonialism," had begun the work of making the lessons of the Cuban Revolution explicit, but Guevara was not available for follow-up work, having embarked in early 1965 on the secret odyssey which was to end in Bolivia. In more ways than one, Debray was the right person at the right place at the right time.

Revolutionary Theory and Practice

The structure of Revolution in the Revolution? is remarkably similar to that of "Castroism: The Long March in Latin America." Prefatory remarks on the relationship between revolutionary theory and practice are followed by criticisms of current forms of struggle in the course of which certain guidelines for the successful conduct of guerrilla struggle emerge; this is followed, in turn, by an analysis of methods of organization and leadership. Nonetheless, there is very little repetition or overlap, a consequence perhaps of the kind of theorizing which characterizes both pieces: to paraphrase Debray's description, theorizing in which the distance separating it from current events is kept to a minimum. Thus while the concerns remain the same on an abstract level, the flux of time and changing events impose new concrete problems.

The discontinuous nature of Debray's writings poses certain problems of interpretation. There is the danger of mistaking the omission of a point emphasized in the early essays for the rejection of that point; and there is also the opposite danger of regarding such an omission as evidence that the old view continues to be regarded with favor. But to recognize these problems is to take the largest step toward avoiding them. The ground rules that must be observed in analyzing *Revolution in the Revolution?* are, first, that it must not be regarded as a magnum opus which supersedes Debray's earlier works in their entirety and, second, that it should not be treated simply as a sequel to these works, e.g., as the product of a division of labor. Of these rules the first has been most often broken. It appears that few of Debray's critics have carefully read the essays and interviews which place *Revolution in the Revolution?* in perspective. In many cases these critics are prepared to believe the worst and have no compunctions about indulging in the facile art of caricature.

A rare example of the violation of the second rule is given by Robin Blackburn in his introduction to a collection of Debray's early pieces. In reaction to unfriendly critics who refuse Debray the benefit of the doubt, Blackburn overcompensates. He errs in overlooking the similarities between Debray's two early essays and *Revolution in the Revolution?* and in exaggerating very questionable disparities. Blackburn argues that the early essays provided the "indispensable complement" to *Revolution in the Revolution?* The latter, he claims, is primarily a "revolutionary call to arms"; it is a combination of "intransigent revolutionary ethics" and the "concrete technics of insurrection." Debray's early essays are said to be primarily concerned with politics, defined as the "theory of the social structure and the contradictions within it which found the revolutionary movement which aims to overthrow it." As such they supposedly set forth the theoretical-political premises of *Revolution in the Revolution?*[10] If there is any substance to the present analysis, both of these characterizations must be judged erroneous. One need only recall Debray's opening remarks in "Castroism" about Marxist-Leninist theory to question Blackburn's identification of "Castroism" with politics defined as Marxist-Leninist social theory; and even "Problems of Revolutionary Strategy" is only marginally concerned with this sort of analysis. Even if we define politics as the theory of revolutionary strategy and tactics, which more accurately describes the two essays, there is not, as we shall see, a qualitative sense in which *Revolution in the Revolution?* is any less a politics and any more a technics of revolution than the two early essays taken together. There certainly are shifts of emphasis and changing themes, but nothing as drastic as a generic division of tasks.

Blackburn supports his argument by noting that Debray originally planned to publish the three major essays together. But this statement should make one ask why, if the essays form an indissoluble entity, Debray did not follow through with these plans. One can only speculate about Debray's reasons. The view taken here is that Debray found the three essays essentially incompatible. When *Revolution in the Revolution?* was published, his only public criticism of the early essays was that they suffered from the widespread error of ignoring the lessons of the Cuban Revolution while exalting foreign models.[11] Given the centrality of the Cuban experience in the theory espoused in his book, quite a lot can be made of this criticism. In particular, it would seem to support the contention that Debray found contradictions in those areas where, contrary to Blackburn's analysis, the essays overlap.

Much misunderstanding about Debray's supposed deprecation or "liquidation" of the role of revolutionary theory could have been avoided if our first rule had been observed.[12] Debray's position in this regard is adequately expressed by his opening remarks in the essay "Castroism," which, after all, were added in 1967 after the publication of *Revolution in the Revolution?* Debray's position seems reasonable at first glance: there is no a priori reason why a rickety structure of strategy and tactics should not be constructed on a makeshift theoretical foundation. Who can say beforehand that the shack won't be capable of sheltering the carpenters of revolution until a better foundation can be laid, especially if it has been done before (in Cuba)? And if carpenters are ordinarily in short supply but are just now on hand in abundant numbers, who can say beforehand that the greater risk cannot be justified, especially if the carpenters are willing, even eager, to assume the risk? Suppose further that foundation-building has been brought into disrepute by a generation of incompetent, time-serving theoreticians. Then one is tempted to throw in one's lot with the daring and orthodox carpenters, especially if one is young; one is not frightened by the knowledge that Leninist methodology is being stood on its head.

Obviously, Debray's methodology carries a higher risk of error; the shack is rickety. Therefore, it is relevant to ask which of Debray's errors are attributable to his shortcut methodology. An answer could take the form of abstract criticism or of concrete counterexample. A good example of the latter is Joao Quartim's *Dictatorship and Armed Struggle in Brazil*, a work in the best Marxist-Leninist tradition.[13] By drawing attention to the disparity between the conclusions reached by Debray and the results of a more solid work which does not short-circuit class analysis, Quartim convincingly underscores the limitations of theory in the genre of *Revolution in the Revolution?* Since this form of methodological criticism relies on concrete theoretical points, however, we will have to postpone our discussion of it until we have examined Debray's text.

Andre Gunder Frank and S. A. Shah attempt a broader argument, which, because of its generality, may be assessed with no more than a glance into Debray's book. Frank and Shah note than an analysis of the class structure in Latin America "would reveal who is the enemy to be fought (the bourgeoisie as well as imperialism), what political weapons he has at his disposal (reformism and temptation), whom the revolution can count on, [and] how it must mobilize these people. . . ."[14] Furthermore, Frank and Shah argue that a correct revolutionary theory would insure that at the first obstacle the movement would not be derailed into reformist culs-de-sac, such as the broad-front line which led to disaster in Brazil and the democratic-peace line in Venezuela.[15]

These assertions, however, are simply non sequiturs when used against Debray and Guevarism. It was not the Fidelistas, after all, who fell into reformist traps but the "theoreticians" of the Brazilian and Venezuelan CPs against whom (among others) Debray's *Revolution in the Revolution?* was directed. Nor did the absence of formal class analysis prevent Debray from identifying the same enemies or recognizing the political weapons that Frank and Shah mention. Nor does Debray differ with most Marxist-Leninists on the question of who must be mobilized; he differs only on the methods for effecting this mobilization. Where Debray and Castroism emphasize the mobilization potential of armed struggle, others emphasize the classical Leninist tools: a program, propaganda, and agitation.

Thus, far from vitiating Debray's conclusions, the kind of analysis counseled by Frank and Shah would probably have left them unchanged. In fact, an analysis of precisely this kind underlies *Revolution in the Revolution?* and the Castroist doctrine. The analysis of Frank and Shah, no less than that of Debray, operates at the continental level, at the level of "Latin American society" and "the Latin American revolution."[16] If Debray's theses are vitiated by an absence of theory, it is primarily an absence of theory on the national level and an integration of such theory into an overall historical analysis of the international class struggle (the Marxist-Leninist tradition). The hallmark of Castroism-Guevarism is not the absolute denigration of all revolutionary theory but the strong adherence to a particular continental theory of revolution. This is not to deny the strong element of pragmatism in Castroism; the preference for a simple continental theory is consistent with the pragmatist's disdain for "grand theory." If this theory is faulty it is because the abstraction involved in formulating theses at this level is too great—so great that truths discovered at this rarified level are too often contradicted by national realities.

Frank and Shah also claim that Debray "counsel[s] revolutionary practice without—or rather with false—revolutionary theory."[17] Despite the interposed qualification, this remark has the same thrust as Clea Silva's facile claim that Debray proposes to "liquidate, once and for all, the role of revolutionary theory"[18] and Huberman and Sweezy's charge that Debray shows no awareness of the importance of "painstaking analysis, from a Marxist point of view, of concrete social situations —the structure of economies, the relations and conflicts among classes, the level of consciousness of classes and strata."[19] The unwarranted nature of these charges becomes obvious when one looks at Debray's other writings from 1966 and 1967. These works are suffused with a concern that the urgent and "painstaking task" of Marxist-Leninist analysis not be postponed any further.

In his interview with Havana students Debray praised this kind of endeavor repeatedly, although sometimes in a gratuitous fashion. Responding to a questioner who wondered how the accumulated knowledge of European parties could be used to advantage by the liberation movements, Debray prefaced his answer with a long tribute to theory:

> . . . there can be no revolutionary practice without revolutionary theory. In Latin America in particular, after the Cuban revolution, it became impossible to pursue a revolutionary course without a great effort to understand the nature of imperialism and the national situation in each country. For reasons that ought to be studied, liberation movements underestimate theoretical work, what can be called theoretical practice. . . . The great danger is to try to palliate this absence of theory with a certain revolutionary verbalism. . . . This is the danger of the formation of a kind of moral language which claims to replace the true language of knowledge. . . . The problem of the moment is to formulate a theory of North American imperialism, to know what it is made of, what means of expression it has, what weight it has in the economy of each Latin American country, what are its tactics, its strategy. In this imperialism has a head start over the people; above all, I think, imperialism sees the tactics and strategy of the Latin American revolution with a certain theoretical lucidity.[20]

Debray went on to warn darkly that the European experience

between 1920 and 1933—a period in which revolutionary crisis had seen the organization of reaction but the ideological weakness, disorganization, and ultimately inglorious defeat of revolutionary forces—had many lessons for the Latin American movement.

In response to another question Debray drew parallels between the Russian defeat of 1905 and the contemporary Latin American scene and speculated about the role of theory in turning the Russian defeat into victory in 1917:

> There is an obvious underestimation of revolutionary theory, that is, the self-criticism and analysis of the enemy and the real environment that men such as Lenin and Mao Tse-tung were able to achieve throughout the Chinese War of Liberation or the Soviet revolution. After the 1905 failure, Lenin publicly criticized and analysed the reason for this failure, and he did so as a mass task, that is, so that the self-criticism reached the masses, and perhaps it was this that allowed the failure of 1905 to be avoided in 1917. This is very important.[21]

To summarize, Debray was asserting, in effect, that whether the post-Cuba Latin American movement suffered the fate of Germany from 1920 to 1933 or was blessed with a period like the Russian years from 1905 to 1917 depended in large part on whether the movement swung around to the Leninist virtues of scrupulous theoretical, ideological, and organizational work or whether it continued to substitute "moral language" for the "language of knowledge." The same sentiment was expressed again at great length in a brief essay written in January 1966 for a Uruguayan Castroist weekly on the role of the intellectual.[22]

Thus all the evidence presented so far points to nothing more than a methodological heterodoxy, i.e., what we previously called a methodological denial of Leninism. This has its origin in the fact that with respect to theory, Debray was in 1966 and 1967 neither an orthodox Leninist nor an orthodox Guevarist; rather (if one will pardon the -isms), he was a Leninist-Guevarist. This description joins the demand for attendance to Marxist-Leninist theory with an immediate revolutionary call to arms. There is nothing unusual about the demand for a unification of theory and practice. The question is one of priorities. The immediacy of the Castroist call to arms demands that some thoroughness be sacrificed for the sake of timeliness—theoretical writing gives way to political writing.

In the essay "Castroism," Leninism-Guevarism bonded the "weakest link theory" and mass struggle in the countryside to the *foco* theory; in the area of organizational forms, it tied a national liberation front and politico-military infrastructure to the insurrectional *foco*. In *Revolution in the Revolution?* the "Leninist" side of the first of these uneasy syntheses falls away entirely; mass struggle and "crisis-watching" go by the board. As for the second synthesis, the national liberation front is demoted from leader to follower, the infrastructure receives no mention, and the Communist party, which had merely been left behind as superfluous in the early essay, is now exposed as a dangerous parasite on the revolutionary body. One might say that in *Revolution in the Revolution?* the syntheses of the early Debray became unstuck in one case and was reversed in the other.

Both changes have implications for the relationship of theory to practice. At best, Debray's methodological denial is nothing more than Guevarism with regrets and genuinely Leninist intentions for the future: it avows the importance of class analysis as a basis for strategical and tactical theory and promises to take it up when circumstances permit—in the meantime the cart must stay before the horse. With the publication of the first essay some doubt was already cast on Debray's intentions by his facile dismissal of theory's time-honored crucible, the Marxist-Leninist party, and by his dismissal of theory's immediate objective, the Socialist political program. As we have seen, *Revolution in the Revolution?* draws even more suspicion in this regard. Let us postpone pursuing this matter, however, until we have more detailed data with which to work.

Forms of Struggle

Although Debray is innocent of belittling the role of class

analysis, the same cannot be said of his attitude toward theories of strategy and tactics, despite the fact that *Revolution in the Revolution?* constitutes such a theory. He prefaces the book's first section (which is devoted to a critical examination of certain military strategies that were not primarily inspired by the Cuban example) with a discussion of the dangers inherent in theorizing about revolutionary warfare. Debray feels that the principal danger, from the combatant's standpoint, is that military writings which originate in another place tend to captivate the mind more than actual, immediate circumstances warrant. Consequently they tend to do more harm than good. They inhibit the imagination, diminishing the capacity to "invent, improvise, make do with available resources, [and] decide instantly on bold moves when . . . in a tight spot."[23] Debray even goes so far as to suggest that during the early months of the Cuban insurrection Castro's ignorance of the writings of Mao Tse-tung was a "stroke of good luck" (p. 20).* While some of what Debray says in this regard is consistent with the Leninist dictum that insurrection must be treated as an art rather than a science, this particular remark carries the unmistakable mark of Guevarist pragmatism. It is one thing to hold that guerrilla activity must be treated as an art; it is quite another thing (verging on anti-intellectualism) to extol the virtues of a tabula rasa state of mind. For Lenin there could be no categorical dismissal of any revolutionary experience, be it ever so remote in time and place from the immediate situation; knowledge of this kind could pose a danger only if it was not complemented by a clear appreciation of the limitations on its relevance imposed by its historical particularity. But such an evaluation presupposes a clear understanding of the particular features of the prevailing national situations. Since that theoretical chore has been pushed to the background by Debray, there remains an internal consistency in his hostility toward attempts to intellectualize revolutionary experiences. The same can be said of the startling way in which he construes the relationship

---

* Hereafter references to *Revolution in the Revolution?* will appear in parentheses.

between tactics and strategy. For Debray, strategy does not precede tactics; the former must be based on the tactical experience of the guerrilla force (pp. 59-60). Again, given the presumed theoretical underdevelopment of the guerrillas, this may well be sound advice; there is undoubtedly a lot of truth to the cliché that a little knowledge is dangerous.

One must ask whether Debray does not violate in practice what he recommends in theory. His stated intention is to theorize about guerrilla strategy and tactics, using the Cuban example to shed light on current problems. One can only conclude that Debray proposes that not all such theorizing be curtailed, only that which derives its inspiration from non-Latin American sources. Debray's analysis of Latin American guerrilla movements, and of the Cuban guerrilla experience in particular, leads him to the conviction that Cuba had great relevance for the rest of the continent, the absence of adequate concrete national analysis notwithstanding. However much theories about guerrilla warfare were likely to be counterproductive, the question of whether studying a particular guerrilla experience would promote or obstruct further revolutionary development was still an empirical one. Indeed, Debray's complaint is not only that his general rule—i.e., that theories of insurrection are likely to do more harm than good —had been ignored too often in the case of other revolutions; he also believes that this rule was automatically and wrongly invoked in the case of Cuba, when careful study would have shown that it was precisely the Cuban experience which constituted an exception. One further complaint is that conceptions about guerrilla warfare which had been imported to Latin America from Europe and Asia escaped the careful scrutiny they deserved because they were disguises for certain political conceptions.

Armed Self-Defense

The first "deviant" military line Debray considers is the tactic of armed self-defense, as it had been unsuccessfully practiced in Colombia by Marulanda, in Bolivia by the miners in 1965, in Peru by Hugo Blanco, in Brazil by Juliao; and as it was being propagandized in Guatemala by Yon Sosa's MR-13.

Debray relates this tactic in a rather free-wheeling way to Lenin's archenemies: economism (restricting the workers' movement to economic demands), spontaneism (reliance on the spontaneous development of the workers' movement), and reformism. Furthermore, Debray seizes upon the fact that except for Colombia all of the experiments with this tactic were organized by one or another variant of Trotskyism. The result is an identification of armed self-defense with Trotskyism and that, in turn, with economism, spontaneism, and reformism. Beyond noting that it could never have come from the pen of Castro or Guevara, this exercise in conceptual assimilation and argument by analogy need not concern us further here.

More substantial are Debray's specific criticisms of armed self-defense, based primarily on the Bolivian debacle and the defeat in Colombia. On the military side, its gravest failure is that it is just what the name implies—a purely defensive tactic. As such it can never accomplish anything more than a partial insurrection. In remaining tied to one locality armed self-defense reduces the guerrilla force to an exclusively tactical role. In denying itself the initiative, it forfeits to the enemy the considerable benefits of mobility and surprise. The self-defense force, composed primarily of poorly armed miners or peasants fighting on home ground, thereby invites encirclement and a carefully prepared attack launched at the moment of the enemy's choosing.

On the political side, Debray argues, the inevitable bloody defeat demoralizes the popular forces. While the self-defense zone is in operation, it allows the government to pose as the guardian of national unity against a cancerous growth, and it serves as an alibi for the inaction of the parties involved—i.e., it promotes opportunism. (The latter criticism is a slap at the Colombian Communist party.) Furthermore, armed self-defense is to be rejected because it does not

> . . . oblige the enemy to "see to it that the situation does not worsen." (Che Guevara) It does not force either representative democracies or oligarchic regimes to reveal their class content openly. Self-defense permits the ruling class to conceal its true character as a dictatorship of violence; it

73

maintains the "equilibrium between oligarchic dictatorship and popular pressure" rather than "rupturing" it. (Che) It enters into and plays the game of the ruling class, promoting divisions in the dominated classes, disguising compromise solutions as victories [p. 30].

The quotations from Guevara are from "Guerrilla Warfare: A Method"[24] and they are noteworthy because they suggest what becomes evident later—that Debray has de-Leninized his foco theory. The passages quoted from Che indicate that Debray has moved to a fuller acceptance of Guevara's famous second thesis in Guerrilla Warfare, viz., that at least some of the conditions for a popular insurrection can be created by the guerrillas. Indeed, what Guevara and, following him, Debray argue goes even further, insisting that this is what revolutionaries must do. The step from possibility to necessity is not a great one when there are few viable possibilities among which to choose. Hence Debray's opposition to armed self-defense: it does not compel the bourgeois state to unmask its repressive essence before the masses; it does not force the ruling class to institute a more inflammatory ruling strategy. In short, the tactic cannot trigger a national political crisis.

Debray's opposition to armed self-defense is not absolute; he does not say that it cannot bear fruit at any point in the revolutionary process, only that it is inappropriate at the beginning. The beginning must be made by a mobile strategic armed force, which in its zone of operations can give the peasantry effective protection, directly and indirectly, by dispersing the regular army. Thus, for Debray, the fact that armed self-defense had been practiced with great success in China and Vietnam does not refute his conclusions; if anything these counterexamples strengthen his argument, for the military preconditions which he requires were satisfied in those countries.

Wilfred Burchett, whose years of close association with the Viet Minh and NLF gives his account of guerrilla warfare in Vietnam a certain authority, agrees only in part with Debray's analysis. Burchett acknowledges that self-defense is not viable in isolation, but his analysis of NLF successes does not support Debray's conclusions about how the isolation must be overcome. Burchett, who attempts to project the views of the many combatants he interviewed, points to preconditions which are not primarily military but political. The isolation of the Vietnamese hamlets was broken by small, armed propaganda squads who organized the inhabitants and coordinated their activities according to the strategy of the National Liberation Front. In this way the self-defense zones became viable even in the earliest stages of the war in South Vietnam.[25]

As was to be expected, Debray's conclusions were not received in silence, particularly not by Trotskyists, whose arguments are too often predicated on distortions of Debray's positions and involve appeals to the authority of sacred, inherited dogma. Almost invariably they find in Debray's works examples of "elitism" and "Stalinism." An example of this distortion as well as of name calling is given by Petras, a Trotskyist sympathizer; he reduces Debray's argument to the "shallow observation that the [Bolivian] miners' defeat 'proves' that the policy of self-defense was wrong."[26] First of all, Debray argues only that self-defense is wrong until a prior condition is fulfilled—the presence of a guerrilla force formidable enough to engage successfully the full force of the regular armed forces. Second, Debray's analysis rests on four other, recent examples besides Bolivia. Finally, it is not so much the miners' defeat as the dramatic finality of it that Debray finds convincing.

Debray can perhaps be faulted for dwelling on the Bolivian miners' revolt, because it offers the most spectacular example of failure. Much less is said about the Colombian peasants in Marquetalia, where, in a more suitable terrain, it took the entire Colombian army three months to uproot the independent peasant republics—and that, only after a similar operation had been defeated two years earlier. Perhaps the fact that Debray's Colombian critics do not press this point is an indication that it is not worth pursuing, for they had no reason to protect Debray. Apparently at the policymaking level of the PCC there was substantial agreement with Debray's conclusions about self-defense tactics. Central Committee member Diego Montaña Cuellar was distinctly apolo-

getic about the defeat of the republics and nonsupportive of
self-defense in a January 1968 article. He wrote:

> The passive concept of "self-defense" could be criticized
> up to 1964. After the organization said "Now we are guer-
> rillas," there surely does not exist in the whole of Latin
> America such a firm, serious and experienced guerrilla force.[27]

In a similar vein Alberto Gomez protested in the pages of
World Marxist Review:

> We never expected the self-defense zones to be impreg-
> nable from the military standpoint. On the contrary, the
> possibility was foreseen that they might fall into enemy
> hands. At the same time, however, we regarded them as a
> base for a future movement, centers of a popular armed
> movement which today are stronger than ever owing to the
> very logic of events.[28]

It is somewhat surprising to find that the Bolivian Trotskyists were more vigorous in their vindication of armed self-
defense than were the Colombian Communists. This posture
stems from the Bolivians' contention that Debray's analysis of
the Peruvian strike is a straw man. According to Guillermo
Lora, leader of Bolivia's Revolutionary Labor party (POR),
the strike was not a result of Trotskyist planning, not a conscious tactic, but the result of governmental provocation and
weak leadership. The presence of POR organizers in the mines
signified nothing more than the fact that once the fighting
had broken out, they had the courage to remain with the
miners to fight out a strike with little chance of victory. The
example which Lora considers noteworthy is the 1952 revolution in which widespread self-defense actions by miners led
to the formation of workers' militias which achieved what no
guerrilla *foco* had ever achieved—total destruction of the regular army. Lora argues, in effect, that in the future a similar
process may lead to a similar result. He vehemently disputes
Debray's contention that the training and equipping of the
regular forces by the United States had succeeded in tipping
the scales forever against such a recurrence. In order to in-
validate this line, Lora boasts, it would be sufficient to point
out that the workers' organizations are also more mature.[29] In

answering in this way Lora brings to an end the substantive debate on armed self-defense and raises a thornier question —the relative weight of political and military factors in the formulation of Latin American revolutionary strategy.

In opposition to the misconceived tactic of self-defense, Debray posits certain putative lessons of the Cuban and Latin American experience. What emerges are theses about the guerrilla *foco* which are 100 percent Guevarist. Guerrilla warfare is divided into three stages: the periods of establishment, of enemy offensive, and of revolutionary offensive. It is in the discussion of the first phase that Debray deviates most widely from his early views. Far from being a time in which the guerrilla stations himself in remote peasant districts to proletarianize himself and politicize the peasants, the period of establishment is one of "absolute mobility" followed by "a longer period of hardening or seasoning by the combatants, the organization of a regular mail service, of supply lines, of relief forces, of arms depots, arriving at the final phase of the true establishment or minimal constitution of a zone of operations." In short, "the technical side grows (armament, communications, production, explosives, training schools for recruits, etc.) in response to the development of guerrilla fire power and its offensive strength" (p. 32).

This passage indicates that Debray's earlier politico-military infrastructure, whose "construction could not be postponed," has not only been postponed but has been reduced to a military infrastructure. The politics of the initial stage have vanished. Debray's views on peasant participation in the first stage of struggle also undergo an abrupt about-face. In "Castroism" he had argued that the security of the guerrilla force demanded on-the-spot political training of combatants and the establishment of strong bonds with the peasant populace, falling just short of open integration. In *Revolution in the Revolution?* Debray argues that the security of peasants and guerrillas demands exactly the opposite, that the greatest feasible isolation be enforced. In order to protect the peasants from government reprisals and the guerrillas from betrayal, unwitting or not, by the peasantry, Debray advises that contacts between the two remain clandestine during this stage.[30]

77

The guerrilla is to be governed by Guevara's "three golden rules": "constant vigilance, constant mistrust, and constant mobility"[31] (p. 42). Of these, mobility is especially important; it is a guerrilla force's "best weapon" (p. 62). Drawing on the Cuban experience, Debray assigns to mobility the role previously held by on-the-spot political preparation: to safeguard against infiltration and betrayal (p. 63).

The Guerrilla Base

The imperative of remaining completely mobile is also at the root of Debray's doubts about the early establishment of a guerrilla base, a tactic used with much success by the Chinese Communists against the Japanese and the Kuomintang and by the Viet Minh against the French. Just as it is wrong for the fledgling guerrilla force to attach itself to a group of peasants, so must it guard against premature attachment to a specific locale. Debray concludes that

> such a base becomes possible only after a first nomadic stage of slow entrenchment in a particularly favorable zone of operations.
> During this time the guerrilla base is, according to an expression of Fidel, the territory within which the guerrilla happens to be moving; it goes where he goes. In the initial stage the base of support is in the guerrilla fighter's knapsack [pp. 64–65].

But Debray does not close the book on the guerrilla base as sharply as he does on the peasant or the armed self-defense base. It is notable that he is uncharacteristically restrained in imputing to the users of this tactic an ideological commitment to foreign models. He says only that "it is not impossible that the Chinese system, as systematized by Mao Tse-tung in *Problems of Strategy in Guerrilla War against Japan*, has reached Latin Americans and superimposed its image on their conception of the Cuban guerrilla struggle" (p. 59).

Debray's choice of a negative example shows the same reserve. In illustrating the pitfalls of guerrilla bases with a concrete case study, Debray does not dwell on the most conspicuous failure, as he does when he morbidly dissects the abject failure of the Bolivian miners. The unsuccessful defense of a Peruvian guerrilla base, under the leadership of Luis de la Puente, in 1965 presented a spectacle every bit as nightmarish as that of the Bolivians,[32] but Debray concerns himself with the almost harmless failure of Guevara to defend a base on the El Hombrito mountain in the second half of 1957.[33]

The reason for Debray's reticence with regard to guerrilla bases is not hard to fathom. To the extent that the decision to employ this tactic is not motivated by blind imitation of foreign models, it is, he feels, a purely military matter and, as such, is not subject to the criticism of those not directly engaged in the guerrilla struggle. "It is not," he says,

> for us to discuss this concept in detail, depending primarily as it does on the concrete conditions of each country and on military decisions for which the guerrilla leadership alone is responsible. . . . Extensive military experience alone can answer questions concerning the guerrilla base or its substitute, the security zone [p. 59]. . . .

Thus, while strategy in the broad, politico-military sense may be open to criticism from the sidelines, military strategy and military leadership are not.

Debray's criticism of guerrilla bases has proved to be the least controversial part of his book. There are several reasons for this. First, there is Debray's lack of assertiveness in the face of purely military matters. Second, the only important example of a guerrilla base was that provided by the Peruvian MIR, which was completely annihilated, making its theoretical defense difficult; the seminal analysis of this failure by Héctor Béjar supports Debray completely.[34] Third, Debray does not step on the toes of the voluble pro-Moscow CPs. On the contrary, the conception under attack is a Chinese innovation.

Pro-Peking groups responded to Debray's criticisms by reaffirming the general applicability of the Chinese model to Latin American conditions. Within this model the guerrilla base is the indispensable rear base of the revolutionary army.[35] Debray's only reference at this time to the problem of a secure rear base had been to say that the guerrilla must carry it on his back. In reality, more is surely needed: the knapsack must be filled and the guerrilla recruited, armed, and trained. If these conditions are not met in the zone of operations (or to the extent that they are not), they must be supplied by a presumably clandestine urban organization, able to assemble the raw material and personnel needed for successful combat and able to build a liaison network. In Peru (under Luis de la Puente) and in Bolivia (under Che Guevara), neglect of organized contact with the urban areas was coupled with a dependence on their support. In fact, dependence on the city was so great that once the lifeline was broken, the guerrillas' fate was sealed.

Armed Propaganda

The contrast between Debray's new conception of the *foco* and the old one is most dramatically displayed in the arguments he directs against the tactic of armed propaganda, as practiced in Vietnam and China. Again, Debray does not reject the tactic absolutely, only during the nomadic stage of guerrilla warfare; and once again he does not deny its utility in Asia. In Vietnam, for example, all the conditions which Debray believes are required for armed propaganda were present: 1) a high peasant population density and an easily recognizable foreign enemy enable the propagandist to remain unobserved in his activity; 2) the propagandists can be supported by "bases of revolutionary support" (p. 50) and a people's army; and 3) the job of propaganda is made easy by the existence of a prevailing climate of war and the fact that the enemy is a newcomer, a foreigner, and an invader, with only the flimsiest justifications for his presence. The first condition provides the agitator with good natural security; the third guarantees quick results in terms of support and recruits for the people's army; and the second arms and trains the recruits, while providing the propagandist with a safe haven and protecting him in his activities. Under these conditions the military pyramid in Vietnam could be built from the bottom up, from a mass base to an elite military force. Paramilitary irregular forces (first guerrillas, later militias) at the villege level fed into semiregular interzonal forces at the regional level which, in turn, sustained a regular army at the national, strategic level. At the apex of the pyramid was the elite corps, the spearhead of the people's army. The activities of these three discrete layers required the coordination of the CP, as did the deployment of the political cadres, who ensured the political conditions of the army's existence.

The situation in "many Latin American countries" (p. 51), on the other hand, permits little natural security due to the sparseness of the peasant population, the cultural barrier separating the guerrilla from the indigenous peasantry, and, in the rural areas, the increased number of highways, airports, sociological teams, religious missionaries, Peace Corps volunteers, etc. Second, there are no regular or semiregular armed forces. Finally, among the isolated peasantry, especially the Indians, the guerrilla is as much a stranger to be automatically distrusted as the enemy. Moreover, Debray asserts, spoken propaganda cannot remove the mental barrier that characterizes the Latin American peasant and contains his revolutionary energy—his fear of the repressive forces and his belief in the myth of their invincibility. This unwarranted reputation can only be abolished through combat. In Latin America, unlike the experience in Vietnam, verbal propaganda does not fall on friendly and receptive ears. Nor, contrary to Debray's earlier views, is the unarmed deed an effective tool in the hands of a foco. An armed deed is the only effective propaganda device. What is even more important to Debray, political activity does not address itself to the fundamental military question, the procurement of arms. This, he tells us, was the "number one political military objective of the [Cuban] rebels" (p. 64). He sees no value in gaining recruits that cannot be armed (p. 53). To bolster this rather abstract argument, Debray notes a "significant detail": Castro did not hold a single political rally in his zone of operations during two years of war (p. 54).

Under these conditions, utilizing armed propaganda prior to the establishment of a powerful guerrilla center involves enormous risks: it provokes the enemy "needlessly," exposes the propagandist and his peasant collaborators to assassination, and reveals the location of a future or possible guerrilla zone, thereby placing the fledgling foco in danger of liquidation (p. 56). This danger to the foco is Debray's central concern.

Where guerrillas and armed patrols work together, the un-productiveness of the latter means a net loss for the revolution. Indeed, Debray regards all ideological disputes involving the guerrillas to be harmful to the revolutionary effort at the outset (p. 56). The problem is not that there is too little political agitation; there is too much. The same attitude toward education or indoctrination is revealed in Debray's summary rejection of political commissars, an integral part of all Communist armed forces since Trotsky conceived them during the Russian Civil War to ensure the loyalty of ex-tsarist officers in the Red Army (p. 114).

On the question of armed propaganda, Debray's contention is that although in Vietnam armed self-defense, armed propaganda, and guerrilla bases could arise together to forge an army of national liberation, in Latin America such an outcome is ruled out by geography, demography, enemy intelligence, and "the social, ideological, and psychological conditions of the peasantry in the majority of Latin American countries" (p. 56). That being the case, armed propaganda cannot be allowed to interfere with the development of the *foco*. The military pyramid, therefore, must be "built from the apex down—the permanent forces first (the *foco*), then the semi-regular forces in the vicinity of the *foco*, and lastly, or after victory (Cuba) the militia" (p. 51). As for the "political army," whose ideological struggle among the people had been so indispensable in Vietnam, Debray can find no role for it until a revolutionary base of support is established among the people. In turn, this political precondition presupposes, as does armed self-defense, the existence of a revolutionary regular army.

This military pyramid is neither coextensive with Debray's earlier organizational pyramid nor inconsistent with it. The notion that the development of the revolutionary armed forces progresses from the *foco* to the regular army and from there to mass armed actions would undoubtedly have been affirmed by the Debray of "Castroism." The differences between that essay and *Revolution in the Revolution?* arise in the conception of the first stage of guerrilla activity. In Debray's earlier work the *foco* retained many of the tasks of traditional Leninist cadres; in his later work such activity is no longer deemed advisable.

In making this evolution Debray's *foco* theory loses its claim to originality. The theory outlined in *Revolution in the Revolution?* is, for all intents and purposes, merely a polished set of arguments to back up the oracular pronouncements of Guevara. One could readily summarize Debray's conception of armed propaganda and self-defense by quoting from Guevara's prologue to Vo Nguyen Giap's *People's War, People's Army*. But in doing so, one cannot fail to recognize how much the argument improves in Debray's hands. In a scarcely credible interpretation of the Vietnamese conception of armed propaganda, Guevara writes that such "propaganda is simply the presence of liberation forces in certain places where they demonstrate their power and combat ability, moving among the people as easily as fish in water."[36] He then divides the liberation struggle into three military stages which begin with a mobile guerrilla *foco*![37] Furthermore, Guevara neglects the absolute primacy given by Giap to the political struggle:

> The liberation struggle has passed through three stages that characterize, in general, the development of the people's war. It begins with small-sized guerrilla units that have extraordinary mobility and are able to mix with the physical and human geography of the region. As time goes by a quantitative process is produced which, at a given time, gives way to the great qualitative leap of the war of movements. . . . Here we have more compact groups dominating entire zones. They have better means and their fighting capacity is much greater, but mobility is their fundamental characteristic. After another period of time the final stage of the struggle is reached. The people's army consolidates and moves into a war of positions. . . .[38]

Here we have a perfect example of how Guevara deals with his fundamental differences with the Marxist-Leninist tradition—he pretends they do not exist. Altogether missing from this schema (which reflects not Giap's but Che's views) are the secret political bases which constituted the rear of the first guerrilla units and which were the embryos of the first liberated zones. Nor does Guevara mention the spontaneous uprisings which preceded the establishment of bases in these areas or the role of self-defense units in the formative stage of the guerrilla struggle. His description-cum-definition of self-defense assumes the prior existence of a people's army:

> A self-defense zone can be defended from limited attacks, provide the people's army with men and provisions, and maintain the internal security of the region. Self-defense is no more than a minimal part of the whole, with special characteristics.[39]

In short, Guevara's propositions about competing forms of struggle are based on a highly dubious reading of Giap. In Debray's hands, however, they are made compatible with a more faithful interpretation of the Vietnamese experience and find a broader and more rigorous set of justificatory arguments. In the process, Debray moves closer to the main bone of contention between Guevarist movements and Communist parties—the role of the party. This is especially true of his discussion of armed propaganda. The main thrust of Debray's criticisms of armed self-defense and guerrilla bases is that positional strategies are alien to Latin America unless they posit a mobile, strategic guerrilla force as a prior condition. The gist of his criticism of armed propaganda is that political agitation in the traditional sense presupposes the dumb propaganda of the gun. This thesis clearly touches a more tender nerve as reflected in the greater volume of criticism, part of which was undoubtedly offered as much in defense of the institution of political agitation as of armed propaganda. Debray's critics did not miss the implication of his argument: to deny political agitation a role in the first stage of the revolution was to abrogate the leadership role of the party. For the moment, however, we will postpone consideration of those objections which have a wider aim and consider only the more technical and limited ones.

Wilfred Burchett has pointed out that Debray's depiction of armed propaganda in Vietnam suffers from some inaccuracies. It appears that while Guevara's interpretation errs in ignoring certain political aspects, Debray overlooks the military side. In fact, the armed propaganda units in Vietnam were created to carry out their mission in the military as well as the nonmilitary sense.[40] This is borne out by the December 1944 directive issued by Ho Chi Minh which defined the function of the armed propaganda units: they were to coordinate the local armed forces and assist them in training and in procuring weapons. They were named the Viet-Nam Propaganda Units for National Liberation in order to emphasize "that [a] greater importance should be attached to the political side than the military side,"[41] but they were nevertheless viewed as the "embryo of the Liberation Army"; and the date of their creation is, to this day, celebrated as the birthday of the North Vietnamese armed forces.[42]

William Pomeroy, a participant in the Philippine liberation ("Huk") movement against the Japanese and Americans, has warned that the Philippine experience with armed propaganda raises serious questions about the efficacy of the propaganda of arms. According to Pomeroy, in the Philippines it was just this kind of propaganda which "needlessly provoked the enemy," leading to inordinate increases in the scale of governmental response. This tended to cancel out the Huks' political work and to lead to military defeat. Since defeat makes for bad propaganda, the propaganda of arms proved counterproductive.[43] Pomeroy further questions the feasibility of leaving political work to the military. The Huk armed forces tended to be less sophisticated than those who did political work as party cadres. Many soldiers were attracted to the Huks out of a craving for adventure and physical challenges. Many of the best fighters had little descipline regarding study sessions, and the exacting conditions of warfare left little opportunity for political education. When political education by party cadres is neglected, Pomeroy argues, there is a tendency for outstanding military cadres to receive from their units loyalty based on personality rather than principle.[44]

Both Pomeroy and two Cuban revolutionaries, Simón Torres and Julio Aronde, have objected to Debray's appeal to the example of Fidel Castro in the Cuban Revolution. Pomeroy's argument is defective in that it attributes to the mountain population of Oriente province (in which the Rebel Army first established itself) "a background of organizational experience and mass struggle."[45] The best historical sources, including Torres and Aronde and Che Guevara, do not support this analysis.[46] Although help given the one or two dozen green survivors of the distaster of Alegría de Pío by the local politician-bandit Crescencio Pérez and his men may have saved the revolution at the moment when it was most vulnerable, what is at issue is whether the politicization of the peasantry was enough to make political agitation unnecessary.[47]

In Cuba, according to Torres and Aronde, two special factors combined to simplify the guerrilla's political task. One of these was the politically virgin state of the Cuban countryside; the other was the peasants' extraordinary familiarity with armed repression.

> What of the countryside? What were the political conditions there? Let us mention a few: absence of a deep ideological effort on the part of imperialism, the bourgeoisie, and the Church; absence of an organized struggle for land, which would imply the existence of definite political conceptions; [and] direct peasant-army confrontation, in which the army upheld the big landowners (rule by machete, evictions, i.e. violence against the peasant masses).[48]

Under these conditions, Torres and Aronde argue, political action

> . . . can be carried out by means of a gun, which breaks the subordination of the peasant to bourgeois power, brutally personified by the *guardia rural*. The political confrontations had already taken the form of direct clashes between the army and the peasantry. In these circumstances, the gun of itself compensates for the lack of political activity and is, in fact, the only thing that can change the relation of forces in this sector of society.[49]

The argument concludes by affirming the need to work politically with the peasant masses because they are not "virgin territory," as they were in Cuba.[50]

It is symptomatic of the rudimentary state of Marxist research in this area that two analysts could use the same premises to arrive at contradictory conclusions. Debray argues that among other factors, the enemy's ideological penetration of the countryside has made the Cuban example even more binding on revolutionaries; Torres and Aronde argue that the resulting loss of innocence among the peasantry has put political propaganda back on the agenda.

The example of Bolivia is instructive. As Quartim has pointed out, the inadequacy of Debray's conception of armed propaganda was rather spectacularly shown by the utter inability of Che's ELN to break out of its isolation from the peasantry. But Quartim is too kind to Guevara. He claims that Guevara did not underestimate, as Debray does, the necessity of supporting the military act by a correct explanation of the objectives of the revolution, and he cites as evidence the September 22, 1967, lecture given by Inti Peredo to a group of fifteen dumbfounded peasants.[51] The fact that this isolated example[52] of non-Debrayist armed propaganda came a scant two weeks before the ELN was destroyed and Guevara was captured indicates that it was hardly a sober implementation of standard policy. The guerrillas were desperate, as they had not been able to recruit a single peasant and were faced everywhere by peasant hostility.[53]

What the ELN appears to have failed to measure in its choice of a zone of operations was the political complexion of its inhabitants. The Barrientos regime had its firmest hold on peasant loyalties precisely in those provinces—Cochabamba, Chuquisaca, and Santa Cruz—in which the guerrillas chose to operate. In Cochabamba, where General Barrientos was a prominent and apparently not unpopular landowner, the ruling party the Front for the Bolivian Revolution (FRB)—won its most crushing victory in the July 1966 elections. In Santa Cruz, Chuquisaca, and in the Beni province (which was at one point considered by the ELN and researched by Debray), the FRB won well over 50 percent of the total vote. All of these areas were undergoing major transformations with the organization of government-sponsored peasant unions, and the peasants were looking to the government for aid.[54] Under these conditions the Guevarist-Debrayist conception of armed propaganda was put to the acid test and failed.

This is not to say that the political inaccessibility of the peasantry completely explains Guevara's isolation. Any account of Guevara's failure which aspires to completeness (which the present account does not) must not neglect the guerrillas' extreme physical isolation. The problem was not only that the peasants were generally unreceptive, they were also scarce.

Nevertheless it was not a question of being boxed into a corner; that very isolation was actively sought. Though Guevara first showed a preference for a more populous region in the Alto Beni, he was pleased by his subordinates' choice of Nancahuazú especially because of its remoteness. After an initial exploration of the area Guevara wrote in his diary: "Apparently the region is seldom frequented. With adequate discipline one could stay there a long time."[55] Isolation in its purest form, in other words, was desirable during the long period of clandestine preparation. Debray does not have much to say about the preparatory stage prior to the opening of hostilities—either about the guerrilla end or about the question of logistics—so one must be careful in attributing specific recommendations to him in this area. But it would be hard to imagine a better way to implement the Guevarist-Debrayist rules of constant vigilance and constant mistrust than to act as Guevara did.

Beyond Mao and Giap

The three tactics repudiated by Debray represent not only three different models of revolutionary warfare, but are also three dominant features of one Asian model. These three tactics were creatively coordinated, notably in China and Vietnam, so as to successfully bring into existence a regular army capable of victory in spite of the staggering technical superiority of the enemy. The great equalizer at every stage was the political mobilization of the numerically preponderant rural masses by a Communist party dedicated to armed insurrection. In concentrating their organizational efforts on the peasantry these parties made an important break with classical Leninism: the industrial working class was effectively abandoned in practice because of the relative military strength of the enemy in the city and the manifest revolutionism of the peasantry. The proletariat was not, however, abandoned in theory; socialism continued to be the goal of the party. Thus, it would probably be more accurate to say that the party merely went into "forced exile" among the peasantry, or, as Isaac Deutscher has put it, the party "substituted" for the working class in the insurrectional phase of the revolution.[56] This strategic innovation, considered heretical in its day, is now generally accepted as a creative adaptation of the Marxist-Leninist method to Asian (and Asia-like) societies. The important bond between Mao and Lenin is a belief in the necessity of a dictatorship of the exploited masses for the transition to socialism, but the germinal form and genesis of that dictatorship could not be more dissimilar. In Russia it grew out of the councils (soviets) of workers and peasants, in and out of uniform, which were dominated by the revolutionary working class (that is, workers adhering to the vanguard party). In China, the revolutionary peasant army extended its areas of domination from isolated guerrilla bases to larger, liberated territories which grew and merged until the whole country was liberated.

In *Revolution in the Revolution?* Debray, in effect, takes the next step beyond Mao, substituting a military *foco* for the vanguard party in the insurrection. He argues that the powerful forms of struggle in which the vanguard party had been the central element were counterproductive in contemporary Latin America; he thus throws the role of the party into question. This argument consumes roughly half of the book. In the second half, Debray drops the subtleties and moves to a frontal attack.

Forms of Organization

In "Castroism" Debray's brief remarks on organization were limited to a blithe assertion that Marxist-Leninist parties were not essential: for the sake of firm political leadership, it was only necessary to have something like the July 26th Movement (an impromptu and heterogeneous affair), or perhaps a broadly based anti-imperialist front. In *Revolution in the Revolution?* the scope of Debray's criticism encompasses all parties, whatever their ideological hue, that have not subordinated themselves in theory and practice to the armed struggle in general and a guerrilla center in particular. All other forms of struggle, Debray argues, whether legal or clandestine, are at best secondary and at worst useless or harmful excrescences on the revolutionary process.

The Superfluity of Parties

Quartim has singled out two "principles" which inform Debray's whole work: "the primacy of the military over the political and the primacy of the countryside over the city."[57] Putting the latter aside for the moment, the former "principle" can be viewed only as an assessment by Quartim of the implications of Debray's stated views; it is not a description of those views. Nor is it accurate to attribute to Debray the "elemental error" of "elevating" the military over the political, as Huberman and Sweezy do.[58] The metaphor of "inversion" used by Torres and Aronde is no better.[59] Strictly speaking, Debray's efforts are geared to reducing the political aspects of the revolution to the military sphere, not to opposing one to the other. He argues, first, that guerrilla warfare is "essentially political" (p. 88) and "totally political" (p. 89); second, that the foco is politically self-sufficient; and, third, that unlike the party, the foco is an indispensable political instrument.

The Countryside. A large part of the discussion of reducing the political to the military occurs in the section on armed propaganda, where Debray purports to show that military action is a necessary and sufficient form of propaganda. The effect of this argument is to curtail mass work among the rural populace. Debray maintains further that a guerrilla movement alone can achieve an alliance between worker and peasant (p. 109). In the mountains intellectuals, workers, and peasants meet, come together in the guerrilla force, and gradually "weld an alliance having the simple force of friendship" (p. 110). That the guerrilla can do this is beyond doubt—it was demonstrated in Cuba. The falsity of the assertion, however, that only the guerrilla movement can forge such an alliance is evident, assuming that it is not vacuously true by virtue of an idiosyncratic definition of the worker-peasant alliance. Even if we accept the unconventionally narrow definition of a worker-peasant alliance as friendship based on direct interaction, counterexamples readily spring to mind: Juliao's Peasant Leagues in Brazil, Hugo Blanco's Peasant Unions in Peru, Popular Action (AP) and the pro-Chinese Communist party in Brazil (PC do B).[60] In the latter two cases the contact was primarily between Marxist-Leninist intellectuals and peasants, with few if any bona fide workers present; but the inclusion of these examples is warranted by the assumption of proletarianization.

Perhaps to avoid these counterexamples Debray revises the definition of proletarianization. He adds that "it [the guerrilla movement] alone can guarantee that the people's power will not be perverted after victory" (p. 109). This is more than a reiteration of the familiar claim that only the mobile guerrilla army can protect the peasantry and, therefore, the worker-peasant alliance; it is an assertion of the superiority of the guerrilla fighter's Socialist consciousness, or, to be more precise, the superiority of guerrilla life in shaping the new Socialist man.

> In order to assume this function [leadership of the toiling masses—the worker-peasant alliance], this historical vicarship, and in order not to usurp a role to which they have only a provisional title, this progressive petty bourgeoisie must, to use Amilcar Cabral's phrase, "commit suicide as a class in order to be restored to revolutionary workers, totally identified with the deepest aspirations of their people" [p. 112].

"The most favorable time and place for this suicide," Debray writes, is not with workers in the factory or on the picket line but

> . . . with the guerrillas, during guerrilla action: here, the small initial groups from the cities have their first daily contact with rural realities, little by little adjust themselves to its demands, and begin to understand from the inside the aspirations of their people; they cast aside political verbosity and make of these aspirations their program of action. Where better than in the guerrilla army could this shedding of skin and this resurrection take place [p. 112]?

What are the mechanisms of this sociological transformation and unification? During the nomadic stage they are shared experience and total interdependence, just as they were in "Castroism." But whereas the guerrilla originally shared the peasant's life, now it is to be the peasant who shares the life of the guerrilla. And interdependence is no longer a relationship between guerrilla and peasant but one just among guerrillas. The most important shared experience is apparently that of facing death. After quoting Lenin for support—to the effect that all of the Bolsheviks' best cadres had been in the Red Army—Debray makes the remarkable assertion that the "best teacher of Marxism-Leninism is the enemy in face-to-face confrontation during the people's war" (p. 111). Needless to say, this not what Lenin intended.

The guerrillas' political experience is not restricted to combat. At a later stage, Debray explains, they deepen their political maturity by carrying through "socialist 'rehearsals'." In a virtual paraphrase of Guevara, Debray writes:

> It [the foco] then tries out and tests tomorrow's revolutionary measures (as on the Second Front in Oriente): agrarian reform, peasant congresses, levying of taxes, revolutionary tribunals, the discipline of collective life. The liberated zone becomes the prototype and the model for the future state, its administrators the models for future leaders of state. Who but a popular armed force can carry through such socialist "rehearsals" [p. 111]?

It is no wonder then that Debray has no use for political commissars in the new guerrilla army. If, as Debray asserts, the experiences of Cuba, Venezuela, and Guatemala demonstrate that "even petty bourgeois or peasants . . . are more quickly and more completely molded by the experience of the guerrilla than by an equal amount of time spent in a training school for cadres" (p. 89), then there is clearly no place for political commissars in the traditional sense: "The people's army is its own political authority. The guerrilleros play both roles indivisibly. Its commanders are political instructors for the fighters, its political instructors are its commanders" (p. 114).

There is plenty of room for doubt concerning the supposed political self-sufficiency of the guerrilla army. The best example of proletarianization that Debray draws on is the ideological transformation of the Rebel Army during the Cuban Revolution. It is true, as Clea Silva has pointed out,[61] that Raul Castro and Che Guevara were Communists when they boarded the ship Granma, but this observation does little more than draw attention to a few of Debray's wildly exaggerated claims; it does not seriously endanger his conclusion. It is noteworthy that except for the columns led by Raul Castro and Guevara, the Rebel Army was hostile to the pro-Moscow People's Socialist party (PSP) and excluded it from participation.[62] It is also significant that Castro fiercely opposed Guevara's conversion of his brother[63] and took a dim view of their political correspondence.[64] But this only indicates that Debray's most exaggerated claim- that combat is the best teacher of Marxism—is unwarranted. Instead, the Cuban experience indicates what one would normally expect —that the best teacher of Marxism is a Marxist. At the same time, the Cuban experience suggests that combat increases the receptivity of the students, and this is perhaps enough to substantiate Debray's claim with regard to political commissars. For under present conditions in Latin America, every new guerrilla force is certain to be better supplied with Marxist-Leninists than was the Rebel Army.

It is probable, however, that the political decisions which confronted the Rebel Army were less complex than those which have confronted its successors. For this reason there is considerable brashness in the confident assertion that specialized political training for select guerrillas, and all that this implies, has been swept from the historical stage. The fact that a certain amount of brashness has a place in polemics need not concern us here. Just as it is expected that to some extent less significant loopholes in a theory be papered over for the sake of a desired effect, so is it the function of critical analysis to expose those loopholes.

The City. What is remarkable about Debray's discussion of the role of the city is not so much what he says as what he chooses to ignore. His discussion centers around the socio-cultural process of "bourgeoisification," the counterpart of proletarianization. The following quotations are representative of Debray's remarks in flavor and content.

> As we know, the mountain proletarianizes the bourgeois and peasant elements, and the city can bourgeoisify the proletarians. The tactical conflicts that are bound to arise, the differences in evaluation and line, conceal a class conflict [pp. 76–77].
>
> Even a comrade, who spends his life in a city is unwittingly bourgeois in comparison with a *guerrillero*. He cannot know the material effort involved in eating, sleeping, moving from one place to another—briefly, in surviving. . . . The city dweller lives as a consumer. . . . These lukewarm incubators [cities] make one infantile and bourgeois. . . . When a guerrilla group communicates with city leadership or its representatives abroad, it is dealing with "its" bourgeoisie [pp. 70–71].

The implication is that whatever functions the urban associates of a guerrilla force may have, they are, by virtue of their "terrain," ideologically unworthy of full partnership with the guerrillas and even less of leadership in the movement. This assessment does more than depose the traditional city-based political elite in favor of a rural military-political elite. The urban population as a whole takes on the aspect of the enemy (the bourgeoisie) and is to be avoided. Even the guerrilla who descends from the mountains to the city to carry out liaison tasks is easily corrupted and poses a danger to the *foco*, for "it is through him that attempts are made to infiltrate the guerrilla unit, willingly or by force" (p. 44). To guard against betrayal, the guerrillas must move their camp immediately after his departure. Even when there is no conscious betrayal, there is the danger of unwitting betrayal. Debray complains about "the terrible abandonment which many *focos* have suffered for months or sometimes for years"—which arises because of the "irreducible difference in conditions of living, [and] therefore in thought and behavior." This neglect is exacerbated by the "hazards of transportation" and "the diffi-

culties caused by encirclement operations or other mobilizations of enemy forces" (pp. 71–72).

For Debray, this settles the question of where the rear of
a guerrilla force must be: in the countryside. Better to do
without a lifeline to the city than to have one which is un-
reliable and which directs traitors and infiltrators to the guerrilla force. How then can the guerrilla keep supplied, given
the fact that contact with the rural inhabitants must also be
avoided? Debray suggests only that the guerrilla force

> make raids on neighboring villages from its own base, by
> vehicle if necessary (seizing and later abandoning a truck),
> in order to obtain foodstuffs and field equipment (knapsacks,
> blankets, clothing, etc.) to create its own supply depots,
> burying or hiding them and thus assuring its freedom of
> action for a few months [p. 72].

In short, the guerrilla contingent must, at least at the outset,
live off the land.

Surprisingly, Debray does not mention arms and recruits
or suggest how they should be obtained. One is left to infer
that they, too, must be gleaned primarily from the countryside. Debray does not make the insupportable claim that this
is what the Rebel Army did; he only suggests that this is what
it wanted to do. Available evidence, however, shows that until
the Rebel Army broke the May offensive by Batista's army,
capturing large quantities of weapons in the process, it depended almost entirely on shipments of arms and recruits
from the city. This was especially true in the critical first
months, during which the guerrillas were saved by the urban
organization. One of the best sources for this information is
Guevara's own account of this period. From the first, the
efficient organization of Frank País in Santiago sent help of
all kinds—food, equipment, arms, and men.[65] On February 1,
a month after the guerrillas had moved to their zone of operations, the first substantial reinforcement arrived.[66] In mid
March, País sent a group of about fifty men to Castro, thus
quadrupling the size of his army.[67] During 1957 only a small
percentage of the guerrillas' arms and munitions were seized
in combat; most of the weapons were obtained in the United

States and smuggled into Cuba. Cars loaded with weapons—six Thompson submachine guns, twenty-four pistols, and six thousand bullets per car—arrived in Havana at the rate of three per week. In addition, an undetermined number of weapons were smuggled into the country hidden in the clothes of young militia women who went to Miami, posing as weekend tourists. In February 1958 arms began to be flown directly to the Sierra Maestra from the United States, Mexico, Costa Rica, and Venezuela; they amounted to well over fifty tons by May 1958.[68]

In view of the Cuban experience, the importance Debray places on everyday military concerns such as supply and recruitment should have led him to place the urban organization at the base of the organizational pyramid (as he had done in "Castroism") and to emphasize its role as the wellspring of arms and recruits. Instead, he dwells on the "class conflict" between the *Llano* (urban wing of the July 26th Movement; literally, "plain") and the *Sierra* (Rebel Army; literally, "mountain") and quotes Castro to the effect that the city "is a cemetery of revolutionaries and resources" (p. 69). In other words, Debray wants neither arms nor combatants to be concentrated in the city. This effectively denies the city a military role.

At first glance, Debray appears to contradict this directive when he concedes that urban terrorism (by which he means primarily sabotage) may have a strategic value—"if it is subordinate to the fundamental struggle, the struggle in the countryside"—in tying down large numbers of enemy soldiers and preventing their participation in the fundamental struggle. This, he notes, was the case in Cuba, where the urban commandos prevented Batista from marshaling more than ten thousand out of fifty thousand men against the guerrillas at any one time. But Debray sandwiches this tribute between derogations: First, he states categorically that "city terrorism cannot assume any decisive role" (p. 75); then he notes that by Castro's reckoning, "the Rebel Army . . . became invincible when it reached a ratio of one to 500." According to this ratio, the urban guerrillas became redundant when the Rebel Army had grown to one hundred men. Debray goes on to applaud

Castro's policy during the Cuban Revolution of demanding, from the start, that all arms be sent to the *Sierra*.

Thus, however desirable the presence of an urban military diversion may appear to be, Debray is clearly disposed to belittle it and, by implication, the urban population and its parties. This bias appears also in his blanket characterization of the Latin American working class as being "of restricted size or under the influence of a reformist trade union aristocracy" (p. 112). Debray believes that the only way to arouse this class and weld it into a revolutionary entity is to present it with the possibility of seizing power in the form of an "invincible" revolutionary army, created and nourished in the countryside. Until then urban struggle can make little headway and inaction, political and military, is the order of the day. The urban masses are fated by their "bourgeoisification" and by the military unsuitability of the city for guerrilla warfare to remain a passive and more or less unwitting audience to the heroism of their army.

The principle of the primacy of the countryside over the city is, as Quartim has correctly observed, one of the two pillars of *Revolution in the Revolution?* This principle was also important to Debray's first *foco* theory, but its role was not as central as in *Revolution in the Revolution?* because the reduction of the political to the military was not a feature of the earlier theory. There the wide-ranging repudiation of the city as a military battleground implied only that the principal locus of armed struggle must be in the countryside; it did not imply the passivity of the urban populace. If, however, it is concurrently argued, as Debray does in his second theory, that politics can be identified with military action, then the absence of military action in the city or of direct involvement in the rural struggle (supply, liaison, etc.) means the absence of politics.

In spite of this Debray insists that "the guerrilla movement, if it is to triumph *militarily* must assemble around it the majority of the exploited classes" (p. 109). How is it to achieve this without a political organization in the cities? Debray suggests only one way: a radio transmitter. In analyzing the Cuban experience he totally disregards the contribution of the *Llano* in this area. He concludes from the Cuban experience that a simple radio station can clarify the aims of the struggle and mobilize the masses more effectively than any urban party organization.

> Even before victory, the radio broke through government censorship on military operations, a censorship such as prevails today in all embattled countries. It is by means of radio that the guerrillas force the doors of truth and open them wide to the entire populace. . . . In short, radio produces a qualitative change in the guerrilla movement [p. 109].

The abnegation of political and military action in the city demolishes more than the traditional Communist party; it assigns the same fate to the political front—the time-honored instrument used by these parties for involvement in armed actions. Debray does not leave it to his readers to make this inference. The proposition that the political front is also an unnecessary excrescence on the revolutionary body in its formative stages is grounded in a critical analysis of the part played by fronts in Guatemala (FUR) and Venezuela (FLN).

The purpose of such organizations is to rally to the armed cause progressive elements of classes outside the Communist movement. Debray scoffs at the futility of Latin American efforts in this regard, noting that the parties have succeeded in doing nothing more than fostering the illusion that alliances existed where in fact none did.

> Considerable energy is thrown into the establishment of a phantom front, composed essentially of members of the party that formed it. Since one party does not make a front, organizations are fabricated out of whole cloth, at the expense of the party itself, and famous progressive "independent personalities" are sought out whose names can be whispered, adding to their mystery. So much energy and effort withheld from the armed struggle in order to supply a showy facade for it, even before it has been consolidated or extended! . . . Magnificent programs are widely publicized abroad but remain unknown [pp. 82–83].

The reason for these ludicrous failures is simple:

> . . . it is necessary to proceed from the small to the large:

to attempt to proceed in the opposite way is pointless. The smallest is the guerrilla foco, nucleus of the popular army. It is not a front which will create this nucleus, but rather the nucleus which, as it develops, will permit the creation of a national revolutionary front. One creates a front around something extant, not only around a program of liberation. It is the "small motor" that sets the "big motor" of the masses in motion and precipitates the formation of a front, as the victories won by the small motor increase [pp. 83–84].

In short, the liberation front, like everything else, presupposes a victorious guerrilla foco.

The Counterrevolutionary Party

We come now to Debray's coup de grâce, the portrayal of the Marxist-Leninist party as unwittingly counterrevolutionary. At first the scope of Debray's remarks is limited to certain reform-ist policies, characteristic of pro-Moscow parties in general and of the Guatemalan and Venezuelan parties in particular, but in the end his attack is carried over to all Marxist-Leninist parties which do not devote their full energies to the initiation of armed struggle in the countryside.

The principle focus of Debray's assault on the conduct of Communist parties in Latin America is their practice of main-taining a legal political existence in the cities while attempting to lead the armed struggle in the countryside. This, according to Debray, sabotages the guerrilla effort in a number of ways. When hegemony over the armed struggle is vested in an urban organization it is necessary for the guerrilla commander, who is only one more member of the Central Committee, to take the enormous risk of descending from the mountains to meet with the other leaders. Debray avers that such trips are bound to lead to disaster:

Sooner or later the guerrilla leader will fall, assassinated on the spot, or tortured, or the victim of "suicide." In rare cases he may be imprisoned, if public opinion can intervene in time. But if he escapes once, he will be caught the next time. Luck or "mysterious fate" may play a role: an auto-mobile accident, for example [pp. 68–69].

There are two thinly veiled references to actual occurrences in this passage. Fabricio Ojeda, the Venezuelan head of the FLN, was betrayed and captured during a stay in Caracas; while in jail, he died—officially, by his own hand. The reference to an automobile accident suggests the fate met by the Guatemalan commander, Turcios Lima.

In addition to, and in part because of, this danger, the guerrilla leader's journey to the city has a disastrous effect on the morale of the guerrilla group. Even when the commander is present, the group's awareness that it is not its own authority leads to certain psychological problems. The guerrillas develop a sense of dependence on the political leadership; "they lose sight of the moral and political principle to count on nothing but your own strength" (p. 70); and they develop an inferiority complex from always being held on a leash. The danger of these attitudes is compounded by the fact that the "bourgeois" political leadership, which cannot comprehend the exigencies of rural warfare, is undependable and incompetent. As a result the guerrillas are bound to be left in the lurch by the urban leadership, a form of betrayal which is no less egregious when it is unwitting.

Debray goes on to deplore the denigration of guerrillas by parties, as manifested in their strategic conduct of the revolutionary struggle. When it is not being neglected, the guerrilla force is the aimless victim of the naive, political juggling acts of a party which treats it as just one more pawn to be manipulated in response to the political machinations of the ruling class. It is likely that Debray had Guatemala, Venezuela, and Colombia in mind when he lashed out at this derogation of the guerrillas' role.

> Che Guevara wrote that the guerrilla movement is not an end in itself, nor is it a glorious adventure; it is merely a means to an end: the conquest of political power. But, lo and behold, guerrilla forces were serving many other purposes: a form of pressure on bourgeois governments; a factor in political horsetrading; a trump card to be played in case of need—such were the objectives with which certain leadership were attempting to saddle their military instrumentalities. The revolutionary method was being utilized for reformist ends [p. 105].

For Debray legal forms of struggle are incompatible with armed struggle; they cannot be integrated into the same revolutionary process. For this reason any attempt to coordinate the two is doomed to failure. In addition to wasting the potential of the guerrilla force by utilizing it for reformist ends, time, energy, and military resources are wasted in an activity which is useless to the guerrilla and which ceases to be of any use to anyone when the party and the legal organizations fall victim to repression.

Harkening back to Lenin's struggles for new organizational forms, Debray attributes the persistence of the Leninist party concept to "the force of tradition" (p. 74). He also hints strongly, however, that the drive to maintain legal options is nourished by opportunism. These efforts, like the establishment of "phantom fronts," are pursued for no other reasons than to justify theoretically the existence of an antiquated institution and to stem the erosion of its revolutionary hegemony by an effective political-military vanguard, the guerrilla foco. For the same reasons the party favors the creation of several focos. The smokescreen behind which this opportunism hides is the "abstract policy" (p. 75) of affirming the necessity to combine all forms of struggle without selecting one form as fundamental and another as subordinate (p. 74).

This policy, Debray argues, "converts the revolutionary movement into a disjointed marionnette" (p. 75). It leads to "uncontrolled actions in the city" (p. 75), by which Debray means actions that are not subordinated to the guerrilla force. (The example he cites is the general strike called by the Llano wing of the July 26th Movement in April 1958.) Furthermore, Debray charges, the policy of multiple forms of struggle leads to the premature creation of many focos. Both of these maneuvers, along with political frontism, are expressions not of the revolutionism of the party but of its jealous competition with the focos for leadership; they are directed not only against the enemy but against the foco as well. For the same reason the strategic goal of the urban forces is precipitation of a coup d'état in the city rather than military destruction of the bourgeois state.

What Is to Be Done?

It is significant that in his denunciation of city leadership Debray lumps the *Llano* of the July 26th Movement, which was decidedly anti-Communist, with contemporary Communist parties. In order to bring such disparate movements into phase ideologically Debray has to depart from the traditional Leninist sociology, which looks for the roots of reformism and ultraleftism in the class composition of the party in question and in the relative levels of political and economic welfare of various strata within the class or classes.[69] For Debray such distinctions are secondary. The fundamental common denominator is the urban setting which "bourgeoisifies" all who remain within its confines. Since no one is immune from this corruptive influence, Debray's antagonists include those groups (Maoist, Trotskyist, and the like) which attempt to exorcise opportunism from existing reformist parties by engaging them in noisy polemics. Not only will the patient fail to recover, the exorcists are fated to succumb in turn. If legal struggle on the ideological front offered some prospect of moving the masses to a revolutionary point of view, things would be different; but since only military activity can awaken the masses, Debray argues, the political *foco* is destined to repeat the classic degeneration from dissident leftism to opportunistic reformism:

> . . . a new revolutionary organization appears on the scene. It aspires to legal existence and then to participation in "normal" political life for a certain time, in order to consolidate and make a name for itself and thus prepare the ground for armed struggle. But lo and behold, it is gradually absorbed, swallowed up by the routine of this public political life. . . . The balance sheet is always positive: functionaries function, printing presses print, delegates travel, international friendships grow, leaders are overwhelmed with work; in brief, the machine is in motion. It has cost dearly and it must be cared for. The organization is "growing stronger."
>
> The prospects of insurrectional struggle diminish, delayed first for a few months then for years. Time passes, with its vicissitudes, and there is an increasing tendency to view the opening of hostilities as a somewhat sacrilegious temptation,

a kind of adventurism, perennially premature. . . . In short, the political organization has become an end in itself. It will not pass over to armed struggle because it must first wait until it establishes itself solidly as the party of the vanguard, even though in reality it cannot expect recognition of its vanguard status except through armed struggle [pp. 120–21].

Thus the absorption of politics by the military is complete; the *foco* is the answer to all political problems, from the mobilization of the masses to the conquest of false ideologies. In Debray's words,

. . . the best way of putting an end to vacillation is to pass over to the attack on imperialism and its local agents wherever conditions are ripe. . . . A successful ambush, a torturer cut down, a consignment of arms captured—these are the best answers to any reformist faintheartedness . . . [p. 126].

The answer to Lenin's question, "What is to be done?," is thus clearly indicated: the task is "to focus all efforts on the practical organization of the armed struggle with a view to achieving unity on the basis of Marxist Leninist principles" (p. 126). In organizational terms this means abandoning political principles for military ones and party discipline for military discipline. The principle of democratic centralism must be suspended once it has presided over the determination of a military strategy and the election of a general staff. Henceforth and until victory is assured, intraparty democracy must be replaced by the military chain of command (p. 103).

Summary

Debray's purpose in writing *Revolution in the Revolution?* was to break down what he saw to be the principal barrier to the further development of the Latin American Revolution —the Communist parties. He argued that the Communist parties' strategies for revolution and their forms of organization were tired old formulas which served only to block the unfolding of a generalized people's war against U.S. imperialism and its native allies.[70] He and his Cuban mentors were not frightened by this staggering contradiction of prior experience, for every revolution has had its share of novelties; and the very recent experience in Cuba had not been contradicted.

For the sake of continuity, the copious literature generated by Debray's writings has, except for specific criticisms, been bypassed. The most devastating critiques, however, are those that address themselves to Debray's methodology and those which interpret the even more recent experience of other Latin American countries to dispute Debray's theses. Let us turn now to these critics for help in evaluating Debray's work.

4

Debray
on the Firing Line

The sensation produced by *Revolution in the Revolution?* was
the result of the supercharged events and controversy that
gave birth to it and of the events which followed its publication, notably Debray's arrest and incarceration in Bolivia.
As a Cuban product of the rivalry between pro-Moscow and
pro-Cuban communism the pamphlet became linked, and
rightly so, with OLAS and Fidel Castro; as an immediate
antecedent to Guevara's capture and assassination in Bolivia
Revolution in the Revolution? was linked with Che Guevara's
dramatic failure. Given these highly placed associations, it
was inevitable that Debray's essay would attract a great deal
of attention.

The fact that Debray, unlike Castro and Guevara, could
be fired upon with relative impunity—without endangering
one's status as friend of the Cuban Revolution—brought out
the worst in some critics with old scores to settle. Debray
became the safety valve for the hostility and frustration that
Cuban gadflies had stirred up for nearly a decade.[1] But disagreement with Debray was not confined to the enemy camp.
From clandestinity and exile, revolutionaries whose experience
contradicted *Revolution in the Revolution?* raised their voices
in opposition. From the same ranks came differing interpretations of Guevara, of the Cuban Revolution, and of Leninism. Since these "friendly" critiques demolish *foquismo*

cleanly, there is no need here to explore the patently hostile literature.

Guevara vs. Debray?

A number of analysts have attempted to drive a wedge between Debray and Guevara, or to turn Guevara against Debray. We have already examined Quartim's efforts in this regard on the question of armed propaganda. Other attempts to make Guevara look more respectable in his weighting of political and military factors have been no more successful. According to Eqbal Ahmad the relation of the early and late Debray to Guevara is just the reverse of that reached here. He maintains that "Castroism," with its emphasis on political preparation and timing, is more, not less, in accord with Guevara's thinking. But the evidence he adduces is rather unpersuasive. On the question of exporting revolution he argues that Castro's and Guevara's

> . . . well-known opinion[s] on the impossibility of exporting revolutions [are] ignored. To the contrary, Debray argues that the fact that peasants may regard the *foco* as a foreign element among them required that guerrillas remain, at first, aloof from the population.[2]

But Debray's sense of "foreign" is clearly metaphorical whereas both Guevara's and Castro's early injunctions against exporting revolutions imply the literal sense of the term. And while neither Castro nor Guevara ever explicitly contradicted himself verbally, both did so in a spectacular way during the Bolivian venture. Ahmad argues further that there is in *Revolution* "no discussion of Che Guevara's earlier contention that guerrilla insurgency cannot succeed against a government which is able to maintain some legitimacy through the pretense of democracy."[3] Ahmad fails to mention that Che's "earlier contention," made in 1960 in *Guerrilla Warfare*, was abandoned by Guevara in 1963 in his "Guerrilla Warfare: A Method."

Ahmad does not deny that Guevara's Bolivian venture was fully in accord with Debray's theory: he seems to believe that Guevara put not his own but Debray's theory into practice. The same contention is made by Quartim,[4] who seizes upon another passage in *Guerrilla Warfare* which appears to place a greater emphasis on peasant mobilization than does *Revolution*. Let us quote the passage by Guevara on which Quartim rests his case:

> The guerrilla fighter needs full help from the people of the area. This is an indispensable condition. This is clearly seen by considering the case of bandit gangs that operate in a region. They have all the characteristics of a guerrilla army. . . . The only thing missing is support of the people; and, inevitably, these gangs are captured and exterminated by the public force.[5]

Quartim believes that this statement shows that Che considered the mobilization of the peasantry to be an indispensable condition for initiating hostilities. Instead, it is more probable that Che considered this a necessary condition for eventual success. Quartim is also wrong in supposing that for Guevara, unlike Debray, the choice of the countryside is dictated more by political factors, such as the possibility of mobilizing the peasants, rather than by strictly military factors (suitability of terrain, etc.). As we have shown, for both Guevara and Debray, the first consideration is the physical survival of the guerrilla center; and for both, political mobilization in the early stages has to be achieved through military action. There are no serious differences between the two writers on this score.

It is more difficult to formulate concisely the relationship between the views of Guevara and Debray on the importance of urban support organizations. As we have seen, Debray's position is that dependence on the city should be kept to a minimum and that the overall command must always reside in the countryside. This view is based on interpretations of Guevara's comments in *Guerrilla Warfare* and on Debray's analysis of the Cuban experience which presumably reflected the viewpoint of Castro and other veterans of the Rebel Army.

On this question there are reasons to doubt that Guevara's position is reflected in *Revolution in the Revolution?* Guevara began arranging for the organization of an urban apparatus in Bolivia early in 1964, more than two years before

Ricardo (who had been in Bolivia in 1963 as a member of the People's Guerrilla Army [EGP]) arrived to begin preparations in the countryside. Tamara Bider Bunker, alias Tania, was charged with creating an urban support organization in accordance with guidelines similar to those later laid down by Guevara in an early 1967 instruction sheet made public in Cuba after his death. Guevara's instructions called for an organization to support the guerrillas by providing supplies, transportation, information, finances, urban action, and contacts with sympathizers.[6]

The impression left by Guevara's careful preparations, viz., that he attached greater importance to urban support than did Debray, is weakened considerably by Che's subsequent behavior. According to Pombo, a Cuban guerrilla sent to Bolivia in July 1966 to assist Ricardo, the urban apparatus was never well developed. It was, in fact, only in an incipient state when Guevara chose to open hostilities on March 23, 1967.[7] It is also noteworthy that when the Bolivian Communist party, which had initially agreed to collaborate in the venture and which was the hub of the urban network, abandoned the guerrillas, Guevara was able to write, as though relieved of a burden, that this development would not tax the guerrillas and would most likely be beneficial in the long run.[8]

Interestingly enough, Debray himself participated in the effort to disassociate Guevara from *Revolution in the Revolution?* In defending himself before the military court in Bolivia against the charge of having intellectually authored Guevara's venture, Debray cited as proof to the contrary the fact that Guevara had his own political commissars, Inti and Coco Peredo, two native Bolivians.[9] Without wishing to argue that Debray was the intellectual author—Guevara as an intellectual author of Debray's book comes closer to the position being taken here—this testimony deserves to be disregarded. Guevara threw together a guerrilla band composed primarily of veteran Cuban guerrillas and Bolivians, some former members of the PCB, some not. Then he put the Peredo brothers in charge of the political education of their novice countrymen and perhaps even bestowed upon the Peredos the title of political commissar. He could, with the same right, have called

Inti Peredo an armed propagandist because he addressed a gathering of Bolivian peasants. Clearly this formality does not imply a difference of any importance between Guevara and Debray. To the contrary, it suggests again that Guevara's Bolivian debacle contradicted Debray's theory only in its outcome.

Voices of Experience

Cuba

The 1969 essay by two Cuban revolutionaries, Torres and Aronde, deserves to be singled out for its contribution to the anti-Debray literature.[10] Torres and Aronde call into question one of the pillars of Debray's theoretical edifice, the Castroist-Guevarist interpretation of the Cuban Revolution. In the process they criticize Debray's unconventional concepts, such as "bourgeoisification," and deplore the overall negative effect of Debray's less credible assertions in the battle against reformist theories, noting that "such theories find the condition for their permanence in the weakness of critics' arguments."[11]

Torres and Aronde argue that Debray's most serious error is his failure to understand the full significance of the July 26th Movement, its internal conflicts, and its relation to the rural guerrillas led by Castro. Debray loosely interprets these internal conflicts in geographical terms. The principal conflict is between the rural guerrilla force, or Sierra, and the urban wing of the July 26th Movement, or Llano. Debray even correlates geographical distinctions with class distinctions, calling the Llano bourgeois and the Sierra proletarian. Torres and Aronde reject this notion as a gross oversimplification. Indeed, the Llano consisted of an amalgamation of diverse interest groups: the national bourgeoisie, petty bourgeoisie, and rank and file militants. One could talk of conflicts within the Llano—between the national bourgeoisie and the militants—or between the Llano militants and the Sierra (on such issues as whether all arms and ammunition should be sent to the Sierra), or between the leadership of the Llano and of the Sierra (on questions of strategy). But one cannot, Torres and Aronde contend, speak of a Llano-Sierra conflict per se. Nor, they argue, did Castro always embody the ultimate authority, as Debray suggests. Torres and Aronde attribute to Fidel a different kind of revolutionary vision than the one Debray outlines. In their view, not only did the revolutionary pyramid have a base at the beginning of hostilities, it was broad enough to embrace members of the upper, middle, and petty bourgeoisie. The apex, which existed apart from this broad front, was also the glue which held it together while maintaining the primacy of the working and peasant classes within the front. Far from insisting upon absolute command, they conclude, Fidel was capable of subordinating the *Sierra* to the *Llano* to preserve the unity of the front as long as the financial support of the wealthy classes was indispensable to the guerrillas.

If we can believe Torres and Aronde, Debray's first *foco* theory is thus a better replica of the Cuban experience than the second, which ironically was inspired by and heavily based on that experience. Debray's Leninist presuppositions, in short, were a better guide than all of the added information, some of it privileged, which he gathered in Cuba.

Peru

Even before the debacle in Bolivia, the fate of the Peruvian guerrillas in 1965 had given mute but eloquent testimony to the hazards of *foquismo*; but the failures of the MIR were not seen in Castroist circles as terribly damning because of the guerrillas' tactical deviations—security zones, armed propaganda, dispersion of guerrilla fronts, and absence of a centralized command structure. What was forgotten, discounted, or denied was that with regard to the urban-rural question the guerrillas were Guevarists, and undoubtedly this also contributed to their failure. According to one sympathetic Peruvian commentator, the orientation of all the guerrilla groups was so rigid that it ignored ready pockets of support in the working-class and student sectors because their strategic model relegated those sectors to a later stage.[12] The leaders commanded the *focos*, leaving behind in the cities "a few embryonic supporter groups" incapable of any significant actions. As a consequence, organized popular support could be choked off by the government's clever policy of selectively repressing only those organizations which voiced support for the guerrillas.[13] Contrary to Debray's thesis, the revolutionary show of force did not have the effect of mobilizing the urban masses. According to ELN chief Héctor Béjar, the expectation that it would was a serious miscalculation:

> Ideologically, our attitude was based on an underestimation of the cities. We thought that if guerrilla warfare began in the midst of the peasant population there was no reason to find a justification for it in terms of bourgeois politics which are foreign, distant and unknown to the peasantry.
>
> This is completely true as far as the peasantry is concerned, but this was not sufficient to impel them to support actively armed rebellion against the system. Under these conditions, the attitude of the urban population was limited to vague sympathy on the part of some, enthusiasm in small —mainly student—sectors, and indifference on the part of the majority.[14]

This greatly strengthened the hand of the government:

> The army, which thus had few problems in its rear, had its hands free to fight us in the interior of the country. There it instituted a general terror to intimidate the civilian population—in which it also succeeded.[15]

Coming from a confirmed Guevarist this is strong criticism.

Uruguay

If Bolivia and Peru have discredited Guevarism's rural orientation by negative example, the relatively successful wave of urban guerrilla warfare, which followed the Bolivian failure, in the more highly urbanized countries of Uruguay, Brazil, and Argentina has tended to discredit that orientation by positive example. The extent of the Guevarist bias against the city is brought into sharp relief when the comments by Debray and Castro about Uruguay are compared with the reality of the Uruguayan National Liberation Front (MLN), better known as the Tupamaros. Debray makes a point of exempting Uruguay from the list of countries in which the conditions are propitious for armed struggle (p. 124). Similarly, the Cuban delegation's report to the OLAS Conference in August 1967 termed the idea of guerrilla warfare in Uruguay and Chile as "absurd"; and Castro scoffed at the idea in his closing address to the conference.[16] It appears that the presumed high level of democracy in these countries was seen as one inhibiting factor, but in view of Guevarist thinking in this area, the decisive factor was probably—at least in the case of Uruguay —the unsuitability of the flat Uruguayan terrain for rural guerrilla warfare. The similarity of the "Switzerland of Latin America" to its European "twin" does not extend to geography. And to the Cubans armed struggle was synonymous with rural guerrilla warfare. As the Tupamaros and urban guerrillas in Argentina have shown, this identification is unwarranted. The low estimate of urban guerrilla warfare which Guevara and Debray encourage in their works has been refuted by experience. The enormous military potential and durability of urban commandos, even in the absence of a rural force, has been clearly demonstrated.

In a 1970 interview, a Tupamaro leader discussed the pros and cons of armed struggle in the Uruguayan urban context:

> It is true that we are operating right in the mouth of the enemy, but it is also true that the enemy has got us stuck in its throat. We are faced with the inconvenience of having to lead a dual life, in which we carry on a public activity— whenever we are able to—yet, in reality, are someone else altogether. But we have the advantage of having a series of indispensable resources at hand which rural guerrillas must engage in special operations to obtain: food, ammunition, weapons, and communications. . . . We the urban guerrillas move about in a city which we know like the palm of our hand, in which we look like everybody else. . . .
> . . . the rate of our losses . . . shows a marked increase. [But] the multiplication of the Movement is so great that it makes for easy, rapid replacement of these losses.[17]

In another interview, one of the founders of the Tupamaros rejected as totally unfounded several of Debray's propositions about the psychology of urban guerrilla warfare which were formulated in "Castroism." According to this anonymous source, the Tupamaros experienced none of the neuroses described by Debray—far from it. What they did experience is just what Debray had categorically denied to the city as a whole, the process of proletarianization, defined as the development of a spirit of comradeship, awareness of self-discipline, and a feeling of dependence on the group.[18] It is interesting that the possibility of such an ideological transformation is unwittingly suggested by Debray himself. Contrary to their role in the first *foco* theory, the masses play no part in the proletarianization of the combatants in the second theory, which defines proletarianization in purely military terms. Consequently, there cease to be any strong reasons why proletarianization should not attend every kind of organized armed struggle. This flatly contradicts the claim that city life "bourgeoisifies" everyone. According to Debray's own premises, there are exceptions; and these have been verified by Tupamaro experience.

It appears then that the urban guerrilla form of struggle may be viable both militarily and ideologically. We have already noted how quickly in the elaboration of revolutionary strategy a possibility becomes a necessity. This is especially evident during the early stages of an insurrection. In the same way, the moment the possibility of urban military success and the compatability of urban and rural guerrilla warfare were demonstrated, *foquismo* in its tidy, Debrayan linearity became obsolete from both a practical and a logical standpoint. Without further criticism, one could say that Debray's model has no future; the only question is what can be salvaged from the wreck. The Uruguayans salvaged a great deal: the immediate transition to people's war; the subordination of all other forms of struggle in favor of armed struggle; political-military unity of command; the avoidance of legal, nonmilitary work; and pragmatism, internationalism, and the "many Vietnams" continental strategy. The Tupamaros have never reduced the functions of the guerrilla to military action in Debrayan fashion, but for years there was a discernible tendency in this direction.[19] In their latest document, issued in July 1973 after more than a year of severe repression and heavy losses, they criticized their Debrayan legacy. In evaluating past mistakes the Tupamaros singled out their underestimation of the "people's tremendous capacity for struggle."[20]

Brazil

Perhaps the most trenchant criticism of Debray has been made by a Brazilian, Joao Quartim. Quartim's views are of special interest here because of the circumstances under which they were formed. He was a militant in a clandestine Brazilian organization, the Revolutionary Popular Vanguard (VPR), during its first year of operation (from January 1968 to February 1969). During this period the VPR grappled with the problem of defining itself with respect to *Revolution in the Revolution?* In October 1968 the VPR rejected Debrayism as a "militarist" deviation and it is primarily on this ground that Quartim rejects him. By "militarism" Quartim, following Lenin, means the view "which considers the decisive confrontation with the repressive apparatus of the ruling class to be the task of the vanguard only, which amounts to the belief that the vanguard can make the revolution in place of the class."[21] The VPR was soon to desert this position, shifting from a rejection of Debray based on antimilitarism to one based on urban militarism. Quartim sees this movement to urban militarism as a regression from Debray, for Quartim judges Debray's strategic emphasis on rural guerrilla warfare to be correct. But he implies strongly that the VPR's deviation was attributable in large part to Debray's popularization of a narrow military viewpoint.

Beyond Debray's intention to undermine the counter-revolutionary influence of the reformist CP's, Quartim finds little of value in Debray's works. His overall view is that the zealous but hapless Debray played directly into the hands of opportunism by encouraging revolutionaries in their self-defeating tactics and by making a laughingstock of revolutionary theory with his outrageous statements. Debray's "less happy formulations"

> offer an unguarded flank to the malicious attacks of the opportunist "left." An example is his notorious sally: "The mountain proletarianizes the bourgeois and peasant elements, and the city can bourgeoisify the proletarians." An amazing stupidity, so easy to refute: the "bourgeoisified" proletarians of Petrograd made the great October revolution, and the

"bourgeoisified" Spanish militia for two years resisted Fascism heroically at the gates of Madrid.

There is worse: it is not only a question of phrases. Behind them lies Debray's Stalinist formulation, with its mixture of dogmatism and brilliant simplicity.[22]

The error which Quartim believes to be central to Debray's theorizing is the interpretation of Latin American reformism. Quartim does not deny that the "temptations and amenities of urban life" may play some role in sapping a party's revolutionism, but he considers the notion that this is the principal determinant "simply ridiculous." Quartim's forceful argument deserves to be quoted at some length.

> The fundamental manifestation of the opportunism and treason of the traditional parties is not the fact that they do not decide to leave for the country, it is not that they prefer to struggle against the enemy *in the town*, but rather that they *do not struggle* against the main enemy. It was not by failing to take to the French maquis that the corrupted bureaucrats of the PCF betrayed the revolutionary proletariat in May 1968.
>
> Debray lacked the theoretical firmness (for we believe he did not lack courage) to get to the bottom of this problem, to say that the traditional Communist Parties are the international instrument of Soviet diplomacy and its strategy of peaceful coexistence. The renegade Prestes [general secretary of the Brazilian Communist party], at the time of the column that bore his name, had the courage to leave for the country. It is obvious that in 1964 it was not because he was "softened up by the hot baths of the town" as Debray says, that he did not repeat the exploit. Prestes possessed the concrete conditions to prepare urban and rural armed struggle in 1964. All the conditions for a revolutionary civil war existed then, as anyone who witnessed the peasant movement or the sailors' revolt in Rio knows very well. If Prestes and his acolytes sabotaged this war and capitulated without firing a shot, it was not because they had failed to read *Revolution in the Revolution?* (the Cuban example was there, before their eyes), but rather because they are servants of the ruling bureaucracy of the Soviet state which, as everyone knows, sabotages by all possible means armed confronta-

tion between the vanguard of the exploited people and US imperialism.[23]

Quartim suggests that at the root of this central misconception is Debray's failure to appreciate the far-reaching implications of the Leninist doctrine of the relationship between revolutionary theory and practice:

> . . . a Marxist starts from the firm assumption that there is no revolutionary practice until there is a revolutionary theory, that the one is inseparable from the other, that it is the *integration* of the two that permits the *revolutionary transformation* of society.[24]

Given this relation between theory and practice, Debray continues, it should have occurred to a Leninist to seek the causes for the opportunism of traditional Communist parties in their programs.

As one may recall, Debray also tried to establish that a cause for the opportunism of the parties was their form of organization. According to Quartim this is another major error; it mistakes cause for effect. Debray forgot, as Lenin never did, "the difference between structural and conjunctural conditions."[25] Consistent with this inversion of the relationship between form and content, Quartim argues, Debray then commits the corresponding error with regard to the revolutionary forces: "He mechanically derives revolutionary politics from military forms of organization."[26] Having imputed the line of peaceful coexistence to the organizational forms of loyal and legal opposition, he bases the revolutionary line on an organizational form suited for unloyal and illegal opposition. A theory so grounded, Quartim argues, will naturally lean heavily to the side of militarism.

As for Quartim's more substantive criticism, he sees Debray committing and encouraging four related errors, all of them expressions or examples of his militarism: first, an "underestimation of the preparatory phase before the guerrilla *foco* opens operations"; second, "a spontaneist conception of the mass movement"; third, a "focist overestimation of the efficacy of armed propaganda"; and finally, "militarism in the

organization of the vanguard and the revolutionary classes."[27]
Let us review these criticisms briefly.

In 1968 in a reply to his critics Debray insisted that it
was not his intention to address himself to problems confronting revolutionary armed struggle where it was not already
underway.[28] As we have seen, this statement is belied by
Debray's work. In addition to what has already been said, we
may quote a specific passage which is nothing if not a pre-
scription for revolutionaries:

> The setting up of military *focos*, not political "*focos*,"
> is decisive for the future. . . . it is a matter of a new *dialectics
> of tasks*. In order to express it schematically let us say that
> one must go from the military *foco* to the political move-
> ment—a natural extension of an essentially political armed
> struggle; but only very exceptionally does one go from a
> "pure" political movement to the military *foco*. . . . In most
> countries where conditions for armed struggle exist it is pos-
> sible to move from a military *foco* to a political *foco*, but to
> move in the opposite direction is virtually impossible [pp.
> 119–20].

In this way Debray excludes politics from the preparatory
phase of guerrilla warfare. To the tactical question of how the
military *foco* should be established, Debray, in effect, replies
that armed cadres must assemble, go into the countryside,
train, and await the forces of the repression.

Quartim makes substantially the same point, terming
Debray's error a "militarist simplification of the tasks of the
vanguard" and a form of opportunism.[29] Among the many
who have fallen into this trap, Quartim includes Che Guevara.

> The Bolivian experience has shown that it is just this mili-
> tarist simplification of the tasks of the vanguard (make war
> in the countryside) that led to an opportunist policy in the
> towns. Because they thought only of the *foco*, the Bolivian
> revolutionaries came to leave the political-military work of
> support for the guerrilla column in the hands of inveterate
> opportunists. These individuals, militants of political organ-
> izations well-known for their incapacity to confront the tasks
> of the revolution seriously, were bound to betray Guevara
> and his comrades.[30]

Quartim finds in this example and others an affirmation of the Leninist proposition that military work must never be divorced from mass work:

> It is not "up to the masses" to rally to the struggle begun and led by the vanguard; it is up to the vanguard to organize itself in such a way as to polarize the revolutionary energy of the masses. If the vanguard is not to be cut off from the concrete process of class struggle, it must achieve—right from the initial phase in which it prepares the guerrilla column—solid anchorage in the objectively revolutionary classes.[31]

It is for this reason that from the beginning a revolutionary organization is needed, capable of "constructing forms of liaison between the vanguard and the masses."[32] And for the same reason the preparatory phase must be centered in the city, for it is there and only there that it can "organize and fortify itself as a vanguard organization,"[33] as vanguard of the proletariat and its allies.

The view that "the masses will by themselves join the guerrilla vanguard and automatically acknowledge the mobile strategic force to be their vanguard," Quartim calls "spontaneism."[34] This is the obverse of organizational militarism; and it manifests itself not only in Debray's neglect of the preparatory phase, but also in his conception of armed propaganda and political fronts. As we have seen, Quartim views Guevara's lamentable experience with the Bolivian peasantry as a decisive rebuttal of Debray's views on armed propaganda. Quartim ridicules Debray's thesis on political fronts by showing its implications when applied to Brazil:

> Transposed into Brazil, Debray's thesis implies the idea that the development of the guerrilla nucleus would by itself permit the creation of a national liberation front unifying all forms of struggle from the Amazon to Rio Grande do Sul. In each State of the country, in each region of each major State, there are today at least several organizations which not only are "for armed struggle," but which have already started to prepare for it either by sending their best cadres into the countryside, or by accumulating the material and means to be able to advance the peoples' war. According to Debray, these diverse organizations should not maintain contact be-

tween one another *before or independently of the consolidation* of their respective guerrilla colums (except if by magic
they could immediately agree on all tactical questions and
effect a unification from one day to the next). Because, says
Debray, "one creates a front around something *extant*, not
only around a programme of liberations." Evidently, as the
foco is not yet something *existent*, there would be neither
the means, nor any reason, to seek at the present time to
unify the principal form of struggle with those that are complementary, and therefore necessary, to the principal form
itself.[35]

Quartim's incisive arguments provisionally answer two
questions which were raised in the previous chapter concerning the efficacy of formulating strategies and tactics for whole
continents. In a critical essay, written in the heat of the
VPR's controversy over Debrayism, Quartim uses two negative examples devastatingly—Bolivia and Brazil. He followed
this two years later with *Dictatorship and Armed Struggle in
Brazil* which serves as a counterexample ruinous to *Revolution
in the Revolution?* Quartim brings to this work the ingredients required for a comprehensive revolutionary theory: revolutionary practice and an intimate knowledge of the politico-
economic history of his country. Space does not permit us to
enumerate the many implicit and explicit criticisms of Debray
that this work offers; nor is it possible here to present a full
exposition of Quartim's strategic alternative to *Revolution in
the Revolution?* We must confine ourselves to a brief description of Quartim's work, interspersed with abbreviated examples of the failure of Debrayism in Brazil.

Dictatorship and Armed Struggle in Brazil contains a
concise and comprehensive revolutionary theory. It begins
with a short political history of Brazil, probably meant more
for foreign readers than Brazilians, followed by a paradigm of
Marxist-Leninist class analysis which is no less exemplary because it is brief. Quartim discovers sources of possible ruling-
class conflicts which Debrayists, blinded by their precepts,
could not take into account. He finds revolutionary potential
in the urban working class and the suburban marginal classes
which would escape those harboring a Guevarist fixation on

the peasantry. And in the peasantry he finds a vast revolutionary potential which, buried deep, requires not a short but a long, continuous tradition of struggle to be brought to the surface.[36] In analyzing the recent history of the Brazilian student movement (from late 1963 through 1969), Quartim finds much that was positive in the intense political debates that wracked the student movement during 1967. They led not to political *focos* and quiescence, as Debray would have had the students believe, but to the evolution of the student movement to revolutionary warfare. Political *focos* did indeed transform themselves into military *focos*; political struggle led to armed struggle.

Quartim turns next to a detailed analysis of the course of armed struggle from the standpoint of strategy and tactics. Predictably it is here that Debray's theses meet their greatest test, and here that they fail. The first and best example of Debrayism preceded the publication of *Revolution in the Revolution?* In 1966 the Revolutionary Nationalist Movement (MNR) launched a *foco* in the Caparáo mountains. It was a clandestine operation, and in no time the guerrillas were subdued by the army. The lesson, Quartim writes, which this experience taught was that "the transition to armed struggle might be immediate but henceforth the rural *foco* would require preparation in the city."[37]

Then came *Revolution in the Revolution?* and the OLAS Conference, which precipitated the breakup of the Brazilian Communist party. Arising from the debris were the Revolutionary Brazilian Communist party (PCBR) which disagreed with the old PCB leadership on parts of the program and on methods of work; the PCBR members preferred the weapon of criticism to the criticism of weapons. The National Liberation Action (ALN) in Sao Paulo, led by Carlos Marighela, disagreed totally with the PCB's program and called for armed struggle, relying completely on the "polarizing effect of armed struggle to regroup the revolutionary cadre of the PCB." The ALN slogan was vintage Guevara: "action builds organization." In Rio State and Parana a Debrayist splinter broke away from the PCB, calling itself the Revolutionary Movement of the Eighth of October (MR-8).

Workers' Politics (POLOP) suffered the same kind of split, with the armed struggle advocates in the states of Minas Gerais and Guanabara combining forces under the banner of the National Liberation Commando (COLIMA). In Sao Paulo they joined with MNR survivors, eventually taking the name Revolutionary Popular Vanguard, VPR.

In 1968 these organizations began to carry out armed actions in the cities. In principle these were logistical actions for the purpose of gathering weapons and equipment for rural guerrilla warfare, but two factors combined to impose a revision in the Debrayist scenario. In the city the armed organizations became rallying centers not only for revolutionary intellectuals, but also for all combative sectors of the people. And the size and combativity of these sectors increased for several years. Meanwhile, difficulties unforeseen by Debray and his Brazilian followers cropped up in the countryside. The MR-8 sent its members thousands of kilometers in search of a suitable territory. Finally they were successful. Arms and equipment were obtained through urban raids; farms were bought for training. But one automobile accident succeeded in cracking the wall of secrecy which had screened all preparatory activities from the public eye. The conspiracy was smashed, and the confession of captured and tortured guerrillas brought heavy repression to the urban wing as well. The MR-8 survived, but it abandoned its orthodox Debrayism.[38]

The Revolutionary Movement of July 26th (MR-26), also known as the Revolutionary Action Movement (MAR), formed from survivors of the MNR, had a similar experience: the torture of arrested members led to government penetration of the urban network and the encirclement and disbandment of the rural foco. Again the survivors became disillusioned with Debray.

The POLOP Opposition and MNR survivors abandoned their search for a foco site after their laborious exploration of the countryside failed to produce a satisfactory spot—one which was wild enough to protect the guerrillas while being of sufficient importance to draw the army into a fight. The choice was made more difficult when seemingly mandatory political considerations were taken into account. One such consideration was the fact that the politically advanced sectors of the peasantry who were consulted by these groups insisted on the need to adapt armed struggle to local conditions. Once freed from their *focist* obsession, the revolutionary cadres turned to mass work among peasants, agricultural wage-laborers, and semiemployed marginal classes living in the suburban slums. In this effort they were greeted with tangible gains, bringing them to the realization that the organization of peasant cells of support and collaboration could and should precede the installation of a mobile strategic guerrilla force. Reality proved to be more complex than Debray had imagined; the POLOP Opposition was irresistibly drawn to another strategy.[39]

Nineteen sixty-nine was the year of urban battles. Here the limitations of what one might call neo-Guevarism (or, equivalently, neo-Debrayism) manifested themselves in actions by the ALN and the newly "militarized" VPR. The urban guerrillas, depending too much on action to do the job of organizing, were unable to grow stronger and pass over the stage of generalized warfare. By concentrating too much on spectacular actions such as the kidnapping of the U.S. ambassador, which brought them wide publicity, they neglected to establish the nationwide network of popular bases of support which the passage to people's war realistically requires, Debrayism notwithstanding. Urban warfare began to be seen not as a precursor to generalized guerrilla war but as a means for the direct assault on state power. Armed propaganda addressed to the whole nation and aimed at demoralizing the regime was preferred to more pedestrian but more substantial forms of armed propaganda, such as the temporary seizure of factories, free distribution of stolen food, reprisals against tyrannical landlords, etc. In this way the guerrillas widened the war without widening their capacity to fight. The momentum they unleashed against themselves soon exceeded the power they could muster to oppose it. Spectacular media events, it seems, do not mobilize the masses as quickly and thoroughly as they do the counterrevolutionary forces.

Quartim does not dispute the Guevarist and neo-Guevarist contention that revolutionaries must be soldiers. In his view, this has become an absolute necessity because of the rise of international socialism as a serious competitor to the international capitalist system. The unbridled competition between capitalist countries has given way to organized competition and a united front against socialism. Thus, Quartim concludes, there will be no more world wars to arm the working classes and then turn them against the bourgeois state, no more spontaneous destruction of the repressive apparatus as occurred in Russia in 1917. In the future, he wrote, all revolutions will have to take the form of long civil wars which combine political and military operations from the start.[40]

Thus, Quartim agrees that preparation for armed struggle should not be postponed, as the reformists propose. But he insists that the mass struggle not be postponed either. He acknowledges that the principal terrain of the people's war will be in the countryside but insists that before it can develop there, it must be given a solid, mass basis in the city. It must be preceded by clandestine peasant organizing, and it must be commanded by a Marxist-Leninist vanguard party capable of directing the overall struggle. The formation of such a vanguard is also an immediate task.

These, then, are the lessons of a Marxist-Leninist interpretation of the Brazilian experience. As they unfold, one is drawn irresistibly to the conclusion that the corner-cutting methodology which carried Debray from one fallacy to the next is itself fallacious.

Confronting Historical Materialism

All of the criticisms considered in this chapter have seized on Debray's contraposition of countryside/proletarian and city/bourgeois. Quartim could hardly believe that Debray was serious. Were the defenders of Madrid "bourgeoisified," were the St. Petersburg proletariat? Did Carlos Prestes become a reformist just because he moved to the capital? Did the PCF undermine the May 1968 revolt because it hadn't trooped off to the French maquis? Of course not. But how is it possible that Debray should voice such absurdities?

Pointing vaguely to Debray's methodological denial of

Lenin does not supply a satisfactory answer. There seem to be other, deeper philosophical problems lurking about. A letter written to Debray in March 1967 by his philosophical mentor, Louis Althusser, shows that indeed this is the case.[41] Althusser notes, first of all, that Debray's argument for the guerrilla *foco* relies totally on a negative demonstration of the falsity and weakness of other strategies. Once a "theoretical space" has been cleared in this way, it is promptly and unceremoniously filled by the concept of the rural guerrilla, without a positive demonstration of its suitability given prevailing conditions in Latin America. The *foco* concept becomes a pure concept; there is no recognition of the *foco's* dependence on historical conditions. It is self-sufficient; it contains within itself all of its own determinants and resolves, through its own powers, all of its contradictions. The psychological attributes of guerrilla life become so many political attributes. Conceptually, the pure concept is sustained solely by a contrived Manichean counterconcept—life in the cities. All of this, Althusser contends, is more Feuerbachian than Marxian, and it is all fallacious. The fundamental error in Debray's reasoning is that "nature occupies the place of history." Guerrillas do not naturally become successful revolutionaries nor city-dwellers inveterate reformists. It is the historical circumstances, Althusser argues, that are decisive. Whether rural guerrilla warfare is viable depends not on its internal virtues but on the historical conditions of the guerrilla's existence.

Althusser acknowledges that, here and there, Debray shows an awareness of the importance of historical analysis, as when he infers from a comparison of conditions in China and Vietnam with those in Latin America that the Asian revolutionary model is unsuited to Latin America. But even here, nature ultimately takes the place of history as Debray concludes that the difference in demographic density is decisive. Had not Marx shown long ago that "demography is not its own light"?[42] Similarly, Althusser notes that in comparing the conditions under which the Chinese and Vietnamese CPs were formed with Latin American conditions, Debray stays on the level of politics and never gets to the heart of things—the economic conditions. Finally, the sole historical support claimed for the *foco* is the Cuban Revolution, but Debray is silent about the economic and political conditions of its success, so that its real import for Latin America remains a mystery.

There is a certain tragic irony in the fact that while Althusser was pointing out how desperately flimsy the *foco* theory was in conception, Debray was experiencing the gruelling and brutal reality of *foquismo* with Che Guevara in Bolivia. After his subsequent arrest and incarceration, Debray began a retreat from the tenets of Guevarism, bringing him squarely back to Althusser's viewpoint. By the time the letter was delivered its mission had already been fulfilled.

5

Orthodox Leninism:
No *Foquismo*

With the Guerrillas in Bolivia

Debray's tenure at the University of Havana lasted six months, beginning in January 1966. While in Cuba he received a letter from Guevara which, according to Debray, invited him for an interview at an unspecified location and stipulated the French publisher François Maspero as the go-between. There must have been more to the letter than that for after returning from his August 1966 rendezvous with Maspero in Paris, Debray went directly to Bolivia, arriving two months before Guevara. He remained in Bolivia during September. Debray has kept silent about his activities during this period, but we know from the diary of "Pombo," a Cuban agent in Bolivia who was kept informed about Debray by Havana, that Debray had at least two missions. He was to make a geopolitical study of the Alto Beni region, which Guevara favored as the location for his future zone of operations, and he was to talk with Moisés Guevara, a Bolivian Maoist and erstwhile mine union leader, whose incorporation into the guerrilla force, along with several of his followers, was being considered.[1]

Debray met with resistance from all sides. The preference of Guevara and Debray for the Alto Beni region caused concern among the Cubans who were supervising preparations, for in July they had purchased a three-thousand-acre farm at

Nancahuazú. To make matters worse, Debray's presence in the Alto Beni interfered with the execution of Guevara's order that another farm be purchased, since the Cubans could not allow themselves to be seen with him. On one occasion Ricardo was compelled to cut short a tour to avoid contact with Debray; on another occasion Debray unwittingly tried to photograph Pombo and his driver. The PCB leader, Mario Monje Molina, objected to the new location because movement from this northern zone to other countries would not be feasible; Monje had agreed to collaborate in Guevara's plan for continental revolution with the understanding that Bolivia was to serve only as a staging area for focos launched elsewhere. Guevara's decision to begin operations in Bolivia was not greeted with enthusiasm. Monje was also incensed over Debray's dealings with pro-Peking splinter groups, fearing that plans were being made to bypass the PCB. Debray's undiplomatic criticism of the party while in Bolivia did not help to improve relations.[2]

Debray returned to Cuba in late September. Guevara arrived in Nancahuazú on November 7, after the plan to relocate in Alto Beni had been scrapped. In February 1967 Debray again set out for Bolivia, arriving at the Nancahuazú camp on March 6. He was accompanied by Coco Peredo, Tania, and Ciro Roberto Bustos, an Argentine recruited by Tania for liaison with guerrillas in Argentina. Due to a misunderstanding on Tania's part, the visitors arrived at the camp two weeks before Guevara's return from a training march.

On March 20 Guevara and his men returned to camp, completely exhausted by the grueling march. He spent the day talking with the visitors-collaborators and discussing their new assignments. Guevara's diary contains the following account of his conversation with Debray:

> He came to stay but I asked him to return to organize an auxiliary network in France, and while on his way there he should go to Cuba, which I know he wants to do, to get married and have a child. I have to write to Sartre and B. Russell to have them organize an international fund to help the Bolivian Liberation Movement. He should also talk to a friend and have him organize everything that he can to help,

especially in the way of money, medicine and electronics, sending an electrical engineer and equipment.[3]

The suggestion by Daniel James that the "friend" to whom Guevara refers was Fidel Castro[4] is supported by the enormity of the aid that this friend was expected to deliver. Where but Cuba could an electrical engineer be found to send to the guerrillas? The request for electronic gear and an engineer also indicates that serious problems in communicating with Havana were already being encountered. (Beginning in April Guevara repeatedly complains in his diary of his lack of contact with Havana.) Debray figured in Guevara's efforts to overcome his isolation in yet another way. He was entrusted with a message to Fidel and was asked to give him a verbal report on the state of the Bolivian campaign.[5] Guevara apparently briefed Debray for this report on March 25.[6]

Any chance that Debray might have had to carry out these missions, however, had already been lost. A week before Che's return, two of Moisés Guevara's men had been captured while deserting from the camp in which the visitors were staying. Three days later another of Moisés Guevara's men had been captured without offering resistance. These men had seen Debray participating in camp chores, including guard duty, and had witnessed a group reading of *Revolution in the Revolution?* in camp.[7] In addition Debray may have made known his intention to serve with Guevara as a combatant. Hence he was already a marked man. His chances of escaping to Cuba deteriorated even further after the guerrilla ambush of an army patrol on March 23. Before this, the Barrientos regime had stubbornly refused to acknowledge the existence of a guerrilla force in Bolivia, despite mounting evidence. The armed action, in which seven soldiers were killed, four wounded, and fourteen prisoners taken,[8] put an end to wishful thinking. The country was put on alert by Barrientos that "Castro-Communists" had "invaded the national territory."

The appeal to nationalist sentiments was effective. The National Confederation of Peasants responded by announcing the mobilization of its membership against "the intervention of foreign elements in the country's internal affairs," and six hundred peasants from Cochabamba volunteered for duty against the guerrillas.[9] In a short time the guerrilla zone was saturated with soldiers; for almost a month no opportunity was found to dispose of Debray and Bustos. Finally, on April 19, in the vicinity of the village of Muyupampa, an opportunity seemingly presented itself when George Andrew Roth, an enterprising newsman in search of a story, found his way to the guerrilla camp. Roth agreed to accompany the two "newsmen," apparently oblivious to the danger involved. In Muyupampa they were promptly seized by the army and jailed.

Retreat from Guevarism

Debray was held incommunicado for two months; meanwhile the Barrientos regime and its CIA advisers used Debray's connections to whip up a propaganda campaign against Cuba. During the early days of his incarceration Debray was severely beaten and tortured. He spent two months in solitary confinement, during half of which he was tied to his bed and deprived of light. In late May he was untied, light was admitted into his cell, and he was provided with writing materials. Expecting to be executed at any moment, the twenty-six-year-old Debray set about writing an essay entitled "In Settlement of All Accounts," which he derisively called his "memoirs."[10] In assessing the last ten years of his life, Debray shows that he is still very much the defiant Guevarist. His portrayal of his adolescent and student life, and of the French culture which shaped or misshaped it, is merciless. He pictures the end result as a physical weakling, an intellectual snob, and a bookworm. He was a thoroughgoing skeptic where emotions such as passion and human virtues such as courage were concerned; he was the disembodied intellect. As a Marxist intellectual he accepted as his due a small niche in the revolutionary directorship, far from the firing line. There was no contact with the rank and file except at carefully staged party meetings and occasional demonstrations. Confrontations with the police were assiduously avoided, the standard watchword being not to respond when provoked.

Cuba, Debray proclaims, brought him face to face with a

new, superior social reality. Cuban Communists showed him that skepticism, serenity, and circumspection are not revolutionary traits but that self-confidence in one's clear-sightedness, passion, warmth, aggressiveness, and courage are. From his experiences he learned what his revered Communist leaders in France had known from their experiences but had concealed —that being a revolutionary means risking torture, hunger, exhaustion, and death. The Cubans taught him that "a provocation that meets with no response will inevitably be followed by another."[11]

Debray takes the same defiant and moralistic tone in his first letter from captivity, written shortly before his trial in October 1967. He condemns the propaganda campaign against Cuba, the tortures and beatings to which he had been subjected, and the publicity afforded his case. He interprets his sudden notoriety as a maneuver, whether conscious or not, of the bourgeois press to divert attention away from the class struggle in Bolivia. And he expresses his continued adherence to Castroism. The statement in which he does so is the best evidence of his sincerity. It reads: "I consider, more than ever, that 'Castroism' is the only realistic and just strategy, emanating from existing conditions, for most of the countries."[12] This is still the unmistakable language of Guevarism, not Leninism: it is contrary to Leninism to allow moral criteria to enter into the choice of strategy or to develop a prejudice for a particular strategy.

Debray admits, however, that he is no longer altogether satisfied with *Revolution in the Revolution?*:

> In the light of the experience of the Bolivian comrades, and of my final conversations with Che, I should probably modify *Revolution in the Revolution?* on a few important points where I am not in complete agreement with him, as I should emphasize others in which I feel he is completely right (such as the condemnation of the Communist Party, for example, which Che found presented too timorously in my book).[13]

What is significant about this statement is not so much Debray's admission that modifications are needed, but the implied admission that he had built *Revolution in the Revolution?* around his interpretation of Guevara's views with no intention of straying from the master. That is why changes in *Revolution in the Revolution?* are mentioned in the same breath as disagreements with Guevara. Where would he substantively modify his book? Wherever he had found Guevara to be in error. Where would he change the book's emphasis? Where initial disagreement had been resolved in Guevara's favor. Before his personal encounter with Guevara and with the realities of guerrilla life, Debray had not had the effrontery to lecture Guevara and Castro on guerrilla strategy. The Bolivian *foco* put Debray on a more equal footing. Debray had participated in its preparation and for a month he had shared the life of a guerrilla. He followed Che's lead in a matter of emphasis, but was moved to disagree with the master on several important points.

If it seems that we have made too much of one sentence, evidence for our conclusions is plentiful. Ten days after Guevara's assassination, Debray told an interviewer, Carlos Nuñez, that Che had not attached much importance to *Revolution in the Revolution?* but that he had been in accord with it, save with regard to the "diplomatic respect" Debray had shown in his condemnation of the CPs. There Che had been a hundred times more severe. Debray explained that Che's dissatisfaction with his book on this score was due to the bitter experience with the Bolivian CP.[14] In January Che had written in his diary that the PCB was "taking up arms" against the guerrillas.[15] Debray's tone in *Revolution in the Revolution?* was, indeed, mild by comparison.

We come now to the question of substantive disagreements between Debray and Guevara. In an interview four days after Guevara's execution, Debray told Marlene Nadle that Che had opened hostilities prematurely, before the guerrillas had recuperated from the training march and before there was sufficient contact with the towns to assure their physical survival.[16] On this occasion he blamed the absence of urban support on betrayals, deceptions, and misinformation. In a subsequent statement made to the court, however, Debray suggested that Guevara's bottomless mistrust of the city and his adamant refusal to risk reestablishing lines of communication with it had been at fault:

> When Bustos and I left the guerrillas, Che was waiting for the arrival of other people from outside, I mean La Paz, real messengers. Unfortunately they never came. No guerrilla could leave the group to do anything in the city, on Che's strict orders. Che's political and military strictness became one of the main reasons for the guerrillas' failure, for after once coming into the jungle, he allowed no combatant to go back to the plains. And as they couldn't go from the plains to the jungle either, there was this terrible misunderstanding, each side waiting for the other to come to decide very urgent matters.[17]

The striking similarity between Guevara's behavior and Debray's espousal of militarism in *Revolution in the Revolution?* was not lost on its author. Debray assured Nuñez that the sections of his book dealing with the role of the city and the relationship between city and countryside would read differently in a new edition. As we have already seen, his forbidding attitude toward the city was not warranted by his own assumptions concerning proletarianization.

During the time of his trial Debray also made several guarded concessions to Leninism. He admitted to having second thoughts about the advisability of launching a guerrilla *foco* without first organizing support for it among the peasantry.[18] And he conceded that the Bolivian experience had shown him the importance of taking the phenomenon of nationalism seriously.[19] These are significant concessions, posing further questions. How will the peasantry be organized, if not by a political party working through legal and illegal channels? At what level of revolutionary theory must nationalism be taken into account: at the strategic level, at which *Revolution in the Revolution?* operates, or at a deeper level? Could class analysis be postponed any further? And if nationalism is normally a tool of reactionary forces, how can it be neutralized or put to the service of the revolution, if not through ideological struggle? In short, must not the Marxist-Leninist party be revived in something like its traditional form?

For understandable reasons Debray did not immediately

pursue these questions. The conditions for launching such an inquiry were lacking both during the traumatic pretrial period and during the trial itself. Since he had been persuaded by Guevara to take an even harsher stance toward the existing parties, Debray was not inclined to grant them any concessions, even if only in the realm of theory. Thus, seven eventful months of captivity found Debray holding fast to the central idea of *Revolution in the Revolution?* with one hand while nurturing the seeds of its refutation with the other. The trial, in its outcome, brought an end to this state of theoretical limbo. The court's charge that Debray had been an important guerrilla under Guevara's command was upheld. An international campaign for clemency, featuring letters from Pope Paul VI and Charles de Gaulle, was to no avail.[20] Debray and Bustos were sentenced to thirty years' imprisonment, the maximum term possible under Bolivian law and more than enough time for reflection.

Debray's first major public concession to Lenin came in a letter written toward the end of 1967. In it Debray strongly affirms the need for a thoroughgoing nation-by-nation class analysis to fill the void which *Revolution in the Revolution?* had tried to bypass. "I am convinced," he wrote,

> that such a basic study is the more necessary and urgent because too much was sacrificed to that other urgency, the urgency of immediate practice at any price. The order of the day is to perform the thankless and fragmentary tasks of theoretical research and historical, economic, and social investigation, using well-proved concepts and not agitational formulas.[21]

In the beginning of 1968 Debray undertook a criticism of *Revolution in the Revolution?* To date it has not been published, but Debray later outlined the massive revisions that he had found to be in order. First, a *foco* must give the city its rightful place as the all-important rear guard of the guerrilla army. Second, it must unite strategy and tactics organically, combining great fundamental objectives with a transitional program geared to the immediate struggle of the masses. Third, it must thoroughly prepare its zone of operations. And fourth, it must be profoundly rooted in the national historical process. Without integration into the historical life of the people, there can be no external intervention.[22] The last point clearly is aimed at the Bolivian guerrilla war and Che's "many Vietnams" strategy rather than *Revolution in the Revolution?*, which had nothing to say about foreign intervention. Indeed, the other three points were surely conceived with Che's experience in mind, as well. Certainly the shoe fits.

Within six months Debray was ready to give way on reducing the political to the military apparatus and, correspondingly, on his blanket repudiation of political parties. In the spring of 1968 he told the interviewer Georgie Anne Geyer:

> I am adding things, . . . I am making them more complete. I am asking now, . . . "What is the political apparatus? —the value of the political apparatus—the value of that which is not purely military?" Fundamentally, I am not changing the idea that the political power should rest on the military leader, but you have to say much more. It is one thing to say that all political power is centered in him, and another to say that he is the maximum leader.[23]

The distinction Debray seems to be making in the last two sentences is between a chief executive and a supreme power, between a Giap or Chu Teh and a Castro or Guevara. By implication the distinction is between the Asian model of insurrection and the Guevarist one, making this concession to Lenin first and foremost a concession to Mao Tse-tung and Ho Chi Minh.

In the same interview Debray showed that he was reexamining the roots of the Leninist model of workers' insurrection, especially in Bolivia. As noted earlier, this model presupposes that the army can become the principal instrument of its own destruction, i.e., that soldiers of the reaction can be persuaded to fill the ranks of a revolutionary army. As the following quotation shows, Debray was now ready to entertain this possibility:

> . . . there are peculiarities to the Bolivian army. When you get closer you see there was a revolution, there are revolutionary officers. One notes that the social makeup of the army is

very different from that in Peru, Argentina, and Brazil. It is obvious that the revolution changed the army.[24]

It is useful on this point to compare the new Debray with the Leninist-Guevarist author of the early essays. In "Castroism" Debray had been similarly impressed by the possibility of a workers' insurrection in Bolivia. He wrote that Bolivia was "the only country where the revolution might take the classical Bolshevik form."[25] After having seen Guevarism fail there, Debray was returning to his earlier appraisal.

By the end of 1968 there was little that bound Debray to *Revolution in the Revolution?* During the first half of 1969 he wrote an essay entitled "Time and Politics," totally devoid of even the faintest trace of his Guevarist past. Guevara is mentioned only twice, and then gratuitously. When the tenets of Guevarism are not ignored, they are contradicted. For his point of departure Debray turns not to Guevara but to European Marxist philosophy in general and to Althusser's philosophy of history in particular.

"Time and Politics" is an inquiry into the philosophical foundations of Leninism and an historical materialist defense of Leninist politics. Its central presupposition is a direct denial of the second postulate of Guevarism—that the conditions for a revolutionary situation can be created by an insurrectionary center. "It is impossible," Debray now maintains, "to provoke or improvise crisis situations artificially; every country, every locality has its own special historical time, its own pace, its speed of development."[26] Debray's interpretation of history is less voluntaristic than previously: crisis situations cannot be created by revolutionary conspirators; at best they are opportunities to be seized for advancing the class struggle.

In order to be seized, an opportunity must be recognized for what it is. Thus, theoretical understanding of the present is a determining factor in the outcome of a crisis. If the present moment is not intellectually mastered, then

> the fundamental problem of "What is to be done?" has no basis and no answer. To master it calls for a considerable knowledge, a necessary abstract theoretical apprenticeship; but if that knowledge and apprenticeship do not ultimately

provide an ability to take a grasp on the here and now, then
. . . we shall have lost the only guarantee now existing that
one day the masses will become the masters of their fate. . . .
If our present is not intelligible, then communism is a
utopia.[27]

This is the most outspoken repudiation of the methodological
denial of Lenin which Debray's earlier essays exemplified. At
the same time it is a clear statement of a second presupposition, one which is completely irrelevant to Guevarism, namely
that instrumental knowledge of the historical process, and
particularly of the present moment, is the best guarantee of
revolution in the future, i.e., of successful intervention in a
revolutionary situation.

Debray contends that only a certain kind of knowledge
can enable the revolutionary, now defined as a politician-
scientist, to seize the moment; that knowledge must be dialectical. Following Lenin, Debray virtually equates Engels's
dialectics or general laws of motion with the unity of oppo-
sites. This "law" holds that the historical development of
natural and social entities is governed by the continuous conflict between contrary elements contained within them. The
opposition of contraries is a "contradiction." The development of an entity is determined by the changing relations of
dominance within each contradictory process: the subordinate
element gains strength, becomes dominant, and splits the
unity apart, giving rise to new entities with new internal contradictions, and so forth. In the analysis of human society a
crisis is the phenomenal form of abstract contradictions. In
bourgeois society, the fundamental abstract contradiction in
the economic sphere is between the forces of production and
the relations of production; in the political sphere, it is between the bourgeoisie and proletariat.

Debray follows his mentor, Louis Althusser, to even diz-
zier heights of abstraction. He borrows the concept of "overdetermination" from Althusser's 1962 essay, "Contradiction
and Overdetermination," a work which he praises lavishly.[28]
Althusser invented this concept to resolve the question of the
relation between the economic base of society and the social
and political superstructure in a way which avoids the charge

of economic determinism, while leaving the economic sphere a determining role. According to Althusser, contradictions in the economic, political, and social sphere condition each other through their continuous modifications of the social structure which generates the contradictory elements. This feedback process is called overdetermination. It causes the contradictions to develop unevenly, so that now this contradiction, now that one, achieves dominance. A revolutionary situation occurs when a large number of contradictions merge, like the ingredients of an explosive, into a "ruptural unity."[29]

Debray subscribes to this model of the Marxian dialectic; it occupies a central place in his analysis of crises. Debray defines a crisis as "a decisive and dangerous moment in the evolution of things."[30] It is decisive because it represents a fusion of contradictions into a "ruptural unity"; it is dangerous to all concerned parties because of the bewildering rapidity with which important contradictions suddenly develop and because a crisis precipitates the division of the people into hostile camps. Debray distinguishes between a crisis and a revolutionary situation. A revolutionary situation is a special kind of crisis, one in which there is a more or less complete polarization into irreconcilable or hostile camps. It is "a situation in which one can no longer remain neutral, in which one must face up to the alternatives: revolution or counter-revolution."[31] Either outcome is possible—a revolutionary situation is also a counterrevolutionary situation. Victory goes to the side which is least dislocated by the crisis and best prepared to intervene in it.[32]

One of Debray's persistent themes in "Time and Politics" is that in a crisis the tempo of overdetermination will always outstrip human powers of comprehension: the supercharged historical process overwhelms the mind of man. Consequently, the decision to act

> . . . is not a deduction, but a gamble, in other words a well-judged leap in the dark. . . . The leap is rational in that it can produce its reasons; it is the end of a chain of reasoning, but an end reached only by way of a discontinuity, by crossing a gap in the reasoning itself; for if reasoning consists in an analysis of conditions as they are, as we perceive them,

then we have made a leap beyond those present conditions, a leap into the future, an anticipation, in short a policy.[33]

Thus, a crisis is "objectively overdetermined but subjectively indeterminate." Though it is inevitable, there is no foretelling its results.[34] Voluntarism is reconciled with determinism, the art of insurrection with the science of politics.

Debray attributes the success of Leninism to its dialectical conception of history. By the same token he ascribes the futility of reformism and *gauchisme*, or ultraleftism, to their undialectical nature. Reformism views history as an inexorable linear approach to a predetermined and preconceived end. Ascension to the millenium is simply a matter of arithmetic, of the continuous accumulation of small changes in the social structure. Progress is measured with reference to the end product: working back from the goal, the position on the line is calculated by comparing the distance already covered with the distance that remains.[35] Radical failure is impossible because the end is inevitable; setbacks are always temporary; an opportunity missed today can be made up tomorrow. Since reformism makes no place for crises, it is no wonder that it is appalled and immobilized by them.

Following Lenin, then, Debray views reformism as the more dangerous deviation. Ultraleftism is a healthy reaction to the paralysis of reformism, but one that is too radical.[36] Because reformists spend their lives piecing together alibis for their inactivity from the writings of the old giants, ultraleftists ignore the giants. Because the reformist is a man steeped in the revolutionary tradition, the ultraleftist abjures the tradition. Because the reformist cultivates a long memory, the ultraleftist has a short one. Thus, to the ultraleftist the past is something upon which one builds, forgetting that the past and present moment also determine what one builds. Hence the familiar pattern:

> Gauchisme demands a "rupture," without knowing of what;
> it is in a void, nowhere and everywhere. The total break of
> the revolution ends up by presenting itself as an absolute;
> the slogan becomes an exhortation to understanding; the
> work of organization is replaced by a moral duty. An undif-

ferentiated protest comes to apply equally to everything, unvarying from one country, one set of circumstances, one social situation to the next.[37]

One cannot fail to be struck by how aptly this characterization of ultraleftism fits Guevara. But there is also a distinct note of self-reproach. Debray does not restrict his definition of *gauchisme* to those "who don't know better." A short memory, he notes, can be "individual" or "political."[38] He does not have to add that his was of the latter variety, Guevara's of the former.

Debray vs. Guevarism

Debray had to serve only three years of his sentence, thanks to a propitious turn in Bolivian politics. In April 1969 Barrientos died in a heliocopter crash. The vice-president, Dr. Siles Salinas, was chosen to serve as president until elections, scheduled for 1970, could be held. Under Siles's moderate rule, the Left, which had been repressed under the military regime of Barrientos and demoralized by Guevara's defeat, was able to reorganize and pose a challenge to the military's candidate, the commander-in-chief of the armed forces, Gen. Alfredo Ovando. In September 1969 Ovando preempted the presidency by ousting Siles in a bloodless coup.[39] To placate the public, Ovando included some civilians in his government and assumed a Left-nationalist orientation. Trade union freedom was restored, neocolonialism condemned, and a wish to establish diplomatic relations with all countries was expressed. On October 7, 1969, the self-styled "revolutionary" government made its most radical move when it seized Gulf Oil's Bolivian properties. To commemorate the event, a day of popular demonstration in support of the action was organized by the Bolivian Labor Central (COB) under the leadership of Juan Lechín.

A day after this momentous occasion—thereafter known as the Day of Dignity—Debray wrote an analysis of the current situation. The account has much in common with his general comments on the military coup in "Castroism," but there is a decisive difference. In "Castroism" the coup was regarded only from a military viewpoint: it was analyzed as a method for seizing power and found wanting because of the insuperable rightist forces acting on the Latin American army from within and without. In "Notes on the Political Situation in Bolivia," Debray is no less impressed with the superiority of the forces from the Right which act upon a well-intentioned coup, but these forces are no longer determinant, only a cause for caution and skepticism. In deciding what must be done the activity of the masses must also be considered. Debray's attitude toward the Ovando regime is governed by the fact that a dialogue had apparently been established between it and the people. A new arena for mass struggle had been opened, and Debray was loathe to remain aloof from it. His strategy for revolutionaries is textbook Leninism:

> Every revolution is a development, and it would be wrong to dismiss this one as petty bourgeois, and withdraw into a tower of Marxist-Leninism, leaving the battlefield and its maneuvers to the rival groups of civil and military bourgeoisie. No; we must first struggle to impose our presence and active participation upon the present political terrain; and then, after that, to take over the leadership, not by any artificial means, but by proving that in the last analysis it is only the mass of people who can make a popular revolution, determine its direction and lead it.[40]

By this time Debray's break with Guevara was virtually complete. It was incomplete only in the formal sense that he had not yet publicly contradicted in an unambiguous way Guevara's first and third postulates in *Guerrilla Warfare*—that in Latin America an irregular popular army can defeat the regular army and that the countryside is the principal terrain of struggle. Debray took care of this a year later. In answer to a questionnaire smuggled into his cell by a journalist, Debray voices his conviction that the Bolivian Revolution can only take the Bolshevik road. Contrary to Che's third postulate, he says that in Bolivia the support of the peasantry will tip the scale, but only the working class can unleash the revolution.[41] He rejects even more categorically Che's first postulate:

> . . . it is very useful to re-read what Lenin had to say after the 1905 revolution about the Army and working with the Army. Lenin stressed that one must continually "work" politically and ideologically with the troops, try to win over as many of them as possible . . . and, during an insurrection, try to surround the repressive detachments with large numbers of people, and immobilize them. . . . [The] famous sentence . . . "militarism can never and in no circumstances be conquered and destroyed except by the victorious fight of one part of the national Army" remains generally valid, especially in the case of Bolivia.[42]

With these two assertions Debray formally completes the break with Guevara. But it is not enough to say that he is now a non-Guevarist. His rejection of Guevarism has taken the form of full acceptance of Leninism; he is an anti-Guevarist. In his answers to the questionnaire Debray manifests this opposition. He asserts that while revolution in Latin America will have to have the same content as the Cuban Revolution, the methods of action will have to be different.[43] In a more biting passage he excoriates the *gauchistes* who refuse to acknowledge conflicts within the army. "Only a childish sectarianism," he declares, ". . . or a metaphysical, moralistic, idealistic concept of class struggle, refuses to recognize and ultimately take advantage of the enemy's secondary conflicts. It would be dangerous, indeed deadly idiocy to reject the possible help of valuable allies whenever and wherever they may be found."[44]

Even more significant than the content of Debray's criticism is its direction. His target, at least in part, is the ELN, which had been reformed under the leadership of the youngest Peredo brother, Chato. Debray's falling-out with Peredo began in December 1969 when the ELN began a campaign of bank robberies in La Paz. Debray was quoted by his lawyer as saying that he disapproved of those acts. To clarify this remark Debray began a short correspondence with Peredo.

Debray's first letter bears the heading "Slow and Sure is better than Hasty."[45] The reply by Peredo opens with a quote from Guevara: "A battle may be won or lost, but it must be fought."[46] These opening sallies epitomize the two unalterably

opposed viewpoints that confront each other in the four letters of the heated correspondence. Equally revealing is the
fact that Peredo's letters end with calls to arms: "Victory or
Death," "Back to the Mountains," "May the War Continue."
Debray's letters restrict themselves to comradely greetings.

In effect, the correspondence is a rehash of "Time and
Politics," with Debray summarily restating his position and
Peredo defending *gauchisme* against Debray's characterizations. The principal bone of contention, prefigured in the
opening remarks, is the timing of the ELN's wave of urban
actions. According to Debray these actions were premature:
the masses were not ready for armed opposition to the Ovando
regime; they had not sufficiently reorganized and had not yet
seen Ovando for what he was. Debray insists that insurrectionary activities must conform to the political level of the
masses and the "rhythm" of political life; they must not be
motivated by abstract moral commitments. And he decries as
a needless waste the death of revolutionaries activated before
conditions for ensuring their survival have been provided.[47] He
even suggests that it would be to the advantage of the popular
forces not to respond to the provocations of the repressive
forces![48]

Peredo, true to *gauchiste* form, sees no meaningful direction in Bolivian history, only an aimless pendulum-like
movement from the right wing to the left, to which only
armed action could give a revolutionary direction. There is no
time for political maneuvering or for providing the best possible conditions for protecting cadres. The growth of the forces
of repression must be matched by the maturation of a revolutionary fighting force, or there can be no liberation. Since
the only effective form of political struggle is military struggle,
the cadres who fall in battle are not wasted; the waste involves
those who do not participate. Revolution, Peredo writes,
means risking one's life.[49]

This exchange starkly and succinctly demarcates the gulf
which separates Leninism and Guevarism, a gulf which Debray straddled in the early works, crossed in *Revolution in the
Revolution?*, and then recrossed decisively in his prison writings. No wonder that in Peredo's last letter to Debray, written

after Debray's release from prison, Peredo had nothing to say except to congratulate him on his release.[50]

Debray's prison term came to an end in December 1970, under the newly formed Left-nationalist regime of General Torres. Talk of amnesty had begun under Ovando, but only as an empty gesture designed to shore up support for a government which was rapidly losing support on both ends of the political spectrum. On October 4, 1970, in full accordance with the Debrayan scenario outlined in "Castroism," Ovando was effectively isolated and fell prey to a countercoup led by the rightist Gen. Rogelio Miranda. But, as if to vindicate Debray's new mass orientation, the union movement led by Lechín forced an alteration in the classic coup-countercoup cycle, an alteration which bore a remarkable resemblance to the Russian Revolution of February 1917. Miranda's coup was planned and executed poorly, allowing the leftist General Torres, whose support in the army was far less than Miranda's, to seize power backed by a general national strike. The outcome of this uprising was a state of dual power, with Torres sharing power with a Popular Assembly, headed by Lechín.[51] It is ironical that a Guevarist revolutionary process put the Guevarist Debray into prison and an ostensibly Leninist revolutionary process secured his release.

When Debray entered prison, he was a thorough Guevarist, but the Lenin in him had been only stifled, not suffocated, during his brief fling with ultraleft heterodoxy. When Che died and a continent-wide quiet descended on the guerrilla front, Debray was cut loose from his moorings, but he did not remain adrift for long. Every repudiation of a Guevarist truth was an affirmation of a Leninist one, and vice versa; every repulsion an attraction, every attraction a repulsion. As early as the end of 1968, his concessions to Leninism had already committed him to a thorough repudiation of Guevarism. The solitude of prison gave Debray the opportunity to rethink the foundations of historical materialism. Having known, as few ever will, the horror of acting "outside" of history and in a human vacuum, Debray reembraced more tightly than ever the necessity of discovering the rhythm of history and the necessity of engaging the masses in any effort to accelerate the long march to socialism. When Bolivia became the scene of mass upheavals and convulsions within the military, it was as though the Bolivian people were restaging the October Revolution. At the same time, the ultra-Guevarist obstinance of the second-generation ELN forced upon Debray the unaccustomed role of public critic of guerrilla warfare.

Thus, not only did Debray's incarceration liberate the Marx and Lenin within him, it liberated the critic of Guevarism as well. One thing was missing, however; the critic of Guevara remained suppressed by the still vivid memory of the man's exemplary personal qualities. Guevara was still treated as though there was no real connection between him and those who are called or call(ed) themselves "Guevarists"— much as Marx had once disassociated himself from "Marxists." With that qualification, we may safely say that the Debray who emerged from prison three days before Christmas 1970 was as orthodox a Leninist as one is ever likely to meet.

6

A New Heterodoxy

During the years from Christmas 1970 until the time of this writing, October 1976, Debray's orthodoxy was to be confronted with exceedingly unorthodox revolutions in Chile and Uruguay. Under their influence we find Debray's orthodoxy weakening. Increasingly, Lenin is asked to share the stage with Salvador Allende, Raúl Sendic (principal founder of the Tupamaros), and other new faces.

In an interview three days after his release from prison, Debray introduced the cast which would prove to dominate his thinking in the years to come. First, the Tupamaros, who are credited with having "finished with the [Guevarist] mystique of the leader" and with being "an example of the predominance of the political over the military." They are applauded for having "made their politics into a praxis, avoiding abstract type polemics of an ideological nature." When questioned further about the political-military relationship, Debray points to Lenin, mentioning that he has discovered that the mature Lenin resembles the early Lenin of *What Is to Be Done?* less than Rosa Luxemburg—something which has escaped attention because the democratic dimension of Lenin's conception of the party and of its relationship with the masses has been covered up by ideological laziness and bureaucratism in the workers' movement. In the same breath, Debray mentions the efforts in Cuba to give socialism a more democratic twist. He then harkens back to Althusser's letter criticizing *Revolution in the Revolution?* for being "abstract" in its treatment of the party and the city-countryside relation. Debray also faults himself for having made light of the general implications of the Vietnam experience and, as a consequence, confusing "the people" with their vanguard in his conception of people's war.

Then the questioning comes around to Chile. It will be recalled that in his 1964 essay, "Problems of Revolutionary Strategy in Latin America," Debray had outlined two possible outcomes for reformist governments in Latin America: abandonment of progressive ideals or military coup d'état, self-betrayal or military betrayal. Looking now at Chile's chances, Debray fears the second alternative, " 'bourgeoisification' from within," while at the same time acknowledging Allende's sterling, statesmanlike qualities.

With that, talk turns to Che Guevara, and the interview ends with a eulogy for the slain hero. Debray classes Che as an "exemplary exponent of Leninism," but this characterization refers to Guevara's personal attributes not to doctrine. The similarity between Che and Lenin which Debray finds so striking is the synthesis of revolutionary theory and practice, which the two so completely embodied. Neither allowed himself to be lured by the raptures of theory for its own sake or succumbed to the mental laziness of the man of action or to the melancholy and despondency common to the theorist. And their extraordinary capacity for self-criticism prevented their theories from straying from their practice and vice versa, while it kept their extraordinary willpower from generating illusions.[1]

The Tupamaros, Salvador Allende, Rosa Luxemburg, the Vietnamese guerrillas, the Cuban leaders, and the omnipresent Che Guevara—all of these disparate thinkers find a respectful niche in Debray's post-prison revolutionary theory. Growing out of exhaustive analyses of the failure of foquismo in general and of the defeats of the Bolivian, Venezuelan, Uruguayan, Guatemalan, and Chilean revolutions in particular, the end product is not easy to describe meaningfully in a few words; whatever else it may be, however, Debray's theory is not orthodox—not orthodox Guevarism nor orthodox Leninism nor orthodox reformism. It has elements of all of these ideologies without being clearly dominated by any of them. The limits of orthodox Leninism are stretched to accommodate *focos* and reformist parties. Let us see how Debray accomplishes this.

Chile: From Reformism to Revolution?

The first test of Debray's orthodoxy came in Chile. He had been flown there from Bolivia and in January 1971 conducted a long interview with the president of two months, Salvador Allende.[2] The interview was published in English, together with a long introduction by Debray, in the widely read *The Chilean Revolution: Conversations with Allende.** A few months after the military coup led by Pinochet drowned the Chilean Revolution in blood, Debray wrote an essay entitled "The Chilean Sieve" which sifts the failed Chilean experiment through a matrix of Marxist-Leninist theses on the state and the conception of revolution that Debray had developed in prison. The two works are perfectly compatible and together afford a penetrating look into the Chilean tragedy and a further glimpse into the Debrayan conception of history.

Overtones of tragedy accompany every line of Debray's analysis. One element of the tragedy was that while in principle no fight is ever lost before it begins, in fact Allende's task was as hopeless as any that history had ever presented to a revolutionary leader. Allende attempted to forge a Socialist revolution from above, without at the beginning being able to count on either a revolutionary situation or a revolutionary vanguard capable of dealing effectively with the inevitable crisis.[3] Allende had been carried into office not by a Leninist party but by a loose electoral coalition, the Unidad Popular (UP), which was composed principally of three ideologically distinct political groupings. Two of these, the pro-Moscow Communist party (PCCh) and the independent Socialist party (SP), had long experience working within the Chilean constitutional system, but effectively none outside it. The Unified People's Action Movement (MAPU) was a leftist offshoot from the Christian Democratic party.

---

* Hereafter referred to as *Conversations*.

Its very diversity meant that the UP lacked the ideological unity required by a vanguard. The three partners shared the ultimate objective of acquiring total state power, and they were agreed that this could be achieved piecemeal through the gradual transfer of power from the bourgeoisie to the exploited classes. The general strategy was to attack the tree of power at its economic roots, using the state to alter the economic infrastructure in such a way as to weaken the bourgeoisie. But here the agreement ended; the UP was split on important particulars. The PCCh slogan was the cautious "consolidate in order to advance." Its strategy was to take over one governmental outpost after the other, using the available political levers to weaken the bourgeoisie and neutralize the petty bourgeoisie, all the while administering a healthy capitalist economy. But, where the Communists wanted to disarm the bourgeoisie within its own institutions, the Socialists meant to discard these institutions piece by piece and replace them with a "new people's state." Their strategy foresaw the necessity of passing through a phase of dual power, during which there would be a progressive transfer of power to representative organs of the mobilized working class, independent of and exterior to the state.[4] In line with this strategy, the SP encouraged the formation of *cordones industriales* (workers' committees established in industrial zones to manage factories seized from their owners and take charge of defense and mobilization within their zones) during the October 1972 truckowners' strike; the Communists opposed the *cordones*. Thus, far from constituting a vanguard, the UP was badly divided.

But however ill-equipped Allende and the UP were to achieve their objective, Debray does not fault the UP for attempting to route the Chilean Revolution through elections. It is Debray's view that in 1970 the UP could not have proceeded in any other direction, and herein lies the other element of tragedy. Debray contents that in Chile in 1970 no revolutionary legitimacy was possible outside of the bounds of representative democracy, nor had it been for half a century. During all that time the class struggle had been confined to the stable framework of bourgeois institutional forms. The working class had no experience with armed struggle, nor did it see a need or use for it in 1970. It equated revolution with a radical change of government.[5] And what was true of the working class was even more true for the middle classes. They had, in fact, been able to impose upon the UP the humiliation of approving a Statute of Constitutional Guarantees as a precondition for inauguration, thereby making the democratic imprisonment of the revolution the formal condition for the proposed revolutionary capture of democracy. Thus, the UP had no choice but to play by rules written by the enemy. The only alternative was to abandon the historic field of battle, and this it could never do.

In his introduction to *Conversations* Debray probes for the source of Chilean constitutional stability, a stability which would be noteworthy even in Europe and which was absolutely astounding in Latin America. He finds the answer in the fact that early on, the development of Chile's economy had thrown a strong, self-confident bourgeoisie into confrontation with a strong, aggressive proletariat. The fact that Chile had been spared heavy foreign penetration early in its development allowed for the rise of a coherent national oligarchy capable of constructing a centralized state apparatus to legitimate its rule and to satisfy its expansionistic hungers. In contrast to much of Latin America, where the state provides the bourgeoisie with a means of subsistence, Debray argues that in Chile it was nothing more than a well-organized instrument of rule, free from the corruption endemic to other countries. Thus, when the working class began to struggle in an organized way against its inhuman living and working conditions, it faced a well-entrenched and ruthless ruling class. A rising tide of violent confrontations, not infrequently taking the form of massacres and lasting almost four decades (from approximately 1880 to 1920), had an exceptional consequence —the union of Socialist theory and the working-class movement. Chile became "the only country on the continent (but in different forms and earlier) in which the parties called working-class because of their ideologies were also organically working-class in their recruitment and social base."[6]

The strength of the proletariat enlightened by Marxism was sufficient to resist every attempt by the bourgeoisie to break it, but it was not sufficient to break the bourgeoisie. The enlightened ruling classes had a knack for neutralizing hostile bodies by assimilation. Threats to the ruling order were made a part of that order, as in the 1920s when the landed oligarchy had given way to a fresh wave of commercial, financial, and industrial bourgeoisie, and again during the Great Depression when a radicalized middle class had been brought into the government as a leading partner in a coalition that included the Socialists and Communists. Furthermore, the major parts of the proletariat were isolated from each other in mining enclaves, and the working-class movement was isolated from the peasantry. The prohibition of union rights kept the majority of workers out of unions and suspectible to bourgeois influence. And the coincidence of the rise of the working class with that of the middle class, and their coalescence into the Popular Front coalition during the 1930s and '40s, "diluted" the working class's pursuit of its own interests by adding those of the petty bourgeoisie.[7] All of these factors militated against the emergence of a coordinated revolutionary dynamic drawing on the combined strength of the working class and an aroused peasantry.

There is nothing in Debray's writings about Chile that could be construed as a criticism of the reformist politics of the Communists and Socialists during this period. Luis Emilio Recabarren, the founder of the Chilean labor movement and of its Communist party (founded in 1912 and given the title "Communist party" in 1922 when it affiliated with Lenin's Third International), is not faulted for building a legalistic bias into the newborn movement. Indeed, the efforts made by the PCCh to transcend the ideological heritage of Recabarren and to fashion a more combative party are disparaged. Debray contends that the Communists were in a "period of retreat and sectarianism" and that the attempt to "Bolshevize" led the party into a "prolonged and sterile isolation."[8] The impression Debray leaves is that all attempts to switch the working class to a more constructive or combative track were doomed to failure by Chile's peculiar economic and social conditions. It isn't that opportunities to avoid the fateful rendezvous with constitutional power had been missed; there simply had been no real opportunities.

It is quite true that, as Debray asserts, Allende was not a reformist in the respect that reformism does not generally attack the political dominance of the bourgeoisie and imperialism as resolutely as Allende did.[9] But this does not alter the reformist character of the fifty-year build-up to the September 1970 electoral victory. Nor does the UP government's timid, legalistic response to the crisis which its victory precipitated brook any illusions about the character of UP leadership. As Debray himself points out, both the Communist and the Socialist strategies presupposed three dubious conditions: first, the dominance of the government in the state; second, full respect for the principle of legality during the period when legality is being used against the bourgeoisie as well as while bourgeois legality is being sacrificed for a Socialist variety; and third, constitutional continuity throughout the period of adaptation of existing institutions to a new social regimen and during the progressive broadening of the UP's support.[10] In sum, the UP wager was that democracy, legality, and constitutionality could survive the alteration and progressive reconstitution of their social basis—that political forms could outlive their content or, indeed, that the former could be the executioners of the latter.

Of course, none of Debray's three conditions for the success of the UP strategy was fulfilled, and Debray evaluates this perversity of history as an illustration of three important laws, or lessons of the past. First, the government does not dominate the state. This is an illusion created in normal times when the army is neutral and obedient. In times of crisis the repressive apparatus—armed forces and police—stands revealed as the commander of the government and the nerve center of the state. Second, Debray argues, legality and democratic institutions can never be more than a limited tool of the revolution. After they have been turned against their creators for a while, the bourgeoisie will itself controvert and subvert them, along with lofty manners, the notion of "fair play," etc. Shaming the bourgeoisie by pointing out its hypocrisy and bad faith (as Allende did until the very end) is an exercise in futility. An eye for an eye and a tooth for a tooth is the only policy. Every extralegal attack on the working class must be met with a counterattack in kind (as was done in Cuba), not with pious phrases. It is, Debray writes, "better to lose the reputation for humanism than power and life. . . . Tears of anger are preferable to crocodile tears."[11]

Finally, Debray concludes, leaning heavily on his prison writings, history does not move in a rectilinear, stepwise manner, ascending to a predetermined end, as reformists would have it. The class struggle is not a process of addition and subtraction; it does not proceed in a continuous fashion from the political and economic domination of the bourgeoisie to that of the proletariat. Rather it passes through a succession of crises leading to points of total rupture, when society is torn in two and the issue becomes very starkly a choice between socialism or fascism, dictatorship of the proletariat or the political dictatorship of the bourgeoisie, Lenin or Kornilov, Allende or Pinochet, liquidate or be liquidated. At such times the methods and even the logic of normalcy are no longer operative. In Chile, petitions against civil war, silly appeals to the humanity of the adversary, pious reproaches, and sentimental homilies were thrown into the faces of an enraged and unblinking reaction only days before the bloody coup. And those within the UP who counted on strong Christian Democratic support and a rupture within the armed forces (because large groups within these entities could rationally expect to fare better under the UP than under military fascism) forgot that in times of crisis, different ordering principles sometimes go into effect, with people tending to identify with and coalesce around "the party," "the nation," or "the army" rather than aligning themselves on the basis of class or occupation.[12]

Besides these general criticisms Debray also faults the UP government for not having been more resolute and forceful at certain decisive junctures, especially when the UP's astounding election gains in April 1971 were not followed up by a call for a plebiscite and acceleration of the revolutionary offensive.[13] Yet Debray, almost alone among Allende's Marxist critics, does not fault him for not having armed the workers.

"What arms?" he asks. Airplanes, tanks, carriers? How would the workers have been trained to use the arms? Would the armed forces have sat idly by and allowed it to take place? And who should have been armed, and when? The necessity of armed struggle had impressed itself on the most class conscious workers as late as the fall of 1972. Moreover, there was never complete solidarity among the proletariat, and the proletariat as a whole was way ahead of the urban and rural petty bourgeoisie, with no possibility of alliance.[14]

In order to have succeeded in the face of all these difficulties, Debray submits, Allende would have required a capable revolutionary vanguard and a fusion of anticapitalist and patriotic sentiments. The failure to build such a vanguard was a consequence of Allende's dual commitment, his adherence to his clashing roles as leader of a people's movement and as president of a bourgeois republic. The fusion of anticapitalist and patriotic sentiments was thwarted by the shrewd, "low profile" strategy of intervention orchestrated by Nixon and Kissinger. The Americans' economic blockade, CIA activities, and maneuvers within the military were well-hidden from the eyes of the Chilean masses and could not, therefore, inflame their nationalistic passions. A direct military intervention might well have unified the Left and brought the peasantry and middle classes into alliance with it.[15] If that had happened, a different, more hopeful revolutionary situation would have been at hand and Chile would have become another Vietnam.

In the introduction to *Conversations* Debray notes that there is a "disproportion in all historical enterprises," a disproportion between the forces that historical actors can unleash and those they can control.[16] He worries that the forces unleashed by Allende could overwhelm him and sweep him from the stage. This, of course, is exactly what happened. But surprisingly, Debray brings a rehabilitated Allende back onto the stage with the assertion that "in Chile only a reformist government could put in motion a revolutionary dynamic."[17] The Chilean masses could not have been aroused in any other way. Debray contends that the only problem posed by the Chilean disaster is "how a popular government that has come to power by reformist means can be transformed into one on the road to revolution." This "leap" or "rupture" was "not possible" in Chile, but, he opines hesitantly, it might be in Western Europe, where conditions are "incomparably more favorable."[18] In those European countries with "a socialist revolution written on their horizon—at least on their mental horizon"—Chile has interjected a "disconcerting dialectic: that it is necessary to act like reformists in order to unleash, beginning with a command post in the State, a growing dynamic of class struggle, and like revolutionaries in order not to be passed over and broken into pieces by that very dynamic."[19] Debray is not exuberant about the choice history has presented him ("the option between the reformist plague and the ultra-left cholera"),[20] and he is frankly struck dumb by the problem he has posed for himself, or rather, that, by his reckoning, history has presented him and France—to follow the Chilean road without ending up at its destination.

Debray wants his essay to end on an optimistic note, but his efforts are rather contrived. First, he admits to a kind of historical irrationalism, declaring that there is no cause for alarm in the fact that a problem posed by history does not yield its solution to theory; history itself will crash through the wall blinding the theorist at a place and time no one suspected.[21] On two other occasions he propounds a "law of surprises" which has the same import: revolutionary theory is destined to be surprised by every important event, "zigzagging from exception to exception."[22] Debray follows up this faint measure of unsubstantiated hope with the observation that history has a habit of breaking through in that "cradle of utopian socialism and crucible of scientific socialism—the true fatherland of socialism"—his own France.[23] And finally he asserts what he has not proved, viz., that the uniqueness of Chile —the very dissimilarity of Chile and France—is a source of "consolation, even certainty."[24]

Debray's scattergun finish raises a flood of unanswered questions and invites a score of easy refutations. One could remind Debray, as Althusser did, that certainties do not come by negative demonstration. And as surely as dissimilarities between France and Chile are grounds for optimism, so are their similarities grounds for doubt and despair. Worse, the whole weight of the Marxist conception of the state and revolution, which was confirmed by the Chilean experience, tips the scales against the "Chilean road," as parts of Debray's analysis have shown. Certainly the Chilean debacle did not come as a "surprise" to most Marxist-Leninists. Furthermore, while the "law of surprises" may hold for distant observers (the "unexpected" wave of revolution in present-day black Africa serving as the most recent example), it does not apply to the architects of those revolutions. There is no evidence that Lenin was surprised by revolution in tsarist Russia, however much his Social-Democratic acquaintances may have been. He was undoubtedly surprised by the spontaneous invention of new forms of organization (soviets) and by the rediscovery of purportedly antiquated or unsuitable forms of struggle (mutinies, street fighting, guerrilla warfare), but he speculated openly on the possibility of a revolutionary seizure of power as soon as the first wave of revolutionism in 1905 had shown him that the revolutionary dynamic could be given a proletarian twist.[25]

It is obvious without further examples that Debray's law, or antilaw, of surprises will not bear close scrutiny. A more serious objection, from a traditional Marxist-Leninist point of view, could be based on Debray's suggestion that the duty of European revolutionary Marxists is to join the reformist parties which command the loyalty of the bulk of the working class. Since the earliest days of Marxism the existence of a distinct, independent party of the revolutionary working class has been held to be a sine qua non of the Socialist movement.[26] Collaboration for specific objectives can take place only between the Marxist party and other parties, none within it. Under no condition may the "proletarian class character" of the party be jeopardized.[27] It would have been inconceivable for the Bolsheviks to share a platform with reformists. One of Lenin's principal activities between 1903 and 1917 was uprooting threats to the party's internal revolutionary Socialist integrity.

Another problem of Debray's advice to be revolutionaries but act like reformists, again from a traditional Marxist-Leninist point of view, is that it appears to demand a conscious policy of deceiving the working class. "Acting like reformists" implies making reformist arguments and promoting reformist policies while suppressing revolutionary ideology. This is far removed from the relationship between revolutionary party and proletariat depicted by Lenin:

> The whole policy of Social Democracy is to *light up* the path that *lies ahead before the masses* of the people. We hold aloft the torch of Marxism and show, by every step the various classes take, by every political and economic event, that life confirms our doctrines. As capitalism develops, and as the political struggle becomes more acute, larger and larger sections of the people become convinced by what we say and by this factual (or historical) confirmation of what we say.[28]

Nothing could be further from the spirit of this passage, written in the context of the debate between Mensheviks and Bolsheviks over an electoral alliance with bourgeois parties, than "acting like a reformist." To the Mensheviks who wanted to lower their political voices in order not to offend the Cadets (a party of the liberal bourgeoisie), with whom they sought an electoral alliance, Lenin replied that one does not sacrifice the instruction of the masses for petty electoral gains, because the most important resource of the proletariat is its class-consciousness, i.e., its understanding of Marxist doctrine and methodology.[29] Putting election to parliament ahead of consciousness-raising was putting the cart before the horse. For Lenin, the only point in participating in elections was to build consciousness; and for this purpose a Duma (parliament) and elections were distinctly inferior to a good uprising. On another occasion Lenin was counseled by the Mensheviks and Jewish Bund to change his call for an uprising to one for a constituent assembly, because the former could not be successfully launched. Lenin answered characteristically, "We must speak the truth; therein lies our strength, and *the masses, the people, the multitude* will decide in actual practice, after the struggle, whether we have strength."[30]

Lenin's fundamental message in these two episodes involving political reform, and in others during the same period, is that the struggle for reforms and the struggle for revolution are not necessarily complementary. At any time the struggle for reforms may interfere with the struggle for revolution, may even be detrimental to it. Lenin valued the Duma as a platform to reach the workers and especially the peasantry outside the organizational scope of the party, and he fought successfully in 1908-9 to purge the Otzovist faction from the party for agitating against participation in it. But the straight and even road that led from one reform to the next did not coincide with Lenin's road to revolution or merge with it at some point in the distance, except by chance. At most, these roads intersected when conditions permitted. The important thing for Lenin was to prepare the proletariat ideologically and technically for the violent seizure of power, and this could not be achieved with deception or lies.

But modern France is not revolutionary Russia. There is one prominent difference that could be used to support Debray's argument. In Russia revolutionary Marxism grew up side by side with reformism and had two revolutionary situations, fed by defeat in war and economic collapse, to help it crowd reformism out of the working-class movement. In France a different process of historical selection allowed the reverse to happen: reformism supplanted revolutionary Marxism. In France, it seems, the Socialist party, led by François Mitterrand, and the French Communist party rob every other organization on the Left of the mass base it needs to grow. In revolutionary Russia the political "market" was competitive; in France monopolies dominate. The Bolsheviks could not be denied a broad working-class base; in France every attempt to challenge the monopolies meets with the same ignominious fate: the "ultra-left cholera" with "closed door meetings and fiery proclamations that never catch fire anywhere."[31] Thus one can no longer follow the Bolshevik example of charting an independent course to socialism; it is necessary to hitch the revolution to reformism. Rather than attempt from without to win reformist workers over to revolution, revolutionaries should burrow into the reformist parties in order to ultimately transform them from within into their opposite. Meanwhile, these parties burrow into the bourgeois state in order to ultimately transform *it* into *its* opposite.

This, then, would appear to be the best rationale for Debray's strategy, and it is not altogether unpersuasive. But it has an important flaw, the same one Althusser detected in *Revolution in the Revolution?*: a strategy must have more to recommend it than the debility of other strategies. In his first assessment of the Chilean Revolution in the Timossi-Cabieses interview, Debray worried that the UP would fall not to the long knives of the reaction but to cooptation by the system; his subsequent analysis shows that, in fact, the Chilean Revolution fell prey to both. The long cohabitation of the working class with bourgeois democracy had robbed it of its survival skills so effectivly that it could not mount a self-defense effort. Could France avoid the same fate? And could the same disease of "bourgeoisification" fail to infect the burrowing revolutionary; that is, is it not more likely that the revolutionary will convert to reformism than that reformist party will turn to revolutionary Marxism? The weight of historical evidence falls heavily against Debray. Until the enormous burden of proof has been lifted, until Debray gives a better indication of what the "incomparably more favorable conditions" are that recommend his project, he stands exposed to the charge that he has once more left the pale of Leninism.

The Tupamaros: From Foquismo to Leninism?

While revolutionary Chile was living out its golden months the Tupamaros were reaching the zenith of an astounding politico-military trajectory. The Tupamaro organization, or as it is also known, the *Movimiento de Liberación Nacional* (MLN), was born around the time of the Venezuelan FALN/FLN and the Guatemalan FAR. But in Uruguay the struggle began in the countryside and moved to the capital. Raúl Sendic, a law student, member of the Socialist party, and principal founder of the Tupamaros, began his political career during the late 1950s as an organizer and fellow worker among the canecutters in the department of Paysandu. Sendic founded a union that succeeded in pressing for a series of beneficial laws, but the laws remained unenforced. In protest, Sendic organized a six-hundred-kilometer "caneworkers' march" in 1962, an election year, to bring the caneworkers into confrontation with the government; but the demonstration was in vain. The government ignored their grievances, and the marchers were fired upon from the headquarters of the Trade Union Confederation.[32]

Having experienced the futility of working within the institutional framework, Sendic and a group of eight compañeros resolved to abandon legal channels and chart a new course for the Uruguayan revolution through direct action. By the Tupamaros' own account, in January 1963 it was decided that a dramatic action—a "risk," "challenge," "test," and definitive "break with the past and the regime"—was needed to unify the group. Thus was the MLN conceived, in the best Guevarist-Marighelan fashion, in the expropriation of arms from the Swiss Colony Rifle Club in July 1963. The founding convention of the MLN was held in January 1966.[33]

Much of the MLN's first five years was spent in secret preparations, punctuated by sporadic expropriations of arms and trucks loaded with food supplies for distribution in Montevideo's slum areas.[34] In August 1966, the Tupamaros marked the attainment of a new "technical-tactical" plateau with their first of many bank robberies.[35] December 1966 brought the first casualty in accidental confrontation with police, followed by a series of police raids which took the life of another Tupamaro. A year later, in another accidental confrontation, a civil guard was shot and given medical treatment by the Tupamaros. A few days thereafter the MLN sent a letter to the daily newspaper *Epoca*, explaining the incident and outlining its policy of sparing police agents who do not participate in the repression.[36]

During the same month, December 1967, President Oscar Gestido died; the task of dealing with a burgeoning economic crisis, resulting from two decades of decline in manufacturing and in the dominant agricultural sector, was passed on to the vice-president, Dr. Pacheco Areco. Pacheco's unpopular strategy for dealing with these problems, featuring a devaluation of the peso and a wage freeze, weighed heavily on the lower-income groups, as did the continuing rampant inflation and chronic stagnation which these measures were designed to correct. On 13 June 1968 Pacheco invoked emergency security measures to cope with the rising tide of popular dissent. Several leftist organizations and newspapers were banned, union leaders arrested, strikes bloodily repressed, censorship imposed, and states of seige declared. Within the government Pacheco clashed repeatedly with the legislature over his predilection for ruling by decree and over the corruptions and inefficiencies of his administration.[37] Thus for the duration of the Pacheco regime, from 1968 to 1971, Uruguay found itself in a genuine political crisis.

The Tupamaros flourished in this climate. After the imposition of Pacheco's emergency measures, the number and scope of their actions took a quantum jump. A general plan was drawn up calling for five major actions in 1968 and forty in 1969.[38] In July the transmitter of Radio Ariel was bombed moments before Pacheco was to deliver a speech. In August Ulysses Pereira Reverbel, the director of the state-owned Power and Telephone Enterprise, an unpopular rightist hardliner and an intimate friend of Pacheco, was kidnapped. Bank robberies, further acts of intimidation against officials of the government and armed forces, bombings, sabotage, and occupations of radio stations were carried out in rapid succession, usually directed against obvious symbols of U.S. imperialism and the allied state apparatus headed by Pacheco. For example, to commemorate the visit of Nelson Rockefeller the General Motors plant was set on fire in the summer of 1969, causing $1 million in damage; and a radio station in downtown Montevideo was seized to broadcast a ten-minute denunciation of Rockefeller and Pacheco.[39] In September, when a strike of bank employees met with management intransigence and escalating threats, the Tupamaros kidnapped a member of the board of Uruguayan banks and made the rapid settlement of the strike in favor of the employees the condition for his release.[40]

In October 1969, the Tupamaros paid homage to Che Guevara on the second anniversary of his death with their daring occupation of the town of Pando. Situated some thirty-two kilometers from Montevideo, Pando had a population of seventy thousand. Forty-nine Tupamaros, divided into six teams, severed communications, overcame the police station and fire department, and robbed the town's four banks of an estimated $240,000 to $400,000. They were ambushed by police on their return to Montevideo and four of their band were killed, five wounded, and sixteen arrested.[41]

In the same month, as if to demonstrate its continued strength and resolve in the face of heavy losses, the MLN held up the Banco Francés e Italiano. One of the keys required to open the safe could not be located, but some documents were stolen that proved the bank was involved in fraudulent activities. During the investigation by the Department of Revenue, the MLN returned to finish the job posing as revenue agents.[42] The capture of incriminating documents became an important political tool in baring the corruption that permeated the country's political and economic institutions.

In March 1970 the MLN accomplished its first successful jailbreak, freeing thirteen MLN women. In April a tobacco company safe containing over $250,000 in gold was stolen. Soon thereafter a team of about thirty Tupamaros occupied a navy garrison and trucked away its arms without suffering a single casualty and without firing a shot.[43]

Throughout 1970 there was a noticeable escalation in police repression, largely through the efforts of secret police chief Héctor Morán Charquero and his U.S. adviser from the AID Public Safety Program, Dan Mitrione. Modern torture tactics were instituted at their behest and under their supervision. Often Tupamaros were shot down in the act of surrendering. In response to this turn of the ratchet the Tupamaros hardened their policy toward the police: Morán was machine-gunned to death in April 1970.[44] In the summer the police were warned that after a truce of fifteen days, all policemen continuing to serve would be treated with less consideration. Then Mitrione was kidnapped in July and held in the "people's prison." The subsequent failure of the government to meet the conditions of his release led to his execution.[45] Pacheco responded with the declaration of a state of seige. A massive dragnet succeeded in catching twenty-four Tupamaro leaders, including Raúl Sendic.[46]

Despite their heavy losses, the MLN soon gave notice that the organization had passed the point where decapitation meant extinction. By the end of the year the MLN was in continuous action, averaging about one operation per day, including numerous acts of armed propaganda, such as occupying theaters to show photographs of the people held in custody in the "people's prison" and occupying factories to issue proclamations.[47] On January 8, 1971, the British ambassador, Geoffrey Jackson, was kidnapped. The ambitious plan for the remainder of 1971 called for setting up a parallel system of revolutionary justice around the "people's prison" and conducting a systematic campaign of reprisals against police atrocities. At the same time plans were made for massive liberations of Tupamaros imprisoned by the government, and the "Plan Tatú," a plan for sending columns of cadre into the countryside to open up a second front, began to be discussed. In addition, the MLN policy toward the November 1971 elections was ironed out. In October 1970 a Broad Front of the Left had been created, uniting Communists, Christian Democrats, Socialists, and leftist splinter groups. The MLN decided to fully support the Broad Front and that actions which might adversely affect its campaign were to be strenuously avoided.[48]

The escape operations, which took precedence over all other activities,[49] were spectacularly successful. In Operation Estrella a team of Tupamaros tunneled five meters from the basement of an MLN hideout to a sewer which led to within ten meters of the dormitory of the Women's Prison (from which the thirteen prisoners had been spirited in 1970). Another tunnel was dug to span the distance from sewer to prison; and on July 30, thirty-eight Tupamaro women were led fifteen blocks through the sewers of Montevideo to freedom.[50] In Operation Abuso 106 Tupamaros surreptitiously burrowed through cell walls and upper-story floors and then tunneled fifty meters under the walls to surface in a nearby house that had been commandeered for the occasion by free Tupamaros. From there they all drove off in fifteen commandeered vehicles. Raúl Sendic and other "old guard" leaders captured in the aftermath of the Mitrione abduction were among those freed.

In one respect, the Tupamaros during this period were the most Guevarist of all the guerrillas: they avoided manifestos, proclamations, and theoretical disquisitions. From 1963 to 1968 the Tupamaros let their actions do all of their speaking for them. Not until June 2, 1968, did a statement of their philosophy appear in print, in the form of an interview. The anonymous interviewee lost no time in revealing the Tupamaro debt to Guevara. The fundamental principle of the MLN was defined as

> the idea that revolutionary action in itself, the very act of taking up arms, preparing for and engaging in actions which are against the basis of bourgeois law, creates a revolutionary consciousness, organization and conditions [emphasis added].[51]

When asked for an example of his assertion, the Tupamaro cited Cuba. One condition of revolution singled out as being within the magnetic field of armed struggle was the mass movement. When questioned about the need for a platform (and by implication, ideological consensus), the Tupamaro reckoned that an acceptance of the principles of the Cuban Revolution, plus the proof by armed struggle that they were attainable, satisfied this need. And he wholeheartedly endorsed the "many Vietnams" strategy for the Latin American continent.

But in this tapestry of Guevarism are important strands of Leninism. The fact that the Tupamaro remains anonymous is in itself significant, for it illustrates the thoroughness with which the MLN had discarded the Guevarist leadership cult. More importantly, the interviewee voices a clear appreciation of the objective conditions fueling the Tupamaro successes and reveals a Leninist conception of the revolutionary's role in a revolutionary situation. The Tupamaro recognizes that Uruguay's economic and political crisis can only deepen and that if a capable revolutionary armed force is not prepared to seize the opportunities for revolution when they present themselves they will be missed. One is reminded of Lenin's exasperated railing at Bolsheviks who were not prepared for and would not take seriously their military tasks during 1905 and

1906, thereby robbing the revolution of the extra push which only armed struggle could give it. Lenin would undoubtedly have applauded the Tupamaro insistence that

> armed struggle is a technique which requires technical knowledge: training, equipment, psychology and practical experience. Improvisation is costly in human lives and in defeats. "Spontaneism" supported by those who speak vaguely about the revolution to be made by the people, is either mere escapism or else involves in trusting to improvisation at the decisive moment in the class struggle.[52]

This interview also gives evidence of something about which the Tupamaros' actions had already dispelled any doubt —that they took their political work among the masses seriously. To be sure, military actions, arms, and goals took a clear precedence over politics at the time of this interview and the 1970 one,[53] but given the Tupamaros' solid entrenchment in the populace—with supporters and collaborators in every pore of society, from the business district to the worst slums —it would be reckless to question their judgment on this score.

One of the important observations Debray made in his two-part analysis of the Tupamaros is that with certain important qualifications (to be introduced later), the MLN's thoroughly Guevarist propositions were verified in Uruguay during this period. In September 1971 Debray contributed a prologue to a book written by the Tupamaros recounting some of the benchmarks of their ascent from 1963 through 1970. Debray points out here that the Tupamaros were the prime movers behind the Broad Front. Standing outside the everyday functioning of the working class, the Tupamaros were nonetheless integrated into it; they were champions of the working class in its union struggles, promoters and "lifeguards" of mass mobilizations; they harrassed and carried out reprisals against the enemies of the people. They heightened the revolutionary consciousness of the masses, educating them in the corrupt functioning of their government, and hastened the crisis of the political system in the process.[54] In all these ways they catalyzed the unification of forces on the Left in much the same way that Debray had postulated in *Revolution in the*

Revolution? Furthermore, Debray submits, the Tupamaros acted as a kind of guarantor of the democratic process in the event of an electoral victory by the Broad Front, and they were the "vertebral column" of resistance against an invasion by Brazil.[55] It will be recalled that one dictum of *Revolution in the Revolution?* is that a *foco* makes a front, not vice versa. At that time Cuba provided the only confirming instance; Uruguay added another.

Debray's concern in his prologue to the Tupamaros' book, written in the month of Operation Abuso at the zenith of the Tupamaro trajectory, is to explain their meteoric ascent. Debray's estimation of the MLN in September 1971 could be contrasted with his analysis of the UP in *Conversations*, composed at a similar high point of the Chilean Revolution: the latter was given the slimmest of chances ("there is nothing to prevent us from hoping");[56] Debray's enthusiasm for the Tupamaros, on the other hand, knew no bounds. He offers no criticism and projects no awesome dangers onto the horizon. No insufficiencies are noted, nor any over- or under-emphases. Unlike *Conversations*, Debray's essay on the Tupamaros provides no footholds for understanding their subsequent decline and fall.

As in 1964 and 1966 Debray was captivated by the Tupamaros and their "new form of undertaking the socialist revolution."[57] His prologue is susceptible to the same criticism that Althusser made of *Revolution in the Revolution?*, that is, of being ahistorical. The Tupamaros, like the rural guerrilla *foco* earlier, are depicted as self-contained entities, inextricably united with each other and bound to the masses by sheer necessity, by the very nature of their task and the organization it entails. There is no discussion of the historical conditions that made the organization successful, only of the elements of that success. In particular, Debray cites the MLN's talent for uniting and harmonizing its contradictory or conflicting characteristics. For example, despite the social and political diversity of the militants, there is ideological unity; despite the internal compartmentalization necessitated by security, the MLN maintains "organic homogeneity"; military hierarchy is founded on democratic decisionmaking; a centralized strate-

gic line is carried out by columns and cells with tactical
autonomy; and the rigorously closed, clandestine organization
utilizes the broadest possible base of support and maintains
close ties with the masses.[58] The necessary transformation of
the individualistic mentalities of the predominantly petty-
bourgeois recruits into a Socialist consciousness—the old problem of proletarianization—is seen, as in *Revolution in the
Revolution?*, as issuing out of the everyday practice of the
organization. Debray goes as far as to second the Tupamaros'
opinion that by their efforts a true state of dual power had
been brought about in Uruguay.[59] How could such an organization fail? Debray leaves no clues.

But fail it did, and within a year after Debray's ringing
hyperboles. In *Las Pruebas de fuego (Trials by Fire)*, written
in 1973, Debray chronicles and analyzes the precipitous decline and fall of the Tupamaros. He finds that the organization he had examined and found in such robust good health
was, in fact, harboring a tumor that would weaken it mortally
just when it most needed its strength. And the disease broke
out precisely where the MLN seemed most secure, attacking
its internal ideological unity. Debray's pathological inquiry
reaches back to the historical conditions to which the early
Tupamaro approach to ideological problems owed its validity.
Uruguay, with its high cultural level and disproportionately
large class of white-collar employees—products of a development from colonial times that was injected repeatedly by
European immigration—was fertile ground for theorizing. At
the same time, the masses recognized that this theorizing was
ordinarily in the service of the dominant classes and reacted
by taking on an anti-intellectual character, which expressed
itself in "spontaneism." In this environment the Uruguayan
Left developed into a proliferation of organizations whose
number was in inverse proportion to the size of the mass vote.
In 1966 twenty-five distinct organizations shared 6.5 percent
of the vote. Small wonder that the Tupamaros equated Marxist theory with sectarianism and eschewed it. Instead, they
rehabilitated another kind of intellectual activity, which they
referred to as "methodology"—"the intelligent creation and
skillful execution of politico-military operation." Through

their actions they cauterized many schismatic wounds that mere disagreements had produced and, in this way, united the many shades of Maoism, Trotskyism, anarchism, Guevarism, and nationalism around a "lowest common denominator"— revolutionary nationalism.

Having revolutionary nationalism as an ideological focus was important in its own right as an ingredient of the Tupamaro success, for in addition to the many divisions among Marxists, there had been the rigid division of long standing between Marxism-Leninism and the national working-class movement. As all their documents show, the spiritual father and symbolic founder of the Tupamaros was not Marx or Lenin but Uruguay's liberator, José Gervasio Artigas. Around him the Tupamaros could bring forces together that had heretofore eyed each other with distrust, even antipathy.[60]

Thus, under Uruguayan conditions the Guevarist virtue of pragmatism (the philosophical foundation of revolutionary nationalism), long a cause of failure in Latin America, became an asset once more. But what begins as an asset may in time become a liability, as Debray's analysis shows.

By Debray's reckoning, the inadequacy of the slogan "actions unite, words divide" became manifest after August 1970, when the Tupamaro leadership was rounded up in the aftermath of the Mitrione execution. Deprived of the firm, prestigious political direction of the old guard, the Tupamaros could maintain neither their political line nor their muchvaunted ideological unity. Two tendencies emerged; a tiny "anti-militarist" faction wanted to create a party with precedence over the foco; it eventually splintered off to go its own way; and enthroned as the new leadership was the militarist "samurai" faction.

The most far-reaching consequence of this change of command was that revolutionary nationalism displaced Marxism-Leninism as the ideology of the leadership.[61] This, according to Debray and the old leadership, expressed itself in a score of "deviations":

militarism, subjectivism, immodesty and ineptitude in self-criticism, incapacity to capture all the aspects of a situation or to evaluate the relations of forces, in other words, adventurism.[62]

In addition to these deviations, usually encountered among ultraleftists, there were the rightist deviations of "liberalism, opportunism and triumphalism." Debray also argues that the new leadership took a more "centralist" view of democratic centralism than did the old leadership, which favored a more decentralized, democratic, mass-oriented party.[63]

Debray shows how all of these negative factors contributed to the disaster of 1972. One of the novelties that had to be dealt with during the period from August 1970 to September 1971 was the unprecedented formation and rise of the Broad Front. The old guard made the proposal that critical support be given the Broad Front, implying on the one hand an effective military truce and on the other an opening of the organization toward the exterior. In "Learn from Them" Debray had asserted that the Tupamaros had solved the problem of integrating a clandestine foco with a public, mass movement. The trick was to maximize contacts without jeopardizing the security of the organization. But this problem had not really been solved, and the new leadership, animated by a spirit of triumph and pride, was too liberal in allowing access to the organization from outside. At the same time some of the barriers of secrecy that had separated different parts of the organization from each other were knocked down. The new constituent parts were reassembled in a more centralized, but not more effective, way. To the contrary, the electoral truce left the Tupamaros sluggish.[64] This, Debray submits, was the consequence of a failure to take heed of a theorem of historical materialism, viz., that there are two adversaries in every struggle and one dare not be so foolish as to be swept up by one's own dynamic and forget to take into account the dynamic of the enemy.[65] A leadership more appreciative of the dialectic of the Uruguayan process would have been alive to the probability of a military buildup, fueled by U.S. aid,[66] and a stepped-up program of infiltration.

The Tupamaros' escape from Punta Carretas in September 1971 served as the warrant for bringing the new Uruguayan military to the front lines of the "antisubversive" struggle: three days after the escape, Pacheco removed prime responsibility for the counterinsurgency effort from the police and delegated it to the joint armed forces.[67] The Tupamaros were poorly prepared to meet this further escalation of the struggle. The old leadership hardly recognized the organization and found it difficult to reintegrate themselves into the Montevideo plan of action. In addition, they found themselves in disagreement with the new direction of the organization. Some, like Raúl Sendic, moved to the interior to begin implementing "Plan Tatú."[68] Throughout the crisis to come, the Tupamaros were to have two heads, which proved to be similar to having no head at all.[69]

The period from September 1971 through March 1972 saw the steady escalation of repression, with the government's Death Squadron emerging as a potent new weapon of systematic terror. The Death Squad gave police the important advantages of clandestinity. Under the cover of secrecy, police could act unlawfully to crush left-wing dissidents and have their crimes attributed to a supposed organization of private citizens. In this way the government could avail itself of terror without losing the appearance of a benevolent democracy. Furthermore, the Death Squad posed a dilemma for the Tupamaros: should they carry out reprisals against it, tit for tat, and have their struggle loftily condemned as political gangsterism, or should they jeopardize their credibility as the armed guard of the people by ignoring attacks against themselves and their supporters?

The presidential election held in November 1971, though a triumph for the Broad Front, was won by the slimmest of margins by Juan María Bordaberry, candidate of Pacheco's Colorado party.[70] Soon after the election Bordaberry made known his intention of giving a high priority to a "frontal attack on subversion."[71] On January 6, 1972, in a Montevideo suburb, the Tupamaros occupied Radio Sarandí and announced the end of the electoral truce. On February 25 they captured Nelson Bardesio, a member of the Death Squad; and in March a sworn statement was taken from Bardesio describing the Death Squad's torture and murder of a suspected

Tupamaro. Meanwhile the Death Squad stepped up its activities against Broad Front activists and compelled the MLN to confront its dilemma. Acknowledging fully the dangers of being drawn off the national political stage and made into a side show, the Tupamaros resolved to deal firmly with the Death Squad but to confine this concern to a secondary status. The MLN was planning a grand offensive of its own in the summer and wanted to use the spring months for preparations. A slow and steady escalation of warfare with the Death Squad, one which would leave the Tupamaros time for readjustment and preparation, was foreseen. As a first step the Tupamaros condemned nine members of the Death Squadron to death. And then, on April 14, 1972, after an intense campaign of protest and denunciations against the Death Squad, different Tupamaro commandos carried out the sentences against four of the nine. The victims were a former subsecretary of the interior, a naval captain, and two police commissioners. The next day, capture of eighteen more members of the Death Squad was announced.[72]

The Tupamaro vision was rudely smashed by the flood of repression that their opening salvo called forth. As their own information should have suggested to them, the Death Squad was a crack shock force of the repressive apparatus; a frontal attack against it was nothing less than a frontal attack against the whole apparatus. The combined weight of the armed forces and police were mobilized instantly and thrown into a full-scale war of annihilation against the Tupamaros. The day after the executions Bordaberry decreed a state of war for the next forty-five days. During the first month 256 Tupamaros were captured, 10 were killed, and 40 underground refuges and depositories were discovered. By early September 1972 these figures shot up to 1,987 captured, 29 killed, and 247 hideouts discovered. Raúl Sendic was captured on September 1. The organization was crushed.[73]

Why did the Tupamaros fare so poorly? Debray's analysis points to the dissension within the ranks and to the cause of that dissension, inadequate politicization of the cadre. From these weaknesses came two ruinous betrayals. One of the traitors, Amodío Pérez, had been an MLN founder and a

champion warrior and organizer. But in the Convention of
March 1972, while he was in prison, he was relieved of his
post for his role in the deterioration of the organization. Heading Operation Gallo from within, Pérez led fifteen Tupamaros
out of the Punta Carretas prison on April 12. But his personality and consciousness could not absorb the shock of his
demotion combined with other personal tragedies. He led the
police to the "people's prison" and to numerous Tupamaro
hideouts and even took part in the interrogation of prisoners.
The other traitor, Mario Piriz, one of the leaders of the "Plan
Tatú," was motivated by greed to carry out his betrayal.[74]

Debray believes the Tupamaros could have shielded
themselves from the threat of betrayals by a more rigid compartmentalization and, even more importantly, by carrying on
an ideological struggle within the bosom of the organization.
The Tupamaros were slow to recognize that the class struggle
had arrived at a point when the words which once would have
divided were now needed to unify.[75]

There is plenty of evidence that the old guard came to
this recognition while still in prison.[76] But the organization
could not be straightened out in time; the pace of events was
already too great. When warfare became total in mid April,
the Tupamaros had scores of militants ready for action on a
plan that would have dealt the armed forces a harsher blow
than had yet been dealt the MLN, but the organization could
not respond. Despite (or perhaps because of) the March
Convention the organization was in the midst of an ideological struggle between the old and new factions, attacking the
mistakes of the "petty bourgeois" period and the conditions
that nourished them. At just the moment when a maximum
counterattack was needed to drive the armed forces back or at
least slow down their advance, the MLN was paralyzed. The
armed forces, encouraged by this lack of response, struck even
harder.[77]

A politico-military *foco*, "methodology," and revolutionary nationalism—these were the constituent elements of the
MLN. All over Latin America for nearly a decade very similar
ingredients had been combined without reaching a flash point,
until in the one-hundred-square-mile urban jungle of Monte-

video they found a suitable set of conditions. But to summarize and paraphrase Debray, the conditions of birth should not—may not—be expected to meet the needs of maturity. As the class struggle developed, the organization and the ideology of the Tupamaros lagged behind the requirements of the revolution. The notion that a state of dual power existed was, Debray now admits, an ultraleft mirage. Historically, dual power means that large masses of people in arms have created a public government and achieved a provisional and limited sovereignty. To reach this stage, Debray now suggests, the Tupamaros needed a Marxist-Leninist party with a legal apparatus. They had already needed it before August 1970. To have avoided the internal weakening they would have had to allow ideological struggle a place in the MLN organization earlier. To keep apace of events, Debray suggests, they needed the guidance of Marxist analysis. When the repression they faced grew formidable, the Tupamaros needed an aboveground apparatus and a political movement, because with these a clandestine army is harder to isolate and excise.[78]

We could interpretively summarize Debray's analysis of the Tupamaro defeat as follows: like so many *focos* before them, the Tupamaros were devoured by the Furies they unleashed. Like Popular Unity in Chile, they had an exaggerated notion of their country's exceptional features and expected to be exempted from certain laws of Marxist theory. Both the Tupamaros and Popular Unity acted as though their exemptions would be valid indefinitely, when, in fact, they expired very quickly. Their revolutions were crushed before any significant progress toward better alignment with Marxism-Leninism could be made. In both cases, by Debray's analysis, revolutionary Marxists within ideologically alien bodies—a reformist Marxist movement in one case and a natural revolutionary movement in the other—were defeated in their efforts to change the ideological direction of their organization (to "proletarianize" it) in midstream, while on a collision course with an aroused reactionary backlash. Debray obviously feels that Allende and Sendic were revolutionary Marxists, but, though they were leaders, their ideology was not the leading ideology. Ironically, if the Cuban Revolution succeeded where the Chilean and Uruguayan ones did not, it was in no small part because Guevara was able to succeed in Cuba where Allende and Sendic failed. Even as a foreigner, Guevara was able to catalyze the implementation of Marxism in the heart of the Rebel Army. Allende and Sendic, both founders of the movements they headed, were thwarted in their attempts to replicate Che's accomplishment.

Preparation for People's War without People's War

Debray published three books on revolutionary theory in 1974. His analysis of the Chilean defeat appears in *The Criticism of Weapons*, volume 1, along with a penetrating analysis of the rise and fall of *foquismo* (broadly defined to cover urban as well as rural guerrilla warfare). The Tupamaros are discussed in the second volume, *Trials by Fire* (volume 2 of *The Criticism of Weapons*),[79] along with case studies of rural *foquismo* in Venezuela and in Guatemala. And Debray's *Che's Guerrilla War*[80] rounds out the picture with a long-awaited analysis of the Bolivian venture. There is much in these works that is novel and brilliant, but those who hope for a rigorous settling of accounts with his *foquista* past will be sorely disappointed. Debray continues to voice criticism of Guevarism; nonetheless, criticism of Guevara himself remains muted. This approach yields a stark contradiction between what Debray claims about Guevara and all of Debray's other claims. To quote Debray: "A political defeat always poses the same question: to know if the defeat was of the fundamental political line or of the way in which it was applied in practice."[81] What Debray does, in effect, is to prove that Guevara's political line was defeated, while loudly insisting that it was not political theory but mistakes of application were at fault.

Debray thereby subverts his avowed purpose in carrying out this exhaustive study of *foquismo*. Debray feared that a new wave of *foquismo* would follow the defeat of the electoral strategy in Chile, just as the first wave had followed on the heels of the mass of electoral disasters a decade earlier in 1963 and 1964. The chances of success for these early *focos*, Debray points out, were compromised from the start by the fact that they were, by design, out of phase with the mass movement. They came along at the tail end of a period of mass agitation, mass participation in elections, and in some cases widespread insurrection, hoping to fill with armed struggle the vacuum left by the receding mass movement. But the shrinking mass base had as its reflection the neglect of the masses in the theory of foquismo and in its forms of struggle and organization. Isolated politically from mass support, the guerrillas' principal struggle quickly became a naked struggle for physical survival, one that inexorably led to premature discovery and military annihilation.[82]

With his "criticism of weapons," Debray wishes to counter any tendencies toward repetition of the mistakes of this period, but he defeats his purpose when he suddenly declares that however much Che's "leap" might have come to the same dismal end, it was a "dialectical" leap nonetheless, one that was in no way "artificial." In the same vein Debray denies that Che's failure "appeared fatal or foreseeable or even probable." "Both right and history were on Che's side," Debray submits.[83]

But by Debray's own account, the historical conditions under which Guevara bypassed traditional theory and forms of struggle were, if anything, even less auspicious than conditions in, for example, Venezuela or Guatemala. When Guevara arrived at the Nancahuazú base on November 7, 1966, the Latin American revolution was at its lowest ebb since 1959. Not only was the mass movement still dormant, but in Bolivia, as in the rest of Latin America, armed struggle was in full retreat.[84] Nineteen sixty-six, the year of the Tricontinental Conference, had been a year of military catastrophe, with many irreplaceable guerrilla commanders losing their lives in the process.[85] And if the other focos were merely out of phase with the mass movement, the Bolivian ELN entered at the absolute nadir. By Debray's own admission, there was a large discrepancy between the mission and the conditions for its success, but confidence in Guevara was so great that everyone involved in the project was confident that Che could bridge the gap.[86]

Given its inhospitable political and physical environment,

it is not surprising that the ELN was on the defensive almost from the first moment. The operation had no "ups and downs," no high points or turning points, only one unbroken, steadily falling decline, much like the EGP disaster in Argentina, also authored by Che. Both of these examples provide evidence that Che's foquismo, the foquismo of *Revolution in the Revolution?*, was too flimsy to stand up to the gale of repression it would inevitably incite. So the Bolivian venture cannot be said to have had a chance despite Debray's claim that it "had history on its side." To say that Guevara had a chance is to argue that it was not Guevara's conception that was wrong, only his execution. But there is no evidence for this position; the end could hardly have come any more quickly. There is, on the other hand, a large body of evidence for the opposite conclusion, and Debray adds to it mightily in his "criticism of weapons."

Revolutionizing the Proletariat

Debray's criticism of armed struggle in Latin America actually extends to a criticism of Marxist theory and politics prior to the Cuban Revolution. Debray finds the nub of the problem of making revolution in the merger of workers' struggles with revolutionary consciousness, of the mass movement with Marxist theory. This was the concern of Lenin in *What Is to Be Done?*, and it is Debray's principal concern in his critique of armed struggle.

Debray suggests an explanation for the historical failure of Marxism in Latin America to make strong connections with the working class. It is, simply, that the Communist parties could not satisfactorily resolve the question of nationalism. They could not tie the essentially bourgeois movement for national independence to a Socialist movement. Nor could they decide what role national liberation should play in the move to socialism or what place Socialists should take in the national revolution.

Debray argues that answers offered by Latin American communism were, from the very first moment, wide of the mark. The parties were founded in the period of the Third Communist International (Comintern), led first by Lenin and then by Stalin. Under the internationalist pressures of the overcentralized Comintern, Latin American Marxism was consistently deflected from its nationalist tasks, with ruinous results. Thus, for example, in the Stalinist Comintern's "third period" from 1927 to 1933, during which all alliances with social democracy were taboo, the obedient Latin Americans shut themselves off from the petty bourgeoisie just as it was being radicalized. Then, from 1933 to war's end, during the Popular Front against Fascism years, the antifascist struggle supplanted, little by little, the anti-imperialist struggle. Finally, during the Cold War and the years of peaceful coexistence between the U.S. and the U.S.S.R., the pacifism of the Soviet line prevented many Latin American parties from preparing for armed struggle.[87]

According to Debray, Latin American communism has consistently ignored or, at best, failed to appreciate the unique feature of Latin America that sets it apart from the "colonial world of imperialism." Latin America, with its century and a half of political independence, its level of institutional organization, and its fundamentally capitalist nature, cannot be lumped with the most recent fugitives from colonialism; but neither can it be lumped with the developed capitalist countries which hold it in economic bondage. The countries of Latin America have already achieved their political sovereignty (with the exception of Puerto Rico and Belice) and are not, therefore, candidates for national liberation struggles in the usual sense. But they have not yet achieved economic "sovereignty" and are not therefore candidates for a European-style Socialist revolution. Latin America is neither Europe nor Asia, though in the past it has been mistaken for first one and then the other. Latin America is the child of the marriage, or one should say rape, of Indoamerica by Europe; and as one might expect, it resembles both parents, but in different proportions and in different ways at various stages of growth. Those who see Latin America through European eyes forget the struggle against imperialism and forfeit the alliances that are available to and needed by the proletariat in the struggle against national oppression. They are attracted by European models of revolution (e.g., the Russian Revolution). Those who confuse Latin America with Asia forget class struggle against the enemy within and end up collaborating with it. They are drawn to the Asian model of revolution.[88] The nub of the problem of revolution in Latin America lies in finding the correct balance—a different balance in each country—between these two extremes. Heretofore only in Cuba had the national revolution, under petty-bourgeois leadership, been successfully routed onto Socialist tracks.

Debray attributes the "Cuban miracle" to Fidel's consistent policy of promoting the widest unity, thereby exploiting to the fullest the special historical condition of Cuba—that of being historically the most neocolonial of the Latin American states. The continual economic presence and political interference of the United States left Cuba with a weak state apparatus and a ruling class totally dependent on and indissolubly tied to U.S. business. Under these conditions the anti-"Yanqui" struggle was readily recognized as a struggle against the national bourgeoisie; the war for national liberation was a civil war. Furthermore, the Cuban proletariat had a tradition of organization vastly out of proportion with the backwardness of the economy. Given these subjective factors, together with a national economic and political crisis, the "Cuban miracle" became a reality.[89]

The fate of the numerous focos that sprang up in the wake of the Cuban Revolution indicated, according to Debray, that it was (and is) too late for bourgeois-democratic revolutions (the first stage of the Cuban Revolution) but too early for Socialist revolution. The national bourgeoisies, Debray argues, are too afraid of socialism to fight for their liberation, but the Socialist forces are too weak to make good the bourgeoisies' fears. This state of uneasy equilibrium, Debray notes, is made to order for a military solution: rule by a nationalist military which stands as a guarantee against Socialist revolution while performing the primordial task of capitalist development, e.g., agrarian reform. Coincidentally, Debray sees military nationalism not only as the logical successor to foquismo but as its historical byproduct. The Peruvian experiment with military nationalism would have been inconceivable without the prior confrontation between the army and its revolutionary countrymen in 1965. And the Torres government in Bolivia was given its impetus by the shock waves sent out by Che's guerrilla war.[90]

Debray implies that, for the time being, the revolutionary road in Latin America can, at best, pass from *foquismo* to military nationalism—from Cuba to Peru—but not from war of the vanguard to people's war—from Cuba to Vietnam. At the same time Debray seems confident that conditions for armed struggle in Latin America have improved and will continue to do so. The possibilities for armed struggle "have not been so great since the advent of the Cuban Revolution." The "objective conditions are . . . today more favorable," Debray writes, than in 1963 and 1964, and the "divorce which was operative then . . . between armed struggle and mass struggle, is not in the least inevitable this time."[91] In short, armed struggle is dead, long live armed struggle. The time for suicidal vanguard wars is past; the time to prepare conditions for people's war has come. Debray renders his criticism of weapons as a contribution to this effort, with the fervent hope that it will not impair "the victory of the people in arms."[92]

Conditions for People's War

But what are the conditions for people's war? Or to express it another way, what are the conditions for survival of a guerrilla army? At a bare minimum, Debray submits, subversion of the enemy's rear is necessary. The revolutionary army must be able to organize popular forces, outside its principal zone of operations, to gather intelligence and attack the enemy's lines of communication, thereby undermining its base of operations and relieving the military pressure on the revolutionary army. In order to get this far two things are indispensable: a successful policy of cadre-building and a revolutionary situation defined by foreign (U.S.) intervention. The experience of China, Russia, Yugoslavia, and Albania has shown that when the struggle for social emancipation and the struggle for national liberation are joined, the cadre work of recruiting and mobilizing the masses becomes many times more effective. The Dominican Republic showed that foreign intervention is not a sufficient condition, but it is a necessary and "optimal" condition.[93]

Debray now sees a rear base of support—a relatively safe haven where the army can be nourished with recruits and supplies and where its morale and politics can be strengthened —as the greatest strategic requirement of the guerrilla army. It will be recalled that in *Revolution in the Revolution?* the question of guerrilla bases was regarded as a purely military one. Debray now discovers it to be an essentially political matter, for a rear support base is inconceivable in the absence of a mass political base of support in the region. In addition, in *Revolution in the Revolution?* Debray argued that differences in population density made the model of people's war inapplicable to Latin America. Debray now harkens back to Althusser's letter, however, to observe that differences in population density are only surface reflections of more profound differences between two distinct socio-economic formations. In China the economic and social "center of gravity" is in the countryside; in Latin America more extensive capitalist development has shifted the center of gravity to the city. Even when the regular army is incapable of uprooting the guerrillas altogether, as in Colombia, the guerrillas can be circumscribed and tolerated because the territory they control and the people they lead are peripheral to the mainstream of the nation's activity; history has pushed them to one side. Debray contrasts this with the exceptional situation in Cuba in 1956. Oriente Province, in which the Rebel Army first operated, was historically the revolutionary and political center as well as the agricultural and economic center of Cuba.[94]

Debray sees a further, seemingly insurmountable problem in Latin America: the unavailability of neighboring revolutionary countries to act as incomparable rear bases, prior to the establishment of liberated territories in the interior of the country. Almost all the examples of successful people's war enjoyed this advantage. China, to be sure, did not, but there the vast extension of land acted as an adequate substitute. In Cuba the Caribbean Sea offered the rebels a window to the outside, one which proved adequate given the ambiguity and indecisiveness of the American and Cuban bourgeoisies in the face of the Cuban struggle. But with the unprecedented preparedness of the "modern nazis"—Debray's term for the U.S. counterinsurgency establishment—these exceptions cannot be repeated.[95]

Debray does not address himself to a question that immediately comes to mind: why prepare for people's war if people's war is impossible? But logically only one reply will do: in the near or distant future, conditions for people's war will be improved by a drastic alteration in the worldwide power relations between socialism and capitalism. The solemn judgment that Debray renders on the present-day power relations brooks no illusions that this turnabout is at hand. His message to all would-be proponents of armed struggle, then, is that they should dig in and wait for more favorable conditions, all the while using existing conditions to carry on with the arduous but indispensable work of revolutionizing the consciousness of the proletariat.

Proletarianizing the Revolutionaries

A recurring theme in Debray's post-prison writings is the delinquency of the *focos* in establishing ties with proletariat. His pathology of this error represents a significant and original contribution to the Marxist theory of organization. The philosophical underpinning of Debray's analysis is a dynamic, interdependent conception of the relation between worker and revolutionary, mass movement and vanguard organization. According to this conception the internal relations of a vanguard are functionally related to the state of its relations with the masses. The tightening of bonds with the masses makes possible the relaxation of relations within the organization, that is, it permits greater internal democracy. Conversely, when ties with masses drop away, the vanguard compensates by tightening up, rigidifying; militarism and centralism supplant ideological struggle and democracy as the backbone of the organization; self-discipline, arising out of profound motivation, gives way to discipline imposed by the organization on its members.[96]

The description by Quartim of the fate of the Brazilian VPR illustrates Debray's point, as do the fates suffered by the

Brazilian ALN, Guatemalan FAR, Venezuelan FALN, and the Tupamaros.[97] The reasons for their isolation from their people differed. The ALN and VPR were archetypal focos and effectively without a political base from the start. The FAR's close ties with the rural poor were severed by a year of intense "pacification" after October 1966. The FALN was isolated by the combined impact of electoral failure, military defeat, the durability of Acción Democrática-style liberalism, and the fact that in turning to socialism the FALN left behind its national revolutionary base. At first the Tupamaros had attracted a wide following among the working classes, but their foquista underestimation of the party apparatus needed to root their actions more firmly in the workers' movement allowed militarism to take over the direction of the organization. However different may have been the causes for isolation, once isolated, each of these organizations responded in the same way: a line of cleavage developed between two tendencies representing two responses to this isolation—a militarist, or "Debrayist," tendency and a politicist, "Leninist," one. The militarist tendency sought to compensate for its weakness

> by making more inflexible the internal cohesion of the movement, by consolidating its stability and unity through disciplinary measures of exclusion and purification, and then the unity and cohesion became hard—but like glass.[98]

And, like glass, the cohesion was shattered by the first hard blow, for,

> whenever the military formation of cadres takes precedence over the political formation, the militants find themselves in mortal danger: not metaphorically. Because the moral factor is the decisive military factor, and the moral factor is inseparable from political education.[99]

One could summarize Debray's analysis very simply with the seemingly trivial axiom that the proletarianization of the revolutionary, like revolutionizing the proletariat (the two are, after all, only different sides of the same process) requires prolonged interaction between revolutionary and proletariat. In addition, there is an unabating need for interparty debate on all major issues, for without it, the revolutionary organization under the combined impact of political and military exigencies cannot be expected to steer a straight course between liquidation of its political or of its military side, i.e., between politicism and militarism.

One would expect, therefore, that Debray would define *proletarianization* in terms of two constituent mechanisms: progressive interaction with the proletariat and ideological struggle. But, surprisingly, in Debray's direct discussion of proletarianization he replaces the conjunction of the two mechanisms with a disjunction; *and* becomes *or*. According to this version there are two kinds of proletarianization—from below, through membership in the class of the proletariat, or from above, from theory, where "theory" denotes "a running balance of the experience of the world's working class."[100] According to Debray, the proletarianization of the European revolutionaries took the former course, while the Bolsheviks took the latter. The former was rationalized by Rosa Luxemburg in *The Mass Strike, the Political Party and the Trade Unions;*[101] the latter by Lenin in *What Is to Be Done?*

Underlying Debray's conception of the genesis of Leninism is a thesis that has been persuasively argued by the Belgian, Marcel Liebman. It contends that Lenin's conception of the revolutionary party in *What Is to Be Done?* is excessively centralized, elitist, and distrustful of the spontaneous, undirected activity of the masses. According to Liebman (and Debray) the revolution of 1905, by and large a spontaneous affair, with its "discoveries" of the mass political strikes, street fighting, and soviets, gave Lenin a deeper respect for the initiative and organizational ability of the proletariat and caused him to repudiate the degree of centralization espoused in *What Is to Be Done?* and other works of the prerevolutionary period.[102]

This is not the place to argue the merits of this thesis, especially since its truth or falsity is peripheral to the real issue. The point is that Debray invokes this interpretation of the formative years of Bolshevism as a vehicle for yet another attempt to drape Lenin's mantle over the theorists of *foquismo* (notably, Che and himself) by pointing out certain similarities between *foquismo* and *What Is to Be Done?* and by suggesting that the two theories are homologous. The theories, Debray writes, arose out of similar sets of conditions, evoked similar responses from the Left, and "shared a common hypothesis [of] . . . the exteriority of the vanguard in relation to the spontaneous movement of the masses."[103] The *foquistas* erred not on the side of heterodoxy but on the side of orthodoxy for

> . . . the guerrilla centre, as we conceived it, was nothing more than a particular version of the party, such as is defined in *What Is to Be Done?*: a little elite group, compact and disciplined, dedicated body and soul to the revolution, subjected to its own rules of conduct, to its discipline and methods of clandestine work, *without organic ties* with the mass movement, abandoned to its sectorial economic struggles [emphasis added].[104]

There are several flaws in Debray's reasoning. First of all, in no significant sense of the word *organic* did Lenin advocate that revolutionaries do without "organic ties" to the mass movement or that they "abandon" the mass movement to its trade unionists. Nor did the Russian Social Democratic Labor party (RSDLP) and then the Bolshevik party ever fit this description. Debray's assertion to the contrary surprisingly disregards that well-established fact. It may, of course, be that by "organic ties" Debray means membership in the proletariat, in which case he is right; nevertheless Debray is still wrong about "abandoning" the mass movement. But even if all of Debray's formal parallels between "primitive Leninism"[105] and *foquismo* were historically accurate, they would still be dwarfed by formidable substantive divergences. None of the differences between Leninism (however "primitive") and *foquismo* has been conjured away: *foquismo*'s methodological denial of Lenin; the reliance on pragmatism in place of historical materialism; the reduction of politics to armed struggle, etc. There is a world of difference between centralization of an organization of theorists, agitators, and propagandists, dedicated above all to educating the proletariat for revolution, and centralization of a military organization primarily dedicated to armed struggle. The fact of centralization in both cases is distinctly secondary. Similarly, Lenin's use of military metaphors in *What Is to Be Done?*, cited by Debray,[106] is less significant than the fact that *foquismo* took these metaphors literally.

Debray's attempt to cast *foquismo* and early Leninism in the same mold is his most adroit synthesis of the two ideologies. In effect, Debray argues that the revolutionaries who clustered around Lenin prior to 1905 constituted a kind of *foco*, a self-professed vanguard in search of footholds in the mass movement. The "only" difference is that the Bolsheviks used theory instead of armed struggle to accomplish this aim. Debray succeeds in presenting certain abstract parallels between early Leninism and *foquismo*, but he grossly exaggerates their significance. These meager parallels shrink to insignificance when confronted with the profound philosophical differences between *foquismo* and Leninism.

Revolution in the Revolution?

On the surface Debray's post-prison writings, taken together, have an eclectic, disorderly character. Despite the resounding defeats of Guevara's rural *foquismo*, the urban *foquismo* of the Tupamaros, and the UP strategy in Chile, Debray gives a vote of confidence to one and all. The defeats of these disparate strategies are attributed to execution, not to conception; conceivably all could have passed on to the stage of people's war. At the same time Debray demonstrates conclusively that the objective conditions for people's war do not now exist, nor, by implication, did they exist in Chile, Uruguay, or Bolivia. How, then, is people's war conceivable in the absence of the very conditions that make it possible?

The only resolution to this apparent contradiction comes from a modified version of the fundamental hypothesis of *foquismo*—that necessary conditions for revolution can be created by a determined *foco*. If we broaden the meaning of *foco* to include noninsurrectionary bodies of revolutionaries, such as the UP in Chile, we have one of the keys to understanding Debray's post-prison conception of revolution. The other key is Debray's emphasis on revolutionizing the masses. He now sees the problem that overshadows and encompasses all the rest to be one of transmitting revolutionary conscious-ness to the populace at large. Debray holds that the Uru-guayan and Chilean *focos* began processes that might have led to the revolutionization of their peoples, but in order to have succeeded, each needed to change character. A revolution may be initiated by a national revolutionary or a reformist *foco*, but it must sooner or later be transformed into a full-fledged Marxist-Leninist organization. By implication there must be Marxist-Leninists within the national revolutionary or reformist movement to take charge of the transformation. In the metaphor of *foquismo*, the small motor may put the big motor of the masses into motion, provided that an even smaller motor is able to shunt the former onto Marxist-Leninist tracks.

In Cuba the Marxist-Leninist revolution took place within the July 26th Movement after it had seized power. By Debray's reasoning this veritable revolution in the revolution must now be placed on the agenda early in the struggle be-cause conditions for such a transformation are much less favor-able: whereas Cuba caught the U.S. napping, now every national revolutionary or reformist struggle is immediately branded as Socialist and attacked accordingly. In order to survive, a movement must quickly live up to imperialism's lofty conception of it.

The upshot of Debray's criticism of the UP and the Tupamaros is that they failed to take measures vigorous enough to effect their internal revolution. Indeed, his investi-gation uncovers so little evidence of progress in that direction that one is justified in questioning Debray's faith in it. Debray's probable reply to such doubts is found in his assess-ment of the singular accomplishment of the Tupamaros and the UP: they awakened their peoples and propelled them down the road to revolution, something that was never any-thing more than a fond dream for the traditional Marxist-Leninist parties.

It is better, Debray is saying, to risk erring on the side of too little Leninism too late than to allow Leninist doctrine to become a barrier between party and populace; better to risk erring on the side of collaboration than erring on the side of sectarianism. The former course may spell defeat of the revolution; the latter blocks its emergence. Debray's view is not merely theoretical: he is active today in France as a member of François Mitterand's French Socialist party.[107] Thus does the *foco* concept attain a permanent place in Debray's latest conception of revolution in its early stages. Even the young Lenin is cast as having inspired a kind of theoretical *foco*. The overall message that emerges from Debray's post-prison writings is that while in the early days of Leninism a theoretical *foco* was a viable tool for forging the union of revolutionary intellectual and proletarian and for beginning the process of revolutionizing the workers' movement, under present conditions the opening wedge requires a new kind of *foco*. Without for a moment neglecting theory, new *focos* may—or must?—begin to the Right or Left of the classical Marxist-Leninist tradition, with armed struggle or the occupation of governmental posts playing the role once played by theory.

7

In Search of
The Correct Synthesis

In a *Time* interview in October 1975 Debray accurately characterized the development of his thought as "a zigzag to find the correct position."[1] This is not meant apologetically because according to Marxist epistemology this is precisely how knowledge develops. Antithesis is called up by thesis and forever bears its stamp. The zigzag of revolutionary theory reflects its involvement in the class struggle. "In a fight to the death," Debray writes, "the important thing is to triumph and there is not time to deliver blows in careful doses."[2] Thus a deviation on the Right from Marxism-Leninism is combatted by an exaggerated swing to the Left. This was as true of Bolshevism as of every other revolutionary movement. *What Is to Be Done?* untempered by Lenin's other writings conduces to militarism; *Left Wing Communism—An Infantile Disorder* leads to opportunism. Debray characterizes "Leninism" as "the resultant of these two diametrically opposed lines of rectification."[3]

But however much he may have erred to the Left or the Right in steering the Bolshevik party to power, Lenin's deflections from the direct course are dwarfed by Debray's, even if we confine our attention to his post-prison writings. To put Debray's zigzagging into perspective, it is useful to dwell for a moment on the continuities of Debray's writings. Central among these is the fact that he is unshakeably loyal to and uncritical of the Cuban line in foreign policy. In his earliest essays Debray praised the spirit of "Castroism" while misperceiving its substance. In *Revolution in the Revolution?* he was not only true to the spirit and letter of Cuban foreign policy, the book itself was an instrument of that policy. It is true that his prison writings backed away from that policy, but not before a similar course was being followed in Cuba. At the same time that Debray was engaging in self-criticism while in prison, Cuba was contributing to the anti-Debray literature in the pages of the American Marxist periodical *Monthly Review* through the efforts of Simón Torres and Julio Aronde. Their article, which appeared in the summer of 1968, gives the impression of a divergence between Debray and Cuba but, in fact, provides further evidence to the contrary.[4]

Debray's post-prison writings clarify and implicitly support the change of direction in Cuban foreign policy after 1968. Debray's analysis of military nationalism as a byproduct of *foquismo*—as the inheritor of the revolutionary energy awakened in the masses by the reverberations of a guerrilla war concluded some years ago—provides a rationale for Cuba's policy toward military regimes. When the relationship between *foquismo* and military nationalism is formulated in this way, Cuba's shift in policy toward reformist governments becomes more understandable and less susceptible to simplistic charges of conservatism or bowing to the Soviet line. It would have been perverse, indeed, for Cuba to renounce the forward-moving process that it had itself put in motion. To use the favorite *foquista* metaphor, to forfeit friendly connections with the "big motor" of the mass movement just because it has consumed or sacrificed the "small motors" which set it in motion, or because it moves more slowly than someone's wish or expectation, would be to indulge in self-flagellation.

Debray's allegiance to Cuba extends even to its altercations with certain prominent personalities; he treats harshly two old-friends-become-enemies, Jean-Paul Sartre and Douglas Bravo. Sartre was one of revolutionary Cuba's first prominent European visitors and admirers, as well as one of the European leftists to whom Guevara had hoped to send Debray for help in organizing international support for the Bolivian guerrilla force. Nevertheless Debray takes Sartre to task for his criticism of Cuba in a case involving a Cuban poet. When Heberto Padilla was arrested and held for thirty-seven days during the spring of 1971 for alleged counterrevolutionary behavior, Sartre participated prominently in the campaign to free the poet. Debray at one point rather gratuitously reveals that "the disgust and loathing of Jean-Paul Sartre before the abominable Stalinist practices of which a Cuban poet in full health and liberty had been victim" had received front-page coverage all over Brazil.[5]

Sartre also opened up *Les Temps Modernes* to Douglas Bravo, who broke with Fidel early in 1970.[6] Bravo's complaint was that after the Bolivian debacle, Cuba and Castro retreated from the internationalism of the mid 1960s; in concentrating on international economic development Fidel turned his back on his duty to support guerrilla warfare throughout Latin America. Castro responded to Bravo's letter on April 22, 1970, with a vicious "clarification," necessitated in large part, he lamented, by the fact that every piece of misinformation about Cuba "is immediately echoed in the bourgeois liberal press of Paris."[7] Castro derided the "philosophical and ideological underdevelopment" displayed by "those pseudorevolutionaries who have discovered a new kind of crime: that of Cuba's trying to attain economic devevlopment" and insisted that

> . . . Cuba has not refused nor will she ever refuse support to the revolutionary movement. But this is not to be confused with support for just any faker. . . .
>
> Now, when the right time comes we will publish the story of some of these fakers, with full details. . . . We have the documents in our possession—on some of these who have been "revolutioncides"—I'm coining a new word—destroyers of revolutions, men who had the opportunity to wage revolutionary war . . . but instead sabotaged it and destroyed it.[8]

Debray's analysis of Venezuela helps explain Fidel's "clarification." Debray reveals that fourteen Cubans, commanded by "Antonio" and accompanied by the Venezuelan revolutionary Leuben Petkoff, landed in Venezuela in July

1966. In early 1967, after suffering "the disaster of Manzanita" in which one Cuban was killed, the platoon commanded by Antonio became separated from the rest. It remained in isolation until found by Petkoff a year later.[9] Petkoff and the Cubans became the center of an "anti-commander" group which felt Douglas Bravo had "betrayed" them, first by his incompetence and then by his "deliberate wish to sabotage the guerrilla effort."[10] In March 1968 this wing split from the supporters of Bravo, "declaring inadmissable the campaigns of denigration directed against the Cuban comrades."[11]

While noting that underneath the recriminations lay fundamental questions of strategy, Debray supports the view of the "anti-command" group and of Fidel Castro that Bravo sabotaged the rural guerrilla effort. It is Debray's view that Bravo never really believed in guerrilla warfare; his position was only slightly different from the PCV, and he cultivated the guerrillas for the same opportunist reasons. Bravo's conception of the revolution, which went by the name of "combined insurrection," was modeled, Debray contends, after the October Revolution, not the Cuban Revolution. The role of the guerrillas in this strategy was that of an armed reserve, a unit not to be risked in battle except in concert with progressive urban and military forces to inaugurate one insurrectionary cataclysm. Accordingly, Bravo spent little time with the guerrillas, remaining in the city for years at a time to intrigue and conspire for control of the PCV, among other things. Consequently, he had no real understanding of or sympathy for the guerrillas' needs. For example, Debray suggests that the separation of Antonio's platoon from the main body of guerrillas would have been shorter had it not been a matter of indifference to Bravo where the guerrillas were or what they were doing before insurrection day.[12] Whether Debray's appraisal is just cannot be determined here, but it should be noted that in a 1971 interview Douglas Bravo makes claims to the contrary. He avers that the Venezuelan revolution had been held back by two erroneous "tactics," one of which aimed at a "revolution in the Russian style" (the very strategy imputed to him by Debray), the other being *foquismo* as espoused by Debray in *Revolution in the Revolution?*[13]

The no-holds-barred attack by Cuba on its old friends stands in stark contrast to its hand-off policy toward its hero, Che Guevara; and here, too, Debray's bearing is irreproachable by Cuban standards. In all of his prison and post-prison writings Debray exemplified the Cuban mood, which was—and continues to be—that Guevara's attributes were such as to automatically disqualify as unworthy any who would criticize his political theory. Guevara was the heroic guerrilla, the super-revolutionary, the existential hero whose whole life was a conscious project pursued with unstinting dedication, honesty, and spirit. His political theory, which called for enormous personal sacrifice, was matched letter for letter by his willingness to sacrifice every living moment and even life itself for the world's exploited and oppressed peoples, of whatever race or nationality. Not only the Cubans, but revolutionaries everywhere have recognized in Guevara the embodiment of Socialist morality—selflessness, internationalism, and humanism. Morally Guevara was a man of the future, Socialist man. As such he was undeniably the peer of Marx, Lenin, Mao, and Ho Chi Minh. It appears that only Socialist men make Socialist revolutions, but unlike these pillars of the Marxist-Leninist tradition, Guevara's bequest to his successors reduces primarily to his exemplary moral stature. Guevara the revolutionary theorist is overshadowed by the principled man of action.

It is no wonder that in their adoration of the man, the Cubans hold his writings above criticism. He is, after all, above reproach, and it is easy to confuse criticism with reproach, the epistemological 'good' with the ethical 'good'. It is often forgotten that a revolutionary bearing may be a necessary condition for revolutionary theory, but it is certainly not a sufficient one. There is more to truth than virtue; there is also correspondence with historical reality. Debray makes just this mistake. In his prison and post-prison writings Debray repeatedly rests his claim that Guevara is the quintessential Leninist on the fact that he embodied the perfect union of theory and practice. But it is not enough that theory be wedded to practice; to be a Leninist, both theory and practice must be rooted in social reality interpreted within the framework of historical materialism. Based on Debray's own discussion, Guevara's conception of history was unabashedly idealistic.[14]

Debray's unwillingness to face up to the consequences of his own thinking lends his post-prison writings an air of evasiveness. Over and over we are led to the brink of the conclusion that Guevara was indeed a Guevarist, only to be brought back at the last moment with a bald negation of what has been proved. The unflattering truth about the deceased hero is suppressed, with the tacit approval of the many mourners present, to guard his memory from well-known tomb desecraters. Debray's reasoning appears to be that it is not important, at least not to revolutionaries, that Guevara's failings be recognized as his as long as they are recognized as failings.

The degree of vacillation in Debray's writings can, in part, be ascribed to the fact that however great his allegiance to the Latin American Revolution, in the final analysis he remains a French intellectual. In late 1974 Debray wrote a novel, entitled *L'Indésirable* (*The Undesirable*), which exposes some of the conflicts inherent in this existential condition. The leading character is Frank, a young Swiss Trotskyist who travels to a fictitious country near the Caribbean to participate in its revolution. The constellation of political forces at work within the country and their interactions follow the general pattern of the Venezuelan and Guatemalan guerrillas: there is a reform-minded Communist party, a National Liberation Front, a rural guerrilla army, a hostile dichotomy between the party and the guerrillas, a split, and finally military defeat.[15]

Debray chose a Swiss and a tropical country in order to achieve the maximum cultural contrast. In his words,

> Latin America is an open world, with open spaces, open hearts and bodies; the world of discovery, of invention, of the excessive, of generosity, facing the European world, closed physically, historically, culturally; a world where individuals are closed, national cultures are closed, the apartments are closed. . . .
> Frank is Swiss, and Switzerland is the closed country par excellence; he comes from that world in which he has lived bottled up in constant introversion . . . and he finds

himself all of a sudden in the world of extroversion, of that which for a European is maximum disorder.[16]

Disgusted by the stagnant closure of Europe, Frank comes to Latin America in order to climb aboard the "train destined for History." But he fails to find accommodations. Disdain for one culture does not guarantee acceptance by an inimical culture. Frank is called "the gringo"; on one occasion a woman who has lost two sons in the struggle compains that he is "bad luck." He is conspicuously out of place and feels it.[17] In the end, when defeat comes, Frank has been frozen out of the movement and finds himself outside of both worlds, the world that he despises and the world that despises him. He is faced with the prospect of returning to Europe. Rather than accept this fate and opt for slow death in the old world, he chooses to end his life in true new world fashion—a Kamikaze assassination of an informer.[18]

As Debray is quick to point out, Frank is not modeled after himself. He is a creature of the imagination and, as a Trotskyist, far from being even a favorite character. But Debray's early prison writings confirm that Frank's old world —new world conflict was drawn from Debray's own deep personal experience. It is equally clear that Debray, like Frank, preferred the new world values and mentality, though perhaps less intensely than the fictional character. (He opted for the fate that Frank repudiates.) This preference was expressed in Debray's writings as an inclination toward the pure, left-wing expression of new world virtue, *foquismo*. Debray was swept off his feet, first by Che and Fidel, then by the Tupamaros. In both cases he was disarmed philosophically by action-oriented pragmatism and seduced into sharp deflections to the Left. He became a kind of free-lance, ultraleft propagandist, and as such he had no equal. Most of Debray's readers were too blinded by his astounding erudition and captivating style to recognize the fallacies that pervade these works until military catastrophe made it clear that something—something fundamental—had to be wrong.

One of those not taken in, even for a moment, was Debray's mentor, Louis Althusser, to whose way of thinking

Debray returned after his *foquista* excursions. Not surprisingly, the works written during these later periods of retreat are more complex and logically superior to his ad hoc Guevarist writings. But we should not confuse Debray with the prodigal son; his is not a simple story of sin and repentance. As a Guevarist Debray contributed significantly to the critique of reformist politics; as an Althusserian Leninist and critic of Guevarism (though not of Guevara) Debray is without peer; and as a synthesizer of Guevarism and Leninism, he has proposed new and provocative relationships between reformism, anarchism, and Leninism. Debray's formidable verbal armory serves for more than obscuring his lapses of rigor; it enables him to penetrate the fog that surrounds the fundamental questions of revolution: what revolution, what is to be done, and with what organization? Whether or not one agrees with his answers to these questions, one can hardly deny that Debray has advanced our knowledge about the nature and role of revolution in modern society.

Notes

CHAPTER 1

1. L. J. Gonzáles and Gustavo A. Sánchez Salazar, *The Great Rebel: Che Guevara in Bolivia*, trans. Helen R. Lane (New York: Grove Press, 1969), p. 76.
2. Ibid., p. 78.
3. Régis Debray, "In Settlement of All Accounts," *Prison Writings*, trans. Rosemary Sheed (New York: Random House, Vintage Books, 1973), p. 200.
4. Ibid., p. 198.
5. In addition to Althusser, Debray mentions by name Garaudy and Figueres; ibid., p. 200.
6. V. I. Lenin, *Left Wing Communism—An Infantile Disorder*, in *Collected Works* (Moscow: Progress Publishers, 1966), 31:66–74.
7. Debray, "Settlement," p. 204.
8. Régis Debray, "Report from the Venezuelan Guerrilla," *Strategy for Revolution*, ed. Robin Blackburn (New York: Monthly Review Press, 1971).
9. Bravo was instrumental in the formation of paramilitary brigades which gave armed support to demonstrations against the dictatorship in January 1958; see Richard Gott, *Guerrilla Movements in Latin America* (Garden City, N.Y: Anchor Books, 1972), pp. 123–34.
10. Régis Debray, "Le Castroisme: la longue marche de l'Amérique," *Les Temps Modernes* (Paris), no. 224, January 1965. The article

first appeared in English in *New Left Review,* September-October 1965, pp. 19–58, and later in Blackburn's collection. The later version incorporates small revisions made by Debray for publication in book form in early 1967. These revisions consist of a new introduction, closing paragraph, several additional footnotes, and a few substitutions of "Castroism" for "Fidelism," although this replacement is not made consistently throughout and is surely of no importance. The new introduction credits not only the Venezuelan guerrillas (whom he mentions first) but also revolutionary militants in Colombia, Ecuador, Peru, Bolivia, Argentina, Uruguay, and Brazil with having contributed to the thoughts that appear in the essay. Régis Debray, "Castroism: The Long March in Latin America," *Strategy for Revolution,* p. 27.

11. "Problems of Revolutionary Strategy in Latin America" first appeared in the *Cahiers Marxiste-Leninistes* series of the Ecole Normale Supérieure. Its first English publication came in 1967 in *New Left Review* 45:13–41. It was reprinted in Robin Blackburn's collection, *Strategy for Revolution,* pp. 113–52.

12. First appeared in a special July-August 1968 issue of the Marxist periodical *Monthly Review* and was reprinted in several anthologies. The present reference is to Régis Debray, "A Reply," *Régis Debray and the Latin American Revolution,* ed. Leo Huberman and Paul M. Sweezy (New York: Monthly Review Press, 1968), p. 147.

13. Debray, "Castroism," pp. 27–28.

14. V. I. Lenin, *What Is to Be Done?, Collected Works,* 5:369.

15. V. I. Lenin, "Letters on Tactics," ibid., 24:43.

16. V. I. Lenin, "The Historical Meaning of the Inner-Party Struggle in Russia," ibid., 15:196.

17. Isaac Deutscher, *Ironies of History* (London: Oxford University Press, 1966), p. 210.

18. Mao Tse-tung, *Selected Works,* 4 vols. (Peking: Foreign Languages Press, 1967), 1:13–104.

19. V. I. Lenin, "The Petrograd City Conference of the R.S.D.L.P. (Bolsheviks): Report of the Present Situation and the Attitude Towards the Provisional Government," *Collected Works,* 24:142.

20. V. I. Lenin, "Guerrilla Warfare," ibid., 11:213.

21. Ibid., p. 214.

22. David A. Crain, "The Course of the Cuban Heresy: The Rise and Decline of Castroism's Challenge to the Soviet Line in the

Latin American Marxist Revolutionary Movement, 1963–70" (Ph.D. diss., Indiana University, 1972), pp. 4–13.

23. Che Guevara, "Social Ideals of the Rebel Army," *Che: Selected Works of Che Guevara*, ed. R. E. Bonachea and N. P. Valdés (Cambridge: M.I.T. Press, 1969), p. 204.

24. Che Guevara, "A New Old Che Guevara Interview," ibid., p. 375.

25. Che Guevara, "Development of a Marxist Revolution," ibid., pp. 246–49.

26. Che Guevara, "Notes for the Study of the Ideology of the Cuban Revolution," ibid., p. 48.

27. Ibid.

28. Ibid.

29. Ibid., p. 50.

30. Che Guevara, "Interview with Laura Bergquist (#1)," ibid., p. 386.

31. Fidel Castro, "The Duty of a Revolutionary Is to Make the Revolution: The Second Declaration of Havana," *Fidel Castro Speaks*, ed. Martin Kenner and James Petras (New York: Grove Press, 1969), p. 104.

32. Crain, "Cuban Heresy," pp. 52–58.

33. Debray, "Problems of Revolutionary Strategy," *Strategy for Revolution*, pp. 140–48.

34. Ibid., pp. 136–40.

35. Debray, "Castroism," p. 30. Apparently the Venezuelan experience with barracks revolts at Carupano and Puerto Cabello in 1962 did much to establish this "absolute law"; ibid., p. 29.

36. Ibid., p. 29.

37. Ibid., pp. 32–33.

38. Ibid., pp. 55–59.

39. Ibid., p. 32.

40. V. I. Lenin, "The Revolutionary Army and the Revolutionary Government," *Collected Works*, 8:562. For more on revolutionary dictatorships see V. I. Lenin, "The Proletariat and Its Ally in the Russian Revolution," ibid., 11:374. Here Lenin traces the belief in the necessity of revolutionary dictatorships as "the old premise underlying the whole tactics [Lenin used the word "tactics" to denote what is today commonly referred to as "strategy"] of the revolutionary Social Democrats." To see how Lenin uses the writings of the young Marx to establish his Marxist orthodoxy, see V. I. Lenin, *Two Tactics of Social Democracy in the Democratic Revolution*, ibid., 9:130–40. Here Lenin

reiterates the view that "major questions in the life of nations are settled only by force."
41. V. I. Lenin, "The Dual Power," ibid., 24:38; cf. V. I. Lenin, "The Crisis of Menshevism," ibid., 11:346.
42. Lenin, "The Crisis of Menshevism," ibid.
43. V. I. Lenin, "Lessons of the Moscow Uprising," ibid., 11:174.
44. Lenin, "The Revolutionary Army," p. 562.
45. V. I. Lenin, "Where to Begin," ibid., 5:17–30; this article addressed itself briefly to the same problems that Lenin dealt with nine months later at great length in *What Is to Be Done?*, pp. 345–529.
46. Lenin, *What Is to Be Done?*, p. 464.
47. Debray, "Castroism," p. 33.
48. Ibid., p. 34.
49. Che Guevara, *Guerrilla Warfare*, trans. J. P. Morray (New York: Vintage Books, 1969), p. 30.
50. Che Guevara, "Cuba: Exceptional Case or Vanguard?" *Che: Selected Works*, p. 62.
51. Che Guevara, "Guerrilla Warfare: A Method," *Venceremos: The Speeches and Writings of Che Guevara*, ed. John Gerassi (New York: Simon and Schuster, 1968), pp. 273–75.
52. Ibid., p. 274.
53. Che Guevara, "The Role of a Marxist-Leninist Party," *Che: Selected Works*, p. 107; Che Guevara, "Socialism and Man in Cuba," ibid., p. 155.
54. Debray, "Castroism," pp. 63–81.
55. Debray, "Problems," p. 135.
56. Debray, "Castroism," p. 38.
57. Ibid., p. 63.
58. Ibid., p. 67.
59. Ibid., p. 68; where Cuba is concerned, this contrast between the ideologically proletarian Rebel Army and the irremediably petty-bourgeois urban leadership is made by Guevara in "Marxist-Leninist Party," p. 107.
60. Debray, "Castroism," pp. 68–69.
61. Ibid., pp. 42–43.
62. V. I. Lenin, "Marxism and Insurrection," *Collected Works*, 26: 22–23.
63. Guevara, "Cuba: Exceptional Case," p. 62.
64. Ibid., p. 61.
65. V. I. Lenin, "The Collapse of the Second International," *Collected Works*, 21:213–14.

66. Guevara, *Guerrilla Warfare*, p. 2.
67. Guevara, "Guerrilla Warfare: A Method," pp. 269–72.
68. Ibid., p. 276.
69. Lenin did not propound a "theory of the weakest link," nor is he responsible for the metaphor, which appears to have been coined by Stalin, who used it to explain why the initial triumph of a Socialist revolution occurred in backward Russia rather than in developed Europe, as most Marxists had expected; he cited a conjuncture of many factors that caused the international chain of imperialist states to weaken and break first in Russia. See Joseph Stalin, *Foundations of Leninism: Essential Works of Marxism*, ed. A. P. Mendel (New York: Bantam Books, 1965). Louis Althusser, in a work much admired by Debray, speaks of a "theory of the weakest link" and claims that "it is obvious that the theory of the weakest link guided Lenin in his theory of the revolutionary party," but Althusser leaves one wondering what this theory consists of beyond the vacuous and abstract instruction to always strike the enemy at its weakest point and the equally vacuous and abstract proposition that disintegration can generally be correlated with weakness. See Louis Althusser, "Contradiction and Overdetermination," *For Marx*, trans. Ben Brewster (New York: Vintage Books, 1970), p. 95.
70. Debray, "Castroism," p. 42.
71. Ibid., p. 44.
72. Ibid., p. 47.
73. Ibid., pp. 43–44.
74. Ibid., p. 39.
75. Hamza Alavi, "Peasants and Revolution," *Socialist Register*, ed. Ralph Miliband and John Saville (New York: Monthly Review Press, 1965), p. 251. V. I. Lenin, *The Proletarian Revolution and the Renegade Kautsky, Collected Works*, 28:301–4.
76. That is to say, the only successful example; the many others ended in failure. Debray, "Castroism," p. 38.
77. Ibid., p. 47.
78. Debray, "Venezuelan Guerrilla," p. 96.
79. Debray, "Castroism," p. 67.
80. Debray, "Venezuelan Guerrilla," p. 96.
81. Debray, "Problems," pp. 135–36.
82. Debray, "Castroism," p. 54.
83. Ibid.
84. Debray, "Problems," p. 124.
85. Debray, "Castroism," p. 55.

86. Ibid., pp. 50–52.
87. Ibid., p. 53.
88. Amilcar Cabral, "Brief Analysis of the Social Structure in Guinea," *Revolution in Guinea: Selected Texts by Amilcar Cabral* (New York: Modern Reader, 1969).
89. Debray, "Problems," p. 133.
90. Debray, "Castroism," p. 80.
91. Indeed, the earliest available record of Guevara's political beliefs indicates that his attitude towards the Apristas was one of open distrust and disdain as early as 1953, when he predicted that Betancourt would "rise to power and betray his people." Hilda Gadea, *Ernesto: A Memoir of Che Guevara*, trans. Carmen Molina and W. I. Bradbury (New York: Doubleday, 1972), p. 4.
92. Debray, "Castroism," p. 71.
93. Ibid., pp. 71–72.
94. An excellent study of the first three years of the Cuban Revolution after the overthrow of Batista which examines their similarities with the Russian Revolution after the overthrow of the tsar can be found in J. P. Morray, *The Second Revolution in Cuba* (New York: Monthly Review Press, 1962).
95. Presumably a dictatorship of the proletariat is what Debray means by "socialist state."
96. Lenin, *Two Tactics*, pp. 52–53.
97. Gerrit Huizer, *The Revolutionary Potential of Peasants in Latin America* (Lexington, Mass.: Lexington Books, 1972), p. 4.
98. Debray, "Castroism," p. 75.
99. Ibid., p. 73.
100. Ibid., p. 72.
101. Gadea, *Ernesto*, pp. 54–55.
102. For a similar sketch of the principal stages in the development of Guevara's insurrectionary theory and strategy, see Donald C. Hodges, *The Latin American Revolution* (New York: William Morrow, 1974), chaps. 1, 5.
103. Che Guevara, "Honoring the Labor Movement," *Che: Selected Works*, p. 196.
104. Che Guevara, "Interview with Jorge Masetti," ibid., p. 363.
105. Guevara, "Social Ideals," p. 198. Cf. Debray: "This is perhaps the greatest paradox of Fidelism: it is by nature both radical (aimed at the capture of power) and anti-sectarian (no party can pretend to monopolize the revolution)"; Debray, "Castroism," pp. 72–73.
106. Guevara, "New Old Interview," p. 374.

107. Che Guevara, "Interview by Telemundo Television," *Che: Selected Works*, p. 381.
108. Guevara, "Cuba: Exceptional Case," p. 59.
109. Che Guevara, "Tactics and Strategy of the Latin American Revolution," *Che: Selected Works*, pp. 78, 81.
110. Guevara, "Guerrilla Warfare: A Method," p. 279.
111. Che Guevara, "Message to the Tricontinental," *Che: Selected Works*, p. 174.
112. Debray, "Problems," p. 128; cf. Debray, "Castroism," p. 74.
113. Debray, "Castroism," p. 80.

Chapter 2

1. Gott, *Guerrilla Movements*, p. 453; Gonzáles and Sánchez, *The Great Rebel*, pp. 77–78.
2. Cecil Johnson, *Communist China and Latin America, 1959–1967* (New York: Columbia University Press, 1970), pp. 162–63. The Chinese made their displeasure of the Cuban-Soviet entente plain in an abrupt turn-about in news reporting from Cuba: in 1964, Chinese papers had assiduously carried the speeches of the Castro brothers and Che Guevara, more regularly in fact than had the Soviet Union; after the Havana Conference, however, no more Cuban speeches were published in China and Soviet coverage picked up. Ibid.
3. Fidel Castro, "Division in the Face of the Enemy was Never a Revolutionary or Intellectual Strategy," *Fidel Castro Speaks*, pp. 111–12.
4. Crain, "Cuban Heresy," p. 117.
5. Ibid., pp. 65–66.
6. Johnson, *Communist China*, pp. 164–67.
7. Cuba, *Política internacional de la revolución cubana: documentos políticos*, 2 vols. (Havana: Editora Política, 1966), 1:89–90, cited in Crain, "Cuban Heresy," p. 141.
8. Johnson, *Communist China*, pp. 167–68.
9. Cuba, *Política internacional*, 1:190, cited in Crain, "Cuban Heresy," p. 155.
10. D. Bruce Jackson, *Castro, the Kremlin, and Communism in Latin America* (Baltimore: Johns Hopkins University Press, 1969), pp. 89–93.
11. Crain, "Cuban Heresy," pp. 143–47.
12. See Fidel Castro, "Communism Cannot be Built in One Country

in the Midst of an Underdeveloped World," *Fidel Castro Speaks*, pp. 189–90; and the introduction by Kenner and Petras, ibid., pp. 181–82.

13. Castro, "Communism in One Country," p. 189.
14. Cuba, *Política internacional*, 1:181-212, cited in Crain, "Cuban Heresy," p. 161.
15. Castro, "Communism in One Country," p. 189.
16. Crain, "Cuban Heresy," pp. 176–77.
17. Cuba, *Política internacional*, 2: 249–53, cited in ibid., p. 167.
18. Crain, "Cuban Heresy," p. 168.
19. The communiqué of this conference is reprinted in Gott, *Guerrilla Movements*, pp. 550–53.
20. Jackson, *Castro, Kremlin, Communism*, pp. 43–44.
21. Crain, "Cuban Heresy," pp. 2–38.
22. Lenin, "Guerrilla Warfare," pp. 222–23; this was Lenin's mistaken assessment of the situation in Russia during the waning moments of the 1905 revolution.
23. Jackson, *Castro, Kremlin, Communism*, p. 47; after withdrawing from armed struggle the PCV admitted to having had illusions of fighting "a revolutionary war for national liberation." Juan Rodríguez, in "The New in the Political Line of the Communist Party of Venezuela," *World Marxist Review* 10 (September 1967): 79, lends some credence to the unsubstantiated claim by Richard Gott that a full revolutionary situation in the Leninist sense was thought to exist in Venezuela; see Gott, *Guerrilla Movements*, p. 140.
24. The chapter of the Tenth Congress' central report dealing with this matter is included as an appendix in Gott, *Guerrilla Movements*, pp. 518–21.
25. Crain, "Cuban Heresy," p. 188.
26. Gott, *Guerrilla Movements*, p. 519.
27. Ibid., p. 256.
28. The commercial agreements included loans from the Soviet Union to the Lleras Restrepo government. Castro's indignation at this act of perfidy boiled over at the OLAS Conference in August 1967 when, in his closing speech, he denounced the loans vehemently, in violation of an agreement that the OLAS resolution condemning Soviet trade policies should be kept secret; see Crain, "Cuban Heresy," pp. 239–41. For Castro's speech see Fidel Castro, *Fidel Castro: Major Speeches* (London: Stage I, 1968), pp. 97–149, or I. L. Horowitz, Josué de Castro, and John Gerassi,

eds., *Latin American Radicalism* (New York: Vintage Books, 1969), pp. 543–79.

29. Régis Debray, *Las Pruebas de fuego: la crítica de las armas*—2 (Mexico: Siglo XXI Editores, 1975), p. 261.

30. Ibid., pp. 260–62.

31. Crain, "Cuban Heresy," pp. 100–101.

32. Debray, *Pruebas de fuego*, p. 301.

33. Ibid., pp. 270–73.

34. Crain, "Cuban Heresy," p. 185.

35. Reprinted in Gott, *Guerrilla Movements*, p. 501.

36. Crain, "Cuban Heresy," p. 186.

37. Gott, *Guerrilla Movements*, p. 89.

38. Debray, *Pruebas de fuego*, p. 281.

39. Ibid., pp. 283–299; NACLA, *Guatemala* (Berkeley, Calif.: NACLA, 1974), p. 185; Crain, "Cuban Heresy," pp. 186–87.

40. See the extract from the declaration of January 1968 in Gott, *Guerrilla Movements*, pp. 507–11.

41. Crain, "Cuban Heresy," pp. 202–4.

42. Unless otherwise noted, the factual basis of the following account of the Venezuelan guerrilla crisis is derived from Jackson, *Castro, Kremlin, Communism*, pp. 46–104, and Gott, *Guerrilla Movements*, pp. 128–213.

43. On July 24, 1966, support of another kind came from Cuba in the form of fourteen Cuban volunteers commanded by "Antonio"; see Debray, *Pruebas de fuego*, p. 64.

44. Quoted in Jackson, *Castro, Kremlin, Communism*, p. 100.

45. Quoted in Crain, "Cuban Heresy," p. 198.

46. Jackson, *Castro, Kremlin, Communism*, pp. 109–10.

47. Ibid., p. 111.

48. Crain, "Cuban Heresy," pp. 199–200.

49. *Granma* (Havana), March 14, 1967 (supplement), pp. 5, 9.

50. Fidel Castro, *Major Speeches*, pp. 112–18.

51. Régis Debray, *La Crítica de las armas*—1 (Mexico: Siglo XXI Editores, 1975), p. 13.

52. Castro, *Major Speeches*, p. 88.

53. Crain, "Cuban Heresy," p. 230.

54. Daniel James, *Che Guevara: A Biography* (New York: Stein and Day, 1970), p. 303.

CHAPTER 3

1. Debray, *La Crítica*, pp. 216–17.

2. Régis Debray, *Revolution in the Revolution?*, trans. Bobbye Ortiz (New York: Grove Press, 1967), p. 12.

3. K. S. Karol, *Guerrillas in Power* (New York: Hill and Wang, 1970), p. 374.

4. Jean Lartéguy, "A Frenchman Held in Seclusion," *Paris Match*, May 13, 1967, p. 104.

5. Debray, "A Reply," p. 141.

6. If further evidence of Cuba's involvement with Debray's book is needed, it should be noted that the first Cuban printing ran to 200,000 copies; see "Foreword" by Leo Huberman and Paul M. Sweezy in Debray, *Revolution?*, p. 7.

7. Roberto Fernández Retamar, "Introduction to the Spanish Edition," ibid., p. 12.

8. Debray, "Castroism," p. 81.

9. Debray was asked by his interviewer, René Depestre, why he wrote *Revolution in the Revolution?* Debray replied: "First, in returning to Cuba, I realized that I had been a victim of a dangerous cliché and that my first two articles suffered from this weakness. I also believed that the Cuban Revolution could not be repeated. I discovered my total ignorance of the Cuban Revolution. Second, when I began to study the Cuban revolutionary process I became aware that in it there were lessons and answers that Latin America needed and that were generally found outside of the Cuban Revolution. That did not mean that it is necessary to take the Cuban Revolution as a reference point or as an absolute model, but that it is necessary to study its lessons and its novelties thoroughly in order to be able to evaluate the native particularities of other revolutionary processes." René Depestre, "Plática con Régis Debray," *Granma* (Havana), February 1, 1967, p. 5 [emphasis added].

10. Robin Blackburn, "Introduction," in Debray, *Strategy for Revolution*, p. 14.

11. Depestre, "Plática."

12. Clea Silva, a Brazilian sociologist, calls this the most serious and dangerous error of Debray's theory; see Clea Silva, "The Errors of the Foco Theory," in Huberman and Sweezy, *Régis Debray and the Latin American Revolution*, p. 22. Frank and Shah are scarcely less harsh when they fault him for failing to see that class analysis is a necessary condition for successful revolutionary practice; see A. G. Frank and S. A. Shah, "Class, Politics and Debray," ibid., pp. 12–17. See also the wildly polemical statements

of the Ecuadorian Maoist Jorge Isaac Arrellano, as quoted in Johnson, *Communist China*, p. 177.

13. Joao Quartim, *Dictatorship and Armed Struggle in Brazil*, trans. David Fernbach (New York: Monthly Review Press, 1971); see especially pp. 114–238.
14. Frank and Shah, "Class, Politics and Debray," p. 16.
15. Ibid., p. 15.
16. Ibid., pp. 13, 15, 17.
17. Ibid., p. 15.
18. Silva, "Errors," p. 23.
19. Leo Huberman and Paul M. Sweezy, "The Strength and the Weakness," *Régis Debray and the Latin American Revolution*, p. 6.
20. Régis Debray, "Interview with Havana Students," *Strategy for Revolution*, pp. 166–67.
21. Ibid., pp. 170–71.
22. Régis Debray, "The Role of the Intellectual," *Strategy for Revolution*, p. 156; this essay first appeared in *Marcha* (Montevideo, Uruguay), no. 1352 (January 1966).
23. Debray, *Revolution?*, p. 21; hereafter references to this work will be given in parentheses in the text.
24. Guevara, "Guerrilla Warfare: A Method," p. 272.
25. Wilfred Burchett, *Viewnam Will Win!* (New York: Guardian Books, 1970), pp. 140–50.
26. James Petras, "Debray: Revolutionary or Elitist?" in Huberman and Sweezy, *Régis Debray and the Latin American Revolution*, p. 108.
27. Diego Montaña Cuellar, "Los problemas estratégicos y tácticos de la revolución en Colombia," *Punto Final*, no. 47 (January 30, 1968); quoted in Gott, *Guerrilla Movements*, p. 253. It should be mentioned that Montaña resigned from the PCC later in 1967 on the grounds that it did not give enough emphasis to the guerrillas; see Gott, *Guerrilla Movements*, p. 255.
28. Alberto Gomez, "The Revolutionary Forces of Colombia and Their Perspectives," *World Marxist Review* 10 (April 1967): 63.
29. Guillermo Lora, *Revalorización del metodo de las guerrillas* (N.p. [Bolivia], Ediciones Masas, 1967), pp. 42–44.
30. Cf. Guevara, *Guerrilla Warfare*: "popular work should at first be aimed at securing secrecy" (p. 10); "the guerrilla fighter will live for days without approaching any inhabited place, avoiding all contact that has not been previously arranged" (p. 41).
31. Guevara termed these three imperatives "the synthesis of our

guerrilla experience." With regard to mistrust, Guevara writes, "at the beginning mistrust even your shadow, friendly peasants, informants, guides, contacts; mistrust everything until you hold a liberated zone." Che Guevara, *Reminiscences of the Cuban Revolutionary War* (New York: Grove Press, 1968), p. 33.

32. See the account of Héctor Béjar, leader of the Peruvian National Liberation Army (ELN), a thoroughly Guevarist guerrilla force which went into action simultaneously with de la Puente's Revolutionary Left Movement (MIR); Béjar's book was awarded the coveted Casa de las Américas Award in 1969. Héctor Béjar, *Peru 1965: Notes on a Guerrilla Experience*, trans. William Rose (New York: Monthly Review Press, 1970), pp. 77–87; see also Gott, *Guerrilla Movements*, pp. 366–71.

33. Guevara's account of the "battle" of El Hombrito in August 1957 reports only two casualties, a wounded soldier and a dead guerrilla. It appears that after a brief skirmish each side withdrew. Guevara's column rejoined Castro and returned to El Hombrito in October. In December he was again engaged in the "battle" of Altos de Cornado with similar results. The sum total of guerrilla casualties was one wounded. After this encounter the base was razed to the ground by Batista's soldiers and abandoned by them and the guerrillas. See Guevara, *Reminiscences*, pp. 151–57, 190–91.

34. Béjar, *Peru 1965*, pp. 75–87.

35. Johnson, *Communist China*, p. 180.

36. Che Guevara, "People's War, People's Army," in *Che: Selected Works*, p. 152.

37. In Vietnam the guerrillas were local tactical forces, not mobile and strategic. Giap contrasts guerrilla warfare with mobile warfare; the latter follows the former. See Vo Nguyen Giap, *People's War, People's Army* (New York: Frederick A. Praeger, 1962), pp. 103–6.

38. Guevara, "People's War," p. 152.

39. Ibid.

40. Burchett, *Vietnam Will Win!*, p. 170.

41. Ibid.; the quotation is from Ho Chi Minh, *On Revolution*, ed. Bernard B. Fall (New York: Signet Books, 1967), p. 138.

42. Ho Chi Minh, *On Revolution*, pp. 137 (editor's footnote), 138.

43. William J. Pomeroy, "Questions on the Debray Thesis," in Huberman and Sweezy, *Régis Debray and the Latin American Revolution*, p. 38.

44. Ibid., pp. 40–43.

45. Ibid., p. 36.
46. "The peasantry's reactions have already been analyzed many times. Immediately after the Alegría de Pío disaster there was a warm sentiment of comradeship and spontaneous support for our defeated troop" [emphasis added], Guevara, Reminiscences, p. 197. Guevara gives a different account to the journalist Jorge Masetti: "The peasants saw us pass by without showing friendship. But Fidel was not disturbed. He would salute them and a few minutes later he would have a more or less friendly conversation going on. . . . Little by little they became our friends." See Guevara, "Interview with Jorge Masetti," p. 365. In an interview broadcast over the Rebel Army's radio station eight months later, Guevara confirms the latter account: "In the Sierra Maestra we began the struggle with a group of men who were almost unarmed, without bullets and almost without any peasant support." See Guevara, "Interview in the Escambry Mountains," Che: Selected Works, p. 367. Whatever their differences, all of these quotations support the view that the guerrillas did not reap the fruits of anything like a "background of organizational experience."
47. This assessment of Crescencio's role is made by Lucas Morán Arce in "Guerrilla Warfare in the Sierra Maestra" (M.A. thesis, University of Florida, 1970), p. 72; and Andrés Suárez in "The Cuban Revolution: The Road to Power," Latin American Research Review, vol. 7, no. 3, p. 12. Suárez charges Guevara with "slighting the role played by Crescencio and his men in saving the survivors from the hands of the army and helping them reach the Sierra Maestra."
48. Simón Torres and Julio Aronde, "Debray and the Cuban Experience," in Huberman and Sweezy, Régis Debray and the Latin American Revolution, p. 46.
49. Ibid., pp. 46–47.
50. Ibid., p. 61.
51. Joao Quartim, "Régis Debray and the Brazilian Revolution," New Left Review, no. 59 (January-February 1970), pp. 72–73.
52. None of the guerrillas who kept diaries mention any other occasions of the ELN giving political lectures to peasants, so it is likely that there were none. The guerrillas did make contact with peasants as early as February 10, 1967, during a training march and several times thereafter, but primarily for logistical purposes. Occasionally guerrilla doctors treated the sick during these brief encounters. There is no reason to believe that Debray would

have had any objections. All we know is that he rated armed confrontations as the most effective form of propaganda and political lectures as the least effective. Medical therapy, like an armed encounter, puts the power of the guerrillas on exhibit. One would expect Debray to favor this kind of propaganda.

53. The ELN began training operations in February 1967. By the end of April Guevara was beginning to show concern over the lack of contact with the peasantry, and the same complaint was repeated with "tragic monotony" (Quartim, "Debray and the Brazilian Revolution," p. 72) until the end. See Che Guevara, *The Diary of Che Guevara* (New York: Bantam Books, 1968), pp. 105–86.

54. Jean-Pierre Bernard et al., *Guide to the Political Parties of South America* (Baltimore: Penguin Books, 1973), pp. 142–45.

55. Guevara, *Diary*, p. 26.

56. Deutscher, *Ironies of History*, p. 106.

57. Quartim, *Dictatorship*, p. 169.

58. Huberman and Sweezy, "Strength and Weakness," p. 7.

59. Torres and Aronde, "Cuban Experience," pp. 45–46.

60. About the Peasant Leagues, Clea Silva writes: "The organization of many peasant leagues in Brazil came about by means of the direct collaboration of the workers who, living in the cities, maintained contact with the rural communities. The peasant was always influenced by the labor movement." Silva, "Errors," p. 23 n. Blanco was an organizer for the Front of the Revolutionary Left (FIR). The AP's organizing efforts in Brazil are described briefly in Jean Marc von der Weid, *Brazil: 1964 to the Present* (Montreal: Editions Latin America, 1972), pp. 43–44.

61. Silva, "Errors," p. 18.

62. Andrés Suárez, *Cuba: Castroism and Communism, 1959–1966* (Cambridge: M.I.T. Press, 1967), p. 27; Suárez, "Cuban Revolution," pp. 17–18.

63. Mohamed Heikal, *The Cairo Documents* (New York: Doubleday, 1973), p. 349.

64. Enrique Meneses, *Fidel Castro* (New York: Taplinger, 1966), pp. 61–62.

65. Morán, "Guerrilla Warfare," p. 51.

66. Guevara, *Reminiscences*, p. 67. According to Morán, there were ten men in this group; see "Guerrilla Warfare," p. 73.

67. Guevara, *Reminiscences*, p. 87. Guevara says there were fifty men, but by Morán's count there were fifty-eight; see "Guerrilla

Warfare," pp. 99–100. It should be noted that Morán was a leader of the July 26th Movement in Santiago.
68. Morán, "Guerrilla Warfare," pp. 140–41.
69. For details see V. I. Lenin, "Differences in the European Labour Movement," *Collected Works*, 16:347–52; "Marxism and Revisionism," ibid., 15:31–39; "The International Socialist Congress in Stuttgart," ibid., 13: 77–79.
70. See Debray, "A Reply," pp. 139–40.

CHAPTER 4

1. Gonzáles and Sánchez, Bolivian journalists who were intimately acquainted with the events in Bolivia, noted this phenomenon in the following terms: "What is an incomprehensible paradox, communists of all persuasions are vying with each other to glorify the memory of the great rebel now that the guerrilla struggle is over, while they train their big guns on the young French philosopher Régis Debray, whom they have stubbornly and repeatedly accused of disloyalty." Gonzáles and Sánchez, *The Great Rebel*, p. 51. Mexico's Lombardo Toledano carried these accusations to their slanderous limit in the pages of *Siempre* when he hinted coyly that the upper-class French "journalist" might well be in the pay of the CIA; see Crain, "Cuban Heresy," pp. 221–22.
2. Eqbal Ahmad, "Radical but Wrong," in Huberman and Sweezy, *Régis Debray and the Latin American Revolution*, p. 73.
3. Ibid.
4. Quartim, *Dictatorship*, pp. 169–71.
5. Guevara, *Guerrilla Warfare*, p. 4.
6. Che Guevara, "Instructions for Cadres Who Work in Urban Areas," in *Che: Selected Works*, pp. 187–91.
7. Marta Rojas and Mirta Rodríguez Calderón, eds., *Tania: The Unforgettable Guerrilla* (New York: Random House, 1971), p. 188.
8. Guevara, *Diary*, p. 57.
9. Régis Debray, "I Regret that I Am Innocent," *Strategy for Revolution*, p. 218.
10. Torres and Aronde, "Cuban Experience," pp. 44–62.
11. Ibid., p. 44. The Cubans also concur with Quartim in charging Debray with "spontaneism" and they join Quartim in his amazement over Debray's naive belief that a radio transmitter can replace the organizational labors of a party; ibid., p. 60.

12. Américo Pumaruna, *Peru: Revolución, Insurrección, Guerrillas* (Lima, Peru: Editiones Vanguardia Revolucionaria, 1968), p. 18.
13. Héctor Béjar, "A Contribution to the Discussion of Guerrilla Tactics in Latin America," *World Outlook*, vol. 6, no. 4 (February 2, 1968), p. 86.
14. Béjar, *Peru 1965*, p. 124.
15. Béjar, "Contribution to Guerrilla Tactics," p. 86.
16. Carlos Nuñez, *The Tupamaros: Urban Guerrillas of Uruguay* (New York: Times Change Press, 1970), p. 35.
17. Donald C. Hodges and Robert E. A. Shanab, *National Liberation Fronts 1960/70* (New York: William Morrow, 1972), p. 291.
18. Maria Esther Gilio, *The Tupamaro Guerrillas* (New York: Saturday Review Press, 1972), pp. 140–43.
19. We will have more to say about this in Chapter 6.
20. Tupamaro document, *NACLA's Latin American and Empire Report*, vol. 7, no. 8 (October 1973), p. 30.
21. Quartim, "Brazilian Revolution," p. 71. Cf. Lenin: "One of the greatest and most dangerous mistakes made by communists . . . is the idea that a revolution can be made by revolutionaries alone. . . . A vanguard performs its task as vanguard only when it is able to avoid isolation from the people it leads and is really able to lead the whole mass forward." V. I. Lenin, "On the Significance of Militant Materialism," *Collected Works*, 33: 227.
22. Quartim, "Barzilian Revolution," p. 68.
23. Ibid., p. 78.
24. Ibid., p. 77.
25. Ibid., p. 69.
26. Ibid.
27. Ibid., p. 68.
28. Debray, "A Reply," p. 139.
29. Quartim, "Brazilian Revolution," p. 69.
30. Ibid., p. 71.
31. Ibid.
32. Ibid.
33. Ibid., p. 75.
34. Ibid., p. 71.
35. Ibid., p. 75.
36. Quartim, *Dictatorship*, p. 139.
37. Ibid., p. 158.
38. Ibid., pp. 173–75.
39. Ibid., pp. 175–77.
40. Quartim, "Brazilian Revolution," pp. 69–82.

41. The letter is reprinted as "Letter from Louis Althusser apropos *Revolution in the Revolution?*" in Debray, *La Crítica*, pp. 238–46.
42. Ibid., p. 243.

CHAPTER 5

1. Harry Villegas Tamayo (Pombo), "Pombo's Diary," in *The Complete Bolivian Diaries of Che Guevara and Other Captured Documents*, ed. Daniel James (New York: Stein and Day, 1968), p. 265.
2. Ibid., pp. 274–76.
3. Guevara, *Diary*, p. 70.
4. James, *Che Guevara*, p. 294.
5. Evidence for this is given in a coded message sent to Castro on May 18, after Debray's capture; the message was intercepted and decoded. See ibid., pp. 359–61.
6. Guevara, *Diary*, p. 82.
7. Régis Debray, "Letter to My Friends," *Strategy for Revolution*, p. 185.
8. Guevara, *Diary*, pp. 80–81.
9. James, *Che Guevara*, pp. 246–47.
10. Debray, "Settlement," p. 171.
11. Ibid., p. 207.
12. Debray, "Letter," p. 187.
13. Ibid.
14. Carlos Nuñez, "Testimonio desde la prisión," *Indice* (Madrid), no. 240 (January 15, 1969), p. 6. Debray made the same point in a letter to the editors of *Monthly Review* a few months after his trial was over: he wrote that Guevara had found his book "too timid for his liking and not radical enough but expressing his own views"; see Debray, "A Reply," p. 147.
15. Guevara, *Diary*, p. 57.
16. Marlene Nadle, "Régis Debray Speaks from Prison," *Ramparts*, August 24, 1968, p. 41.
17. Quoted in Gott, *Guerrilla Movements*, p. 460; A faulty translation of the same passage can be found in Debray, "I Regret," p. 224.
18. Nadle, "Régis Debray Speaks," p. 41.
19. Nuñez, "Testimonio," p. 6.
20. Gonzáles and Sánchez, *The Great Rebel*, p. 149.

21. Debray, "A Reply," p. 143.
22. Debray, *La Crítica*, pp. 237–38. Debray's recollection of his critique here differs with that given to two journalists shortly after his release from prison in 1970; at that time he left out the point concerning the preparation of the zone of operations and substituted the predominance of the political over the military. See Jorge Timossi and Manuel Cabieses, "Régis Debray habla en libertad," *¡Ahora!* (Santo Domingo), no. 375 (January 18, 1971), p. 32.
23. Georgie Anne Geyer, "Why Guevara Failed: An Interview with Régis Debray," *Saturday Review*, August 24, 1968, p. 15.
24. Ibid.
25. Debray, "Castroism," p. 38.
26. Régis Debray, "Time and Politics," *Prison Writings*, p. 130.
27. Ibid., p. 90.
28. Ibid., pp. 102, 108.
29. Louis Althusser, "Contradiction and Overdetermination," *For Marx*, pp. 89–116; see also "On the Materialist Dialectic," ibid., pp. 200–18, and the "Glossary," ibid., pp. 252–53.
30. Debray, "Time and Politics," p. 146.
31. Ibid., p. 127.
32. Ibid., p. 128.
33. Ibid., p. 106.
34. Ibid., pp. 113, 109.
35. Ibid., pp. 92–93.
36. Ibid., pp. 96–97.
37. Ibid., p. 136.
38. Ibid., p. 135.
39. Bernard, *Guide to Political Parties*, pp. 146–47.
40. Régis Debray, "Notes on the Political Situation in Bolivia," *Prison Writings*, p. 21.
41. Régis Debray, "Some Answers to Questions about a Failed Uprising," ibid., p. 58.
42. Ibid., p. 48.
43. Ibid., p. 63.
44. Ibid., p. 45.
45. Régis Debray, "Correspondence with Chato Peredo," *Prison Writings*, p. 65.
46. Ibid., p. 72.
47. Ibid., pp. 68–70.
48. Ibid., p. 81.
49. Ibid., pp. 65–77.

50. Ibid., p. 84.
51. Bernard, *Guide to Political Parties*, p. 148.

CHAPTER 6

1. Timossi and Cabieses, "Régis Debray habla," pp. 26–32.
2. Régis Debray, *The Chilean Revolution: Conversations with Allende* (New York: Random House, 1971), pp. 13–128.
3. Debray, *La Crítica*, p. 281.
4. Ibid., pp. 249–50.
5. Ibid., pp. 279–80.
6. Debray, *Conversations*, p. 32.
7. Ibid., pp. 33–36.
8. Ibid., p. 39.
9. Debray, *La Crítica*, pp. 285–86.
10. Ibid., p. 251.
11. Ibid., pp. 254–58.
12. Ibid., pp. 259–67.
13. Ibid., pp. 284–85.
14. Ibid., pp. 268–78.
15. Ibid., pp. 281–83.
16. Debray, *Conversations*, p. 56.
17. Debray, *La Crítica*, p. 288.
18. Ibid., pp. 290–91.
19. Ibid., p. 289.
20. Ibid., p. 291.
21. Ibid., pp. 290-91.
22. Ibid., p. 14; Debray, *Conversations*, pp. 121, 55.
23. Debray, *La Crítica*, p. 291.
24. Ibid.
25. In December 1906 Lenin wrote, "The victory of Social-Democracy in the present Russian revolution is *quite possible*. It is our duty to inspire all adherents of the workers' party with confidence in *this* victory: it is impossible to fight successfully if one renounces victory beforehand [original emphasis]." Lenin, "The Proletariat and its Ally," p. 374. This quotation provides a counterexample for the "law of surprises" in that Lenin is paraphrasing an appraisal by Kautsky of the chances for a Socialist revolution in Russia.
26. For example, in a letter dated 1889 Engels wrote: "For the proletariat to be strong enough to win on the decisive day it must—

and this Marx and I have been arguing ever since 1847—form a separate party distinct from all others and opposed to them, a conscious class party." Frederick Engels, "Engels to G. Trier in Copenhagen," *Karl Marx and Frederick Engels: Selected Correspondence* (Moscow: Progress Publishers, 1965), p. 409.

27. Ibid.
28. V. I. Lenin, "How Plekhanov Argues about Social-Democratic Tactics," *Collected Works*, 10: 475.
29. V. I. Lenin, "Preface to the Russian Translation of W. Liebknecht's Pamphlet 'No Compromises, No Electoral Agreements,'" *Collected Works*, 11: 402–3.
30. V. I. Lenin, "No Falsehood! Our Strength Lies in Stating the Truth," ibid., 9: 299.
31. Debray, *La Crítica*, p. 288.
32. Nuñez, *Tupamaros*, p. 11.
33. Debray, *Pruebas de fuego*, p. 160.
34. Nuñez, *Tupamaros*, p. 17.
35. *Los Tupamaros en acción: actas tupamaras*, p. 92. Debray estimates that between $30,000 and $50,000 per month are required to keep an underground apparatus functioning—hence the frequency of bank robberies; see Debray, *La Crítica*, p. 131.
36. "The Tupamaros in Action," *The Tupamaros: Urban Guerrilla Warfare in Uruguay* (New York: The Liberated Guardian, n.d.). This unsigned article was originally published by OSPAAAL in *Tricontinental* (Havana), no. 17 (March-April 1970), pp. 45–60.
37. Bernard, *Guide to Political Parties*, pp. 512–13; Nuñez, *Tupamaros*, p. 44; José Diaz, "The Situation in Uruguay," *The Tupamaros: Urban Guerrilla Warfare in Uruguay*, p. 6. This article first appeared in *Tricontinental*, no. 9 (November-December 1968).
38. Gilio, *The Tupamaro Guerrillas*, p. 127.
39. "The Tupamaros in Action," pp. 41–46.
40. Alain Labrousse, *The Tupamaros* (Middlesex, Eng.: Penguin Books, 1973), p. 71.
41. *Actas Tupamaras*, pp. 147–48; Gilio, *The Tupamaro Guerrillas*, pp. 101–25; Labrousse, *The Tupamaros*, pp. 73–77.
42. *Actas Tupamaras*, pp. 185–91; Hodges and Shanab, *National Liberation Fronts*, p. 293.
43. *Actas Tupamaras*, pp. 191–98; Labrousse, *The Tupamaros*, pp. 80–83.
44. Labrousse, *The Tupamaros*, pp. 78, 152–54; Nuñez, *Tupamaros*, pp. 46–47; *Actas Tupamaras*, pp. 198–205.

45. Labrousse, *The Tupamaros*, pp. 99–112.
46. Debray, *Pruebas de Fuego*, p. 161.
47. *Tres evasiones de Tupamaros: actas tupamaras/2* (Buenos Aires: Distribuidora Baires S.R.L., 1973), p. 21.
48. Ibid., p. 21; Tupamaro document (unsigned), "The Tupamaros: 1972 and Beyond," *CILA Dossier* (Montreal: Editions Latin America, n.d.), p. 19. This is a reprint of a report given to *Punto Final* (Chile) by members of the MLN leadership.
49. *Tres evasiones*, pp. 22–23.
50. Ibid., pp. 19–54; Gilio, *The Tupamaro Guerrillas*, pp. 184–85.
51. "Thirty Questions to a Tupamaro," reprinted in Labrousse, *The Tupamaros*, p. 131.
52. Ibid., pp. 134–41.
53. Hodges and Shanab, *National Liberation Fronts*, pp. 282–95.
54. *Actas Tupamaras*, pp. 35–41 passim. In *Las Pruebas de fuego* (p. 119), Debray mentions his prologue by the title "Learn from Them," but the title is unaccountably omitted from the Spanish edition.
55. During the months before the elections the military dictatorship of Brazil geared up for an eventual Broad Front government with maneuvers on the Uruguayan border, known as "Operation Green Poncho"; "Operation Thirty Hours" explored the possibility of Brazilian occupation of Uruguay in the event that a compatible Uruguayan government was unable to contain the Tupamaros. See NACLA, *Latin America & Empire Report*, vol. 9, no. 4 (May-June 1975), pp. 16, 44–45.
56. Debray, *Conversations*, p. 57.
57. *Actas Tupamaras*, p. 7.
58. Ibid., pp. 24–34.
59. Ibid., p. 18.
60. Debray, *Pruebas de fuego*, pp. 182–97.
61. For this reason the Tupamaros refer to this period as "petty bourgeois"; ibid., pp. 161–65.
62. Ibid., p. 164.
63. Ibid., pp. 164, 161.
64. Ibid., pp. 122–29.
65. Ibid., p. 158.
66. The statistics tell the story of U.S. involvement in the renovation of the Uruguayan military. Mitrione was killed in August 1970. In 1971 the Foreign Military Sales (FMS) program took orders from Uruguay for a record $2 million in military equipment. This was over eight times the 1970 figure. If past practice is a

guide, most of these purchases were paid for by credits made available to the buyer by FMS. See NACLA, *Latin America & Empire Report*, vol. 9 (March 1975), p. 26. At the same time the AID Public Safety Program more than doubled its aid to the Uruguayan police; see NACLA, *The U.S. Military Apparatus* (Berkeley, Calif.: NACLA, 1972), p. 58.

67. Debray, *Pruebas de fuego*, p. 122.
68. Ibid., p. 162.
69. Ibid., p. 160.
70. The Broad Front polled 18 percent of the vote, the National party 40.5 percent, and the Colorado party 41 percent. But, according to Debray's figures (which differ from those of Bernard, *Guide to Political Parties*, p. 516), the majority of Bordaberry's votes were not cast for him but for the candidates of factions controlled by the Colorado party; thus, the votes cast for the Broad Front actually exceeded those cast for Bordaberry. See Debray, *Pruebas de fuego*, pp. 133–34. Gott, in an epilogue to Labrousse's *The Tupamaros* (p. 129), reports that "few independent observers doubted that the bulk of the [Broad Front] votes had gone to the [progressive] candidate of the Blancos [National party], Wilson Ferreira Aldunate."
71. Labrousse, *The Tupamaros*, p. 129.
72. Debray, *Pruebas de fuego*, pp. 149–53; CILA Dossier, pp. 33–35.
73. Debray, *Pruebas de fuego*, p. 166.
74. Ibid., pp. 174–75.
75. Ibid.
76. See the "Plan 1972" in CILA Dossier, pp. 24–28; and Debray, *Pruebas de fuego*, pp. 142–48.
77. Debray, *Pruebas de fuego*, p. 159.
78. Ibid., pp. 234–41.
79. First appeared under the title *Les Epreuves du feu* (Paris: Editions du Seuil, 1974).
80. Régis Debray, *Che's Guerrilla War*, trans. Rosemary Sheed (Middlesex, Eng.: Penguin Books, 1975).
81. Ibid., p. 118.
82. Debray, *La Crítica*, pp. 23, 74, 131–33; Debray, *Che's Guerrilla War*, p. 144.
83. Debray, *Che's Guerrilla War*, p. 25.
84. Ibid., p. 104.
85. Debray, *La Crítica*, p. 222.
86. Ibid., p. 218.
87. Ibid., pp. 37–43.

88. Ibid., pp. 44–50; Debray, *Pruebas de fuego*, pp. 216–17.
89. Debray, *La Crítica*, pp. 53-67.
90. Ibid., pp. 67–74.
91. Ibid., p. 23.
92. Ibid., p. 24.
93. Ibid., pp. 75–96.
94. Ibid., pp. 107–20.
95. Ibid., pp. 121–24.
96. Ibid., pp. 185–87.
97. Quartim's analysis of the VPR appears in the introduction to his article "Régis Debray and the Brazilian Revolution." A discussion of the weakness of the ALN can be found in Quartim, *Dictatorship*, pp. 83–242 ff., and in Debray, *La Crítica*, pp. 147, 165–66. Debray's extensive investigations into the defeat of the FAR and FALN constitute the first and third chapters of *Las Pruebas de fuego*. A detailed and up-to-date account of the course of the FAR is contained in NACLA, *Guatemala*, pp. 176–207.
98. Debray, *La Crítica*, p. 185.
99. Ibid., p. 196.
100. Ibid., p. 191.
101. See Rosa Luxemburg, *The Mass Strike, the Political Party and the Trade Unions* (New York: Harper & Row, 1971).
102. Marcel Liebman, "Lenin in 1905: A Revolution that Shook a Doctrine," *Monthly Review*, April 1970, pp. 57–75.
103. Debray, *La Crítica*, p. 148.
104. Ibid., p. 157.
105. Ibid.
106. Ibid., p. 149.
107. *Time* (International Edition), October 6, 1975, p. 13.

Chapter 7

1. *Time* (International Edition), October 6, 1975, p. 13.
2. Debray, *Pruebas de fuego*, p. 191.
3. Ibid.
4. Torres and Aronde, "Cuban Experience," pp. 44–62.
5. Debray, *Pruebas de fuego*, p. 151.
6. Ibid., p. 108.
7. *Granma* (EWR) (Havana), May 3, 1970, p. 4.
8. Ibid.
9. Debray, *Pruebas de fuego*, pp. 63–82.

10. Ibid., p. 82.
11. Ibid., p. 87.
12. Ibid., pp. 88–94.
13. Georges Mattel, "Entrevista con Douglas Bravo," ¡Ahora! (Santo Domingo), no. 385 (March 29, 1971), p. 52.
14. See Chapter 5.
15. Régis Debray, L'Indésirable (Paris: Editions du Seuil, 1975).
16. Ernesto Gonzáles Bermejo, "Régis Debray: Literature and Politics Are Activities without Any Relation," Diorama de Cultura, Excelsior (Mexico City), November 9, 1975, p. 3.
17. Debray, L'Indésirable, pp. 263, 70.
18. Ibid., p. 269.

Bibliographical Note

I have included below a bibliography of sources consulted in the present study. Several of these sources, in turn, contain excellent bibliographies pertinent to selected aspects of our study. David Crain's 1972 doctoral dissertation, "The Course of the Cuban Heresy: The Rise and Decline of Castroism's Challenge to the Soviet Line in the Latin American Marxist Revolutionary Movement, 1963–70," is an exhaustive history of the polemic between Cuba and traditional Marxist-Leninist movements during the decade after Cuban insurrection. Its correspondingly exhaustive bibliography includes an annotated list of newspapers and periodicals—some in English—through which Cuba, the U.S.S.R., and revolutionary movements in Latin America make their views public. Richard Gott's mammoth 1971 work, *Guerrilla Movements in Latin America*, is the single best history of the decade of rural guerrilla warfare in Latin America. It makes lavish use of direct quotations from hard-to-get documents and includes a number of these as appendices. Its bibliography is broken down according to the following subjects: general, Cuba, Che Guevara, Régis Debray, the Sino-Soviet dispute, OLAS, Guatemala, Venezuela, Colombia, Peru, and Bolivia. It contains a chronology of guerrilla warfare in Latin America from 1958 to 1969.

A good complement to Gott's book is John Gerassi's *The Coming of the New International*, which contains declarations, interviews, and writings by many of the most prominent rural guerrilla leaders. It also contains "Thirty Questions to a Tupamaro." *National Liberation Fronts 1960/1970* by Donald Hodges and Robert Shanab includes interviews with urban guerrilla leaders from Brazil and Argentina and another interview with a Tupamaro leader. Alain Labrousse's *The Tupamaros* and Major Carlos Wilson's *The Tupamaros: The Unmentionables*, together with the aforementioned sources, afford a penetrating look into the most renowned of the urban guerrilla organizations.

The works of Debray listed by English titles in the present bibliography are available in English, those listed by their Spanish titles are available in French and Spanish, and those listed in French are currently available only in French. I have the assurance of Debray's French publisher, Editions du Seuil, that *La Crítica de las armas—1* and *Las Pruebas de fuego: la crítica de las armas—2* will soon appear in English.

Most of Che Guevara's written works are available in English. All of his book-length writings have been translated. The best and most complete English compilation of his essays, speeches, interviews, and letters is that of Rolando Bonachea and Nelson Valdéz, which contains, in addition, a complete bibliography of his publications and speeches. A few items not included in this work can be found in John Gerassi's collection *Venceremos: The Speeches and Writings of Che Guevara.* As for secondary literature, the most useful bibliographies are those of Che's first wife, Hilda Gadea; two Bolivians, L. J. Gonzalés and Gustavo A. Sánchez Salazar; and the American Daniel James. The former two biographies are unabashedly sympathetic; the latter unabashedly hostile. The only mass publication analysis of Guevara's thought that deserves to be mentioned is the slim *The Marxism of Che Guevara* by the Frenchman Michael Lowy. But as its title suggests, Lowy is blind to the anarchist spirit and content of Guevara's revolutionary theory.

The collected works of Lenin are available in English, but these forty-five, unindexed volumes may not provide the easiest access to Lenin's essential writings on revolution. For those interested in gaining an overview of specific areas of Lenin's thought, the Moscow publisher (Progress) has brought out several useful collections by subject areas. The bibliographical entries for Lenin other than his *Collected Works* are those collections pertinent to the present study. *On Scientific Communism* includes fragments by Marx and Engels. In a similar enterprise George Thompson has counterposed representative quotations from Marx, Engels, Lenin, and Mao to sketch out the elements of Marxist-Leninist revolutionary theory. A. Neuberg's *Armed Insurrection* expounds the theory of insurrection of the early Third International. Neuberg is a composite of pseudonym for a number of prominent revolutionaries of the period, including Ho Chi Minh.

Sources

Aguilar, Luis E., ed. *Marxism in Latin America*. New York: Alfred A. Knopf, 1968.

Alavi, Hamza. "Peasants and Revolution." In *Socialist Register*, edited by Ralph Miliband and John Saville. New York: Monthly Review Press, 1965.

Althusser, Louis. *For Marx*. Translated by Ben Brewster. New York: Vintage Books, 1970.

————. *Lenin and Philosophy*. Translated by Ben Brewster. New York: Monthly Review Press, 1971.

Bambirra, Vania, ed. *Diez años de insurrección en América Latina*. 2 vols. Santiago: Prensa Latinoamericana, 1971.

Béjar, Héctor. "A Contribution to the Discussion of Guerrilla Tactics in Latin America." *World Outlook*, vol. 6, no. 4 (February 2, 1968), pp. 86–88.

————. *Peru 1965: Notes on a Guerrilla Experience*. Translated by William Rose. New York: Monthly Review Press, 1970.

Bernard, Jean-Pierre, et al. *Guide to the Political Parties of South America*. Baltimore: Penguin Books, 1973.

Blanco, Hugo. *Land or Death: The Peasant Struggle in Peru*. New York: Pathfinder Press, 1972.

Burchett, Wilfred. *Vietnam Will Win!* New York: Guardian Books, 1970.

Carr, E. H. *The Bolshevik Revolution*. 3 vols. Middlesex, Eng.: Penguin Books, 1966.

Castro, Fidel. *Fidel Castro: Major Speeches*. London: Stage I, 1968.

————. *Fidel Castro Speaks.* Edited by Martin Kenner and James Petras. New York: Grove Press, 1969.

————. *Revolutionary Struggle 1947–58: Selected Works of Fidel Castro*, vol. 1. Edited by Rolando E. Bonachea and Nelson P. Valdés. Cambridge: M.I.T. Press, 1972.

CILA Dossier. Montreal: Editions Latin America, n.d.

Connor, James E. *Lenin on Politics and Revolution: Selected Writings.* Indianapolis: Pegasus, 1968.

Crain, David A. "The Course of the Cuban Heresy: The Rise and Decline of Castroism's Challenge to the Soviet Line in the Latin American Marxist Revolutionary Movement, 1963–70." Ph.D. dissertation, Indiana University, 1972.

Debray, Régis. *The Border & A Young Man in the Know.* Translated by Helen R. Lane. New York: Grove Press, 1968.

————. *Che's Guerrilla War.* Translated by Rosemary Sheed. Middlesex, Eng.: Penguin Books, 1975.

————. *The Chilean Revolution: Conversations with Allende.* New York: Random House, 1971.

————. *La Crítica de las armas—1.* Mexico: Siglo XXI Editores, 1975.

————. *L'Indésirable.* Paris: Editions du Seuil, 1975.

————. *Prison Writings.* Translated by Rosemary Sheed. New York: Random House, Vintage Books, 1973.

————. Prologue to *Los Tupamaros en acción: actas tupamaras.* Mexico: Editorial Diógenes, 1972.

————. *Las Pruebas de fuego: la crítica de las armas—2.* Mexico: Siglo XXI Editores, 1975.

————. *Les rendez-vous manqués.* Paris: Editions du Seuil, 1975.

————. *Revolution in the Revolution?* Translated by Bobbye Ortiz. New York: Grove Press, 1967.

————. *Strategy for Revolution.* Edited by Robin Blackburn. New York: Monthly Review Press, 1971.

Depestre, René. "Plática con Régis Debray." *Granma* (Havana), February 1, 1967.

Deutscher, Isaac. *Ironies of History.* London: Oxford University Press, 1966.

Engels, Frederick. "Engels to G. Trier in Copenhagen." *Karl Marx and Frederick Engels: Selected Correspondence.* Moscow: Progress Publishers, 1965.

Gadea, Hilda. *Ernesto: A Memoir of Che Guevara.* Translated by Carmen Molina and W. I. Bradbury. New York: Doubleday, 1972.

Gerassi, John, ed. *The Coming of the New International.* New York: World Publishing Co., 1971.

Geyer, Georgie Anne. "Why Guevara Failed: An Interview with Régis Debray." *Saturday Review,* August 24, 1968, pp. 14–18.

Gilio, Maria Esther. *The Tupamaro Guerrillas.* New York: Saturday Review Press, 1972.

Gomez, Alberto. "The Revolutionary Forces of Colombia and Their Perspectives." *World Marxist Review* 10 (April 1967): 59–67.

Gonzáles Bermejo, Ernesto. "Régis Debray: Literature and Politics Are Activities without Any Relation." *Diorama de Cultura, Excelsior* (Mexico City), November 9, 1975, pp. 2–4.

Gonzáles, L. J., and Sánchez Salazar, Gustavo A. *The Great Rebel: Che Guevara in Bolivia.* Translated by Helen R. Lane. New York: Grove Press, 1969.

Gott, Richard. *Guerrilla Movements in Latin America.* Garden City, N.Y.: Anchor Books, 1972.

Guevara, Che. *Che: Selected Works of Che Guevara.* Edited by R. E. Bonachea and N. P. Valdés. Cambridge: M.I.T. Press, 1969.

———. *The Diary of Che Guevara.* New York: Bantam Books, 1968.

———. *Guerrilla Warfare.* Translated by J. P. Morray. New York: Vintage Books, 1969.

———. *Obras completas.* 4 vols. Buenos Aires: Distribuidora Baires S.R.L., 1974.

———. *Reminiscences of the Cuban Revolutionary War.* New York: Grove Press, 1968.

———. *Venceremos: The Speeches and Writings of Che Guevara.* Edited by John Gerassi. New York: Simon and Schuster, 1968.

Heikal, Mohamed. *The Cairo Documents.* New York: Doubleday, 1973.

Ho Chi Minh. *On Revolution.* Edited by Bernard B. Fall. New York: Signet Books, 1967.

Hodges, Donald C. *The Latin American Revolution.* New York: William Morrow, 1974.

———, and Shanab, Robert Elias Abu. *National Liberation Fronts 1960/70.* New York: William Morrow, 1972.

Horowitz, I. L.; de Castro, Josué; and Gerassi, John, eds. *Latin American Radicalism.* New York: Vintage Books, 1969.

Huberman, Leo, and Sweezy, Paul M., eds. *Régis Debray and the Latin American Revolution.* New York: Monthly Review Press, 1968.

Huizer, Gerrit. *The Revolutionary Potential of Peasants in Latin America.* Lexington, Mass.: Lexington Books, 1972.

Jackson, D. Bruce. *Castro, the Kremlin, and Communism in Latin America.* Baltimore: Johns Hopkins University Press, 1969.

James, Daniel. *Che Guevara: A Biography.* New York: Stein and Day, 1970.

————, ed. *The Complete Bolivian Diaries of Che Guevara and Other Captured Documents.* New York: Stein and Day, 1968.

Johnson, Cecil. *Communist China and Latin America, 1959–1967.* New York: Colombia University Press, 1970.

Karol, K. S. *Guerrillas in Power.* New York: Hill and Wang, 1970.

Labrousse, Alain. *The Tupamaros.* Middlesex, Eng.: Penguin Books, 1973.

Lartéguy, Jean. "A Frenchman Held in Seclusion." *Paris Match,* May 13, 1967, p. 104.

Lenin, V. I. *Against Dogmatism and Sectarianism in the Working Class Movement.* Moscow: Progress Publishers, 1971.

————. *Against Revisionism, in Defense of Marxism.* Moscow: Progress Publishers, 1970.

————. *Collected Works.* 45 vols. Moscow: Progress Publishers, 1961–70.

————. *National Liberation, Socialism & Imperialism.* New York: International Publishers, 1968.

————; Marx, K.; and Engels, F. *On Scientific Communism.* Moscow: Progress Publishers, 1967.

Liebman, Marcel. "Lenin in 1905: A Revolution that Shook a Doctrine." *Monthly Review,* April 1970.

Lora, Guillermo. *Revalorización del metodo de las guerrillas.* N.p. (Bolivia): Ediciones Masas, 1967.

Lowy, Michael. *The Marxism of Che Guevara.* Translated by Brian Pearce. New York: Monthly Review Press, 1973.

Lukács, Georg. *Lenin: A Study on the Unity of His Thought.* Cambridge: M.I.T. Press, 1970.

Luxemburg, Rosa. *The Mass Strike, the Political Party and the Trade Unions.* New York: Harper & Row, 1971.

Mao Tse-tung. *Selected Works.* 4 vols. Peking: Foreign Languages Press, 1967.

Mattel, Georges. "Entrevista con Douglas Bravo." ¡Ahora! (Santo Domingo), no. 385 (March 29, 1971), pp. 52–54.

Memagalos, Florence. "Régis Debray: The Prophet of Castro Communism." In *The Soviet Union and Latin America,* edited by J. Gregory Oswald. New York: Praeger Publishers, 1970.

Meneses, Enrique. *Fidel Castro*. New York: Taplinger, 1966.
Morán Arce, Lucas. "Guerrilla Warfare in the Sierra Maestra." M.A. thesis, University of Florida, 1970.
Morray, J. P. *The Second Revolution in Cuba*. New York: Monthly Review Press, 1962.
NACLA. *Bibliography on Latin America*. Berkeley, Calif.: NACLA, 1973.
——. *Guatemala*. Berkeley, Calif.: NACLA, 1970.
——. *Latin America & Empire Report*, vol. 9. Berkeley, Calif.: NACLA, 1975.
——. *Research Methodology Guide*. Berkeley, Calif.: NACLA, 1970.
——. *The U.S. Military Apparatus*. Berkeley, Calif.: NACLA, 1972.
Nadle, Marlene. "Régis Debray Speaks from Prison." *Ramparts*, August 24, 1968, pp. 40–42.
Neuberg, A. *Armed Insurrection*. London: New Left Books, 1970.
Nuñez, Carlos. "Testimonio desde la prisión." *Indice* (Madrid), no. 240 (January 15, 1969), pp. 2–6.
——. *The Tupamaros: Urban Guerrillas of Uruguay*. New York: Times Change Press, 1970.
Partido Communista de la Argentina. *No puede haber una revolución en la revolución*. Buenos Aires: Editiones "UNIDAD," 1967.
Pumaruna, Américo. *Peru: Revolución; Insurreción; Guerrillas*. Lima, Peru: Editiones Vanguardia Revolucionaria, 1968.
Quartim, Joao. *Dictatorship and Armed Struggle in Brazil*. Translated by David Fernbach. New York: Monthly Review Press, 1971.
——. "Régis Debray and the Brazilian Revolution." *New Left Review*, no. 59 (January-February 1970), pp. 65–82.
Rodríguez, Juan. "The New in the Political Line of the Communist Party of Venezuela." *World Marxist Review* 10 (September 1967): 78–82.
Rojas, Marta, and Rodríguez Calderón, Mirta, eds. *Tania: The Unforgettable Guerrilla*. New York: Random House, 1971.
Solioni, Humberto. *Interview with Douglas Bravo* (1970). New York: Pathfinder Press-Merit Pamphlet, 1970.
Stalin, Joseph. *Foundations of Leninism: Essential Works of Marxism*. Edited by A. P. Mendel. New York: Bantam Books, 1965.
Suárez, Andrés. *Cuba: Castroism and Communism, 1959–1966*. Cambridge: M.I.T. Press, 1967.
——. "The Cuban Revolution: The Road to Power." *Latin American Research Review*, vol. 7, no. 3, pp. 5–29.

Thompson, George. *From Marx to Mao Tse-tung: A Study in Revolutionary Dialectics*. Letchworth, Hertfordshire (England): Garden City Press, 1971.

Time (International Edition), October 6, 1975, pp. 12–13.

Timossi, Jorge, and Cabieses, Manuel. "Régis Debray habla en libertad." *¡Ahora!* (Santo Domingo), no. 375 (January 18, 1971), pp. 26–32.

Tres evasiones de Tupamaros: actas tupamaras/2. Buenos Aires: Distribuidora Baires S. R. L., 1973.

Tupamaro Document. *NACLA's Latin America and Empire Report*, vol. 7, no. 8 (October 1973), pp. 30–31.

The Tupamaros: Urban Guerrilla Warfare in Uruguay. New York: The Liberated Guardian, n.d.

Los Tupamaros en acción: actas tupamaras. Mexico: Editorial Diógenes, 1972.

Vega, Luis Mercier. *Guerrillas in Latin America: The Technique of the Counter State*. London: Pall Mall, 1969.

Vo Nguyen Giap. *People's War, People's Army*. New York: Frederick A. Praeger, 1962.

Weid, Jean Marc von der. *Brazil: 1964 to the Present*. Montreal: Editions Latin America, 1972.

Wilson, Carlos. *The Tupamaros: The Unmentionables*. Boston: Branden Press, 1974.

Index

231